Spiral of Entrapment

SPIRAL OF ENTRAPMENT
Abused women in conflict with the law

Hallie Ludsin & Lisa Vetten

*The Centre for the Study of
Violence and Reconciliation*

Funded by the
Foundation for Human Rights

First published in 2005 by Jacana Media (Pty) Ltd.
5 St Peter Road
Bellevue 2198
Johannesburg
South Africa

© Hallie Ludsin & Lisa Vetten, 2005

All rights reserved.

ISBN 1-77009-054-1

Cover design by Triple M
Set in Stone Serif 9/12.5
Printed by Pinetown Printers

See a complete list of Jacana titles at www.jacana.co.za

ACKNOWLEDGMENTS

THIS BOOK HAS BEEN MANY YEARS in the making and many people, at different times and in different ways, have contributed to its development. We would like to thank Kailash Bhana, Tessa Hochfeld, Julia Kuhn, Shereen Mills, Collet Ngwane, Kameshni Pillay and Veronica Sigamoney who all contributed to earlier versions of the book. Lilly Artz, Helene Combrinck, and Lebo Malepe also provided advice and comments on some of the drafts. Vanessa Kottler and Ilze Olckers gave us helpful editorial guidance at different stages. We are indebted to Women's Human Rights Resources (WHRR) of the Faculty of Law at the University of Toronto, who undertook the initial research and writing of the sections on international law and approaches to clemency. Bobby Rodwell compiled the various case studies in the book and we thank her for her time. Lorraine Wolhuter and Johan Kriegler reviewed the book in its final form. Their incisive and constructive comments helped refine our thinking and arguments.

Our thanks to the Ford Foundation, which funded some of the initial research for this document, as well as to Davina Cohen, who raised additional funding through a performance of the Vagina Monologues in New York. We should like to thank the Foundation for Human Rights in particular for providing the funds that enabled us to finish the book.

Lastly, our most important acknowledgements go to those women who have shared their experiences with us over the years and entrusted us with their cases and futures. This book is dedicated to all of you.

CONTENTS

PART ONE: The psycho-social context of abused women's lives 9

Introduction 10

Chapter 1. Societal responses to domestic violence in South Africa 16

Chapter 2. Psych-social explanations for the impact of abuse 49

Chapter 3. When abused women kill 83

PART TWO: Legal Defences and mitigation of sentence for abused women who kill 97

Chapter 4. Defences for women protecting their lives 98

Chapter 5. Defences for women who lost control 154

Chapter 6. Post-conviction relief 170

Chapter 7. Evidentiary requirements 186

ENDNOTES 197

PART I

The psycho-social context of abused women's lives

INTRODUCTION

YOU ARE 16 AND PREGNANT. Your parents insist you marry the father. You are 14 and have played truant from school for the day to be with your boyfriend. Your very traditional parents are outraged and insist you be married as soon as you are old enough. You meet a man who assaults you during your courtship but you marry him anyway, expecting no better; this is how your father treated your mother.

You and your husband have been together some time. He beats you on the head with his gun. You and your children live on bread and coffee because he locks up the other food for his exclusive consumption. Your children beg the neighbours for food. You are locked in the bathroom for days at a time. He kicks you, slaps you and punches you. He rapes you, calls you "whore", "bitch" and "cunt" and interrogates the children to find out where you have been and who has visited you during the day. His sexual abuse of you results in your hospitalisation. You stuff a dishcloth in your mouth when he beats you so that your children will not hear your cries. Your daughter calls her doll "bitch" because that is what her father calls all the females in the household. He takes your money, he gives you no money and he stops you from working. He shows up at your job and causes a scene, accusing your manager of sleeping with you. You are asked to leave to prevent further embarrassment.

You leave many times but he finds you every time and weeps, promising this time will be different. The local shelter is full and cannot take you in. Your parents have no space to take you in. Your parents are dead. You approach the police but your husband is a police officer. The police are afraid of your violent husband. There is no law to protect you; it is 1992 and there is no law allowing for a husband to be prosecuted for the rape of his wife. It is 2001 and police commissioner Jackie Selebi says the police do not have the resources to implement the Domestic Violence Act.[1] You have no work experience, nowhere to go and children to feed, clothe and shelter. Your family is sick of you and does not wish to hear about your problems any longer.

You are caught in a spiral of entrapment, choices diminishing with every failed turn for help. Words die in your mouth. It is as if a barrier has come down between you and the world, which stares back, uncomprehending. If the presence of a heartbeat is the criterion by which we distinguish the living from the dead, then you are alive, but to all other intents and purposes, you have become a stone – inert, inanimate and insentient. Only by amputating all sense of self, all feeling, all hope, are you able to exist. And then one day he threatens to harm – even hurts – one of the children, or beats you so badly that you fear next time he will kill you, or threatens to have you gang-raped, or humiliates you once too often. In that moment you see very clearly that you will never be able to escape him, that you have become nothing and that this is what you will remain for the rest of your life. And so, in a desperate act of self-preservation, you kill him – because it is either he or you.

This introduction, a composite of the lives of Anieta Ferreira, Elsie Morare, Sharla Sebejan, Meisie Kgomo, Harriet Chidi and Maria Scholtz, tries to convey some sense of the slamming brutality of domestic violence. This is crucial to understanding the context in which battered women act when they kill their abusive partners.

While the majority of battered women kill in the course of defending themselves against an attack by their partners, there is another, smaller group who, like these women, kill while their abusers are passive, or hire third parties to carry out the killings for them. Because the former group's behaviour conforms with what the law understands either as self-defence or temporary non-pathological criminal incapacity, this group is generally able to draw successfully upon the criminal defences to murder. It is the latter group that challenges not only the criminal justice system but also common societal understandings of domestic violence. Not only do they confound popular perceptions around how battered women are supposed to behave but they also call into question the adequacy and effectiveness of law enforcement responses to domestic violence. Their matters also illustrate how the criminal justice system supplies defences created by men, for men and based on men's experiences.[2]

The Supreme Court of Appeal began grappling with some of these challenges when it heard Anieta Ferreira's appeal against her life sentence, which it subsequently replaced with one suspended for six years. Importantly, the court understood that battered women's decisions to kill should be evaluated from neither a male perspective nor an objective perspective but

> "by the court's placing itself as far as it can in the position of the woman concerned, with a fully detailed account of the abusive relationship and the assistance of expert evidence such as that given here. Only by judging the case on that basis can the offender's equality right under s 9(1) of the Constitution be given proper effect."[3]

This is the purpose of this book: to provide a fully detailed account of the complex emotional and social landscape inhabited by battered women, the nature of the state and social assistance available to them and how to use this information to defend an abused woman accused of murdering her abusive intimate partner. The book was compiled as a guide to judicial officers, prosecuting and defence counsel, police investigators, expert witnesses such as psychologists and social workers, and women's activists faced with the criminal trial of one of these battered woman. It seeks to fill gaps in the understanding of these cases by outlining the social context in which abused women act by exploring:

- why abused women do not leave their abusers;
- why women's options to stop the abuse are limited and sometimes non-existent; and
- the psychological impact of abuse on battered women.

The book also informs defence counsel of new ways to argue traditional criminal defences on behalf of these women, focusing particularly on the types of evidence necessary to support the defences. For expert witnesses it explains what information they should include in any expert report.

Part 1 of the book provides the psycho-social context and background to battered women's actions. Chapter 1 defines domestic violence and sets out its prevalence in South Africa. It then discusses societal and cultural factors contributing to the occurrence of domestic violence before outlining state and civil society responses to the problem. This chapter includes an overview of research monitoring the implementation by members of the criminal justice system of legal remedies to address domestic violence. We also examine the societal, economic and cultural factors which constrain women's choices. As the chapter explains, individual women's lack of resources, unhelpful and even hostile attitudes on the part of law enforcement officials and overall insufficient responses by society to abuse, all contribute to trapping women within abusive relationships. It concludes with the story of Anne Riberts which illustrates the difference good help and support can ultimately make to some abused women's lives.

Chapter 2 provides a more individualized focus upon both the perpetrators and the victims of domestic violence. It is introduced with "Thembi's" life story, an example of how children are affected by domestic violence and the subsequent loss of both parents – one to death and the other to prison. It then sets out the key theories explaining the impact of domestic violence upon women and attempts to locate abused women within a shared set of experiences. It highlights how, while there is much that abused women have in common, the experience and impact of abuse will remain unique to each woman, as will many aspects of the strategies they adopt to cope with their circumstances. It also includes research on the psychology of abusers. The research on abusers is particularly important because it underscores that abuse is a method of control rather than a disconnected series of random acts performed by out-of-control men. It also highlights the real dangers women face in trying to leave. Anieta Ferreira's story ends the chapter, demonstrating how lethal the combination of isolation, violence, and entrapment can ultimately be.

Taken together, these two chapters provide the background to understanding what leads abused women to kill, the subject of chapter 3. This chapter begins by summarizing how women come to see themselves as trapped within the relationship, their choices ever diminishing. It sets out the process by which women come to be caught in the spiral of entrapment. All three of these chapters provide the information essential not only to understanding the context of these women's lives but also for creating a foundation for the inclusion of the experiences of abused women who kill in traditional criminal defence law.

Part 2 of the book details the technical aspects of defending abused women who kill. Currently there is only one reported case in South Africa in which an abused woman, who killed her abuser in a non-confrontational situation, argued self-defence and her defence failed. The remainder of these women either argued non-pathological criminal incapacity or simply pleaded guilty to murder.[4] Part 2 of this book challenges traditionalist thinking that effectively excludes women from access to self-defence, forcing them either to plead that they didn't know what they were doing, or knew they were doing something wrong, when they killed the person who made their lives a living hell. As Part 1 explains, the effective exclusion results from gender bias because the way women defend themselves does not look like the way men defend themselves.

Chapters 4 and 5 discuss critically each of the existing defences to murder and how they can be expanded to end the inherent male bias that currently exists within criminal defence law. In particular, these chapters explain how to include non-confrontational killings within the defences, punctuating the discussion with examples from around the world in which abused women succeeded with the defences. Chapter 4 explains self-defence and putative self-defence for women who killed because they believed they had no other choice in order to escape the abuse. Chapter 5 describes non-pathological criminal incapacity and the insanity defence for women who have killed because they lost control. Provocation is discussed within non-pathological criminal incapacity or as part of sentence mitigation.

Chapter 6 discusses post-conviction remedies for women convicted for the murder of their batterers. The first section of the chapter considers sentence mitigation for women who are convicted for murder. It explains the Criminal Law Amendment Act 105 of 1997, which sets out a mandatory minimum sentence for premeditated murder and the standard used to derogate from it. The chapter looks at the recent success in *S v Ferreira*, and uses the decision to highlight the importance of the social context evidence contained in Chapters 1 through 3 to sentence mitigation. The remainder of the chapter considers the possibility of clemency and suggests tactics towards achieving it.

Chapter 7 summarizes the types of expert and non-expert testimony necessary for abused women to access these defences. It emphasizes the need for evidence of the history of abuse between the accused and the deceased, the history of violence against the accused, the deceased's history of violent behaviour against others, and testimony on the social context of abuse and its effects on the accused. The book concludes in

Chapter 8 with a few brief remarks about the process of defending an abused woman who kills. With all of this information, we hope to arm women's advocates with the tools necessary to give women who kill their abusers real access to criminal defences and post-conviction relief.

CHAPTER 1

Societal responses to domestic violence in south africa

Contents	Page
A. DEFINING AND DESCRIBING DOMESTIC VIOLENCE	17
B. THE SOCIAL CONTEXT IN WHICH DOMESTIC VIOLENCE TAKES PLACE	20
1. The Macro-system: Cultural norms and values regarding women, marriage and the family	22
2. Institutional responses to domestic violence	27
(a) Legal responses to domestic violence before 1998, including the Prevention of Family Violence Act 133 of 1993	27
(b) The Domestic Violence Act 116 of 1998	29
(i) Protection orders	29
(aa) The application process	29
(bb) Court hearings and breaches of the protection order	31
(c) Criminal charges	33
(i) The role of the police	34
(ii) Problems with implementation of that role	34
(iii) Why women drop charges	36
(iv) Conclusion	37
(d) Health care workers	38
(e) Civil society organisations	39
3. Personal networks: communities, friends and family	40
4. Access to economic and tangible resources	41
(a) Private maintenance: Direct relief from the abuser	44
(i) Emergency financial assistance under the DVA	44
(ii) Maintenance order under the Maintenance Act	44
(iii) Maintenance order under the Divorce Act	45
5. Conclusion	45

ABUSED WOMEN DO NOT make decisions about their lives in the abstract, or according to fixed rules. Rather, their choices are made within contexts shaped by social beliefs and values, personal circumstances and access to resources. Competing obligations and responsibilities to others may also form part of this context. Part A of this chapter begins by briefly defining domestic violence and reporting its prevalence in South Africa. It then proposes a model for understanding the textured, contradictory and multi-layered influences at work in abused women's lives. Part B describes the socio-cultural context of domestic violence, highlighting how many norms and values effectively set up women for abuse. The chapter describes domestic violence legislation as well as its implementation by the police and courts. It also analyses the responses of civil society, friends and family to women's need for help. While South Africa recently has made real efforts to alleviate the blight of domestic violence, the chapter highlights how much still has to be done to ensure that meaningful and effective options are put in place for women to end the abuse.

A. DEFINING AND DESCRIBING DOMESTIC VIOLENCE

Domestic violence can be understood in at least two ways. The first is to understand domestic violence as a form of control where methods can include physical, sexual and psychological abuse or economic abuse or any combination of these.[5] Defining domestic violence as a systematic method of control points to the instrumental nature of such abuse. Essentially, control is the goal and the individual acts of abuse and violence is the means the abuser uses to ensure the victim's compliance with his demands.[6]

Until recently, society and the law viewed domestic violence as consisting of physical violence only. South Africa's Domestic Violence Act (DVA) (Act 116 of 1998) goes a long way toward appreciating how multi-faceted abuse is. It does so by formally recognizing control as a key feature of domestic violence[7] and that such violence can also include physical, sexual, emotional, verbal and psychological abuse. It also defines emotional, verbal and psychological abuse broadly, describing it as a pattern of degrading or humiliating conduct towards a complainant including repeated insults, ridicule, or name-calling; repeated threats to cause emotional pain; or the repeated exhibition of possessiveness or jealousy which is such as to constitute a serious invasion of the complainant's privacy, liberty, integrity or security. Other behaviours that may form part of this pattern of control include isolating the woman from her family and friends,[8] as well as various forms of economic abuse such as the inadequate provision, or withholding, of food, clothing, shelter and medical care.[9] Coercive behaviour may also be directed towards children, property, pets or others. The threat and/or use of violence towards children is another powerful means of ensuring abused women's compliance.[10]

Another way to understand domestic violence is to see it as a form of objectification, treating or making into a "thing" something that is not really a thing. Treating human beings as things or objects may take many forms, including:

- instrumentality – treating the object as a tool of his or her purposes;
- treating the object as lacking in autonomy and self-determination;
- treating the object as lacking in agency as well as in activity;
- treating the object as interchangeable with other objects of the same type and/or objects of other types;
- treating the object as violable or lacking in boundary integrity, as something that it is permissible to break up, smash, break into;
- treating the object as something that is owned, can be bought, sold etc;
- treating the object as something whose experiences and feelings (if any) need not be taken into account.[11]

Domestic violence inflicts profound and far-reaching consequences upon victim's lives. Victims suffer from fractures and disability, chronic pain syndromes, lacerations and abrasions, suicidal behaviour and self-harm, alcohol and drug abuse, depression, complications in pregnancy (including miscarriage), gastro-intestinal disorders, ocular damage and eating and sleep disorders.[12] HIV infection is another consequence, with South African women in abusive or controlling relationships twice as likely to be infected with HIV than women in non-violent relationships.[13] Still other women die at their partners' hands. Approximately half of all South African women murdered in 1999 were killed by their intimate partners.[14]

Prevalence of domestic violence in South Africa
Domestic violence is considered to be one of the most under-reported crimes in South Africa. Indeed, no official national statistics regarding the prevalence of domestic violence exist, largely because law enforcement includes acts of domestic violence within a range of criminal charges such as assault, pointing a firearm, intimidation or attempted murder (among other things). No study has disaggregated domestic violence from police statistics for these other crimes. Instead, we have to turn to community-based prevalence studies to extrapolate such figures. These studies find that domestic violence is a major problem that, in one form or another, affects as many as one in two women in some parts of South Africa.

One study surveying 1306 women in three provinces found that 27% of women in the Eastern Cape, 28% of women in Mpumalanga and 19% of women in the Northern Province had been physically abused in their lifetimes by a current or ex-partner.[15] The same study investigated the prevalence of emotional and financial abuse experienced by women in the year prior to the study and found that 51% of women in the Eastern Cape, 50% in Mpumalanga and 40% in Northern Province were subjected to these types of abuse.[16] Another study, undertaken with a sample of 168 women drawn from 15 rural communities in the Southern Cape, estimated that on average 80% of rural women are victims of domestic violence.[17] Interviews conducted with 1 394 men working for three Cape Town municipalities found that approximately 44% of the men were willing to admit that they abused their female partners.[18] National figures for intimate femicide (men's killing of their intimate female partners) suggest that this most lethal form of domestic violence is prevalent in South Africa. In 1999 8,8 per 100 000 of the female population aged 14 years and older died at the hands of their partners - the highest rate ever reported in research anywhere in the world.[19]

Although widespread, domestic violence is, at the same time, a hidden phenomenon and as a consequence, poorly understood. In the absence of accurate information about the problem, its causes and effects, people typically resort to seemingly commonsensical explanations for its occurrence. As a consequence a whole mythology, which typically blames the victim and suggests there is something deviant about her,[20] has grown around the nature of abuse and its victims.[21] Most of these misconceptions arise from a fundamental misunderstanding of the reasons why women remain in abusive relationships. Lack of understanding leads people to think that women must somehow enjoy, or derive pleasure from the abuse, or alternatively that the violence cannot be that serious.

Abusive behaviour is also mystified, with people believing that abusers are mentally ill and/or unrelentingly brutal and vicious. The popular notion that it "takes two to tango" or that women provoke the abuse is another set of ideas that diminish the abuser's responsibility for his behaviour. The belief that alcohol is the primary cause of marital aggression[22] is another way in which the abuser's responsibility may be denied. Given popular, racialized assumptions around who drinks excessively and who does not, this view usually implies that it is primarily poor and/or black men who abuse.

Overall these various assumptions promote the idea that domestic violence is a purely individual problem caused by defects in the characters of the people concerned. In thinking this way, societies avoid thinking about how their institutions and practices contribute to the occurrence and perpetuation of domestic violence. Both the remainder of this chapter and the next chapter challenge these misconceptions, first by describing the broader socio-cultural context in which abuse occurs and the nature and effectiveness of social support offered to abused women; and, secondly, by sketching broadly the dominant psycho-social theories explaining the effects of domestic violence.

B. THE SOCIAL CONTEXT IN WHICH DOMESTIC VIOLENCE TAKES PLACE

The context of any particular woman's life is made up of both social and individual factors, which affect the occurrence of and responses to abuse. These factors must be considered individually, in combination with one another, and as part of a social phenomenon.[23] In the sections that follow we first set out a broad framework for categorizing the various factors that make up women's particular situations and then provide research illustrating these various circumstances. This information provides an important social context for understanding individual women's reasoning and responses to violence, the subject of Chapter 2.

The various elements playing a role in developing individual women's psycho-social contexts and influencing the choices open to them in responding to the abuse, can be classified under the following headings:

- The macro-system refers to larger *societal and cultural blueprints* informing men's and women's behaviour and their relationships with one another. These will also differ according to people's socio-economic backgrounds, their education and their religious beliefs;
- Larger community networks, comprising institutions, their policies and practices, add another layer to a contextualized approach to domestic violence. These include the various agencies making up the criminal justice system, mental health and health agencies and other bodies or organizations in the battered woman's community concerned with domestic violence. How the woman is treated by both her personal and larger community network impacts greatly on whether she will continue to seek help;
- The micro-system refers to *women's personal networks of family, friends, workmates and neighbours,* to name a few. These may be extensive or minimal and they may also offer varying degrees of support to women, which may also change over time. For instance, workmates may initially provide important support but, if women do not leave their partners as workmates may believe they should, then this support may dwindle over time;
- The *economic and tangible resources* that abused women may (or may not) have access to, such as money, housing, transportation, income, credit, clothing;
- Women's *individual personal histories*, including their emotional, physical and behavioural strengths and limitations, as well as prior, significant events in their lives and the consequences of those events.[24]

How the woman is treated by both her personal and larger community networks impacts greatly on the extent and nature of help she may seek, as will her personal history, socio-cultural background and access to resources. The remainder of the chapter presents research fleshing out the first four dimensions of this framework. It also shows that the combination of a lack of resources, indifferent or stereotypical understandings of domestic violence, its victims and perpetrators, combined with limited social support leaves women with few effective options to combat the violence in their relationships.

1. The Macro-system: Cultural norms and values regarding women, marriage and the family

South Africa may well be a culturally diverse society; nonetheless its various groups demonstrate remarkable cross-cultural agreement on the subordinate status of women. While some of the forms this second-class status takes may vary across cultures, the outcomes still place women in positions where they are subject to their male partners' authority and control. Dobash and Dobash's observations on marriages in the United Kingdom would thus seem to apply equally to South African marriages or marriage-like relationships.

> "It is still true that for a woman to be brutally or systematically assaulted she must usually enter our most sacred institution, the family. It is within marriage that a woman is most likely to be slapped and shoved about, severely assaulted, killed, or raped. Thus it is impossible to understand violence against women without also understanding the nature of the marital relationship in which it occurs and to which it is inextricably related."[25]

Traditionally, South African society and its state institutions have treated the home and family as private, with what happens between family members deemed beyond the realm of outside intervention. Indeed, until relatively recently, the marriage contract was treated as a private matter outside the scope of law enforcement. While more recent legislation has sought to make law enforcement responsible for intervening in abusive relationships, many sections of society continue to see domestic violence as a private problem.

Placing and keeping families within the realm of what is private carries a number of far-reaching consequences. First, for a long time it has allowed abusers to act with relative impunity by escaping punishment for abusing their wives. Marital rape, for example, became a crime only with the enactment of domestic violence legislation in 1993. Secondly, treating domestic violence as a private matter encourages the application of private solutions to the problem,[26] rather than encouraging victims to have recourse to public assistance such as counselling agencies or the criminal justice system. Finally, as an expression such as "keeping it in the family" illustrates, not only does secrecy then come to surround family affairs, but many feel that shame is brought upon the family when its problems are aired publicly. Indeed, openly discussing "family problems" may be seen as reducing the status of the family in community eyes. As a consequence women become the keepers of family respectability and must then also bear the brunt of any breach of privacy. Those women who do speak about their abuse may then be stigmatised for "washing their dirty linen in public." The effect of this belief is paradoxical: women should "break the silence" and "speak out" (or be considered weak or accepting of the abuse) but at the same time be willing to accept community and family censure for so doing.[27]

Studies have also highlighted how communities see women as both dependent upon and weaker than men. In such communities, women without men are seen as deficient, while women who attempt to exercise some power in their relationships are seen as having brought the abuse upon themselves for having threatened their partners' authority.[28] Failing to behave as a proper woman – by drinking, nagging or not keeping the house clean for instance – may not only result in women being stigmatized by their communities but is also thought to justify abuse.[29] The belief that children need both parents is strongly held by many communities – to the extent that women who leave their partners or have them removed from their homes may be stigmatized for having failed to maintain the highly valued family structure.[30]

Women's nurturing qualities are also thought to make them particularly suited to healing troubled family relationships. Thus the emotional and social responsibility for keeping families together falls primarily on women, who also carry primary responsibility for making relationships work – an obligation further cemented by the romanticized notion that "love conquers all." Where men are categorized as emotionally inept or inarticulate in relationships, women are expected to be the communicators and facilitators of emotional expression. When women are unable to bring about this harmonious state of affairs, they may feel a sense of shame and failure and see themselves as not having loved enough or hard enough. Many others will similarly judge them for having failed as wives.[31]

Aspects of African customary law follow the same trend towards a general acceptance of domestic violence as part of a man's authority. Two practices thought to enhance women's risk of domestic violence are *lobola* (dowry) and a patriarchal property system that places wealth solely within the hands of men.

Under customary law, it is generally accepted that a couple cannot marry unless they have reached agreement about payment of *lobola* or a dowry by the groom to the bride's family.[32] Some men (and women) view payment of bridewealth as endowing them with ownership of their wives.[33] Ownership then entitles them to treat their wives as they please.[34] Interviews with 1306 women in the provinces of Mpumalanga, Eastern Cape and Limpopo found that between 94% and 98% of the sample agreed that it is culturally expected that a woman should obey her husband,[35] while between 59% and 63% agreed that it was culturally accepted that if a wife did something wrong her husband had the right to punish her.[36] When asked if it was accepted that a man owned his wife once he had paid lobola for her, 76%–84% of women agreed with the statement.[37] Twenty-three per cent of women interviewed in the Eastern Cape and as many as 58% of women in Limpopo province thought if a man beat his partner, it was culturally accepted that he loved her.[38]

Under customary law, when a woman marries, she is absorbed into her husband's family. Disputes that arise then are expected to be resolved by his family, who often prove to be unsympathetic.[39] Failing this, she could then turn to the traditional courts. Unfortunately, pressure is exerted on the abused woman by her own family to avoid this option. If a wife wishes to divorce or leave her husband, her family may be required to return the full amount of *lobola*. While customary law excuses a family from repayment in cases of domestic violence, this "only provides the wife with a justification for leaving in cases in which the violence is so severe that it 'makes cohabitation dangerous or impossible'."[40] In a poverty-ravaged country, many families are unable to return the *lobola*, which means the woman's family may be unwilling to allow her to return. As a result, some features of customary law practices increase the likelihood that the woman will remain trapped in the relationship.

The attitudes of adherents to customary law and their families suggest that female subservience to men, masculine entitlement to punish women under some circumstances, as well as male ownership of women are an entrenched feature of cultural norms. In fact, these attitudes are so entrenched that the Supreme Court of Appeal justified the reduction of the mandatory minimum sentence of a man convicted of raping his wife on the basis that "It is clear from his evidence that at the time of the incidents the accused honestly (albeit entirely misguidedly) believed that he had some 'right' to conjugal benefits."[41]

In conclusion, many cultural norms make it women's responsibility to alter their behaviour to prevent abuse, or change the situation, while simultaneously exonerating men both from responsibility for the abuse as well as for behaviour change. The consequence of these various cultural beliefs promotes the development in battered women of at least two sets of rationalizations that effectively set them up for abuse. The first, described as an appeal to the salvation ethic, is based on the belief that the abusive man is at heart a good person whose violent behaviour arises from specific, resolvable problems. His recovery is dependent on his female partner persevering to help him overcome his problems. The second, the appeal to higher loyalties, is another rationalization strongly informed by societal values – such as staying together for the sake of the children. Some religious advisers also tell women that ending a marriage may incur eternal damnation.[42] In other words, many sections of South African society place a higher value on maintaining the family than on the safety of women and children, making the pain and humiliation of women's abuse secondary to the primary goal of saving or fixing abusive partners.[43]

The table appended below summarises some of the factors at the macro-level that have been identified as contributing to domestic violence:

Unicef chart: factors that perpetuate domestic violence[44]

| Cultural | - Gender-specific socialization
- Cultural definitions of appropriate sex roles
- Expectations of roles within relationships
- Belief in innate superiority of males
- Values that give men proprietary rights over women and girls
- Notion of the family as the private sphere and under male control
- Customs of marriage (bridewealth/dowry)
- Acceptability of violence as a means of resolving conflict |
|---|---|
| Economic | - Women's economic dependence on men
- Limited access to cash and credit
- Discriminatory laws regarding inheritance, property rights, use of communal lands and maintenance after divorce or widowhood
- Limited access to employment in formal and informal sectors
- Limited access to education and training for women |
| Legal | - Lesser legal status of women either by written law and/or by practice
- Laws regarding divorce, child custody, maintenance and inheritance
- Legal definitions of rape and domestic violence
- Low levels of legal literacy among women
- Insensitive treatment of women and girls by police and judiciary |
| Political | - Under-representation of women in power, politics, the media and in the legal and medical professions
- Domestic violence not taken seriously
- Notions of family being private and beyond the control of state
- Risk of challenge to status quo/religious laws
- Limited organization of women as political force
- Limited participation of women in organized political system |

2. Institutional responses to domestic violence

Women generally speak out about the abuse they experience.[45] Most make several attempts to seek help, first from informal, personal networks such as family and friends and then through formal assistance from police, courts, doctors and social workers.[46] The next section of this chapter concentrates on the different legal remedies, state responses, and social and personal network responses to women seeking help. It shows that women often are met with hostility, bias, indifference and/or helplessness, leaving them with little effective help to avoid abuse.

(a) Legal responses to domestic violence before 1998, including the Prevention of Family Violence Act 133 of 1993

Since 1993 South Africa's government has attempted to deal with the problem of domestic violence primarily through law reform and the criminal justice system. Although the system has come a long way toward addressing abuse of women, problems with legislation, lack of enforcement and entrenched attitudes that accept domestic violence, have hindered women's ability to access the legislative remedies effectively and prevent further abuse. These failures are particularly damaging because women learn from experience and from one another whether the law will protect them from violence or not. If the legal system is unresponsive towards victims of domestic violence, they will be discouraged from using it.

Before the passing of the Prevention of Family Violence Act in 1993, women could try to protect themselves through interdicts and peace orders. However, the interdicts were expensive, while violations of peace orders resulted in light punishment and were not well enforced.[47] The process for receiving a peace order required a woman to complain to a magistrate or court of her fear of future harm. If the court agreed that a peace order was necessary, it would require the abuser to pay a recognizance fee which he would forfeit if he violated the peace order within a six-month period. If the abuser failed to pay the recognizance fee he would be imprisoned. Until 1992, breach of a peace order resulted in the loss of a recognizance fee amounting to R50, or one month's imprisonment. In 1992 the penalty was increased to a maximum of R2 000 or six months' imprisonment.[48]

South Africa first attempted directly to protect women from domestic violence through the Prevention of Family Violence Act (PFVA). It worked on an interdict system. The process for obtaining an interdict was easier and faster than for a peace order. A magistrate had the discretion to issue an interdict to stop the abuser from assaulting or threatening the applicant, and/or from entering the home. With this order, the magistrate issued a suspended warrant of arrest that came into effect if the abuser breached the terms of the interdict. The magistrate could imprison an abuser for up to 12 months for breaching the interdict. Importantly, the legislation removed the common-law exemption for marital rape, an exemption husbands could claim to avoid prosecution and conviction for raping their wives.[49]

Despite the advances in legal protection against domestic violence, the Act was of limited use to abuse victims. First, the Act created primarily a civil remedy to domestic violence, seemingly trivialising the abuser's criminal actions. The police could arrest an abuser under the Act and criminal penalties could be imposed only after there had been a breach of the interdict. Even then, punishment for a breach was limited. The process of obtaining the interdict included sheriff's fees for serving it, transportation to and from courts and wages lost due to time spent in court, all of which discouraged applicants.

Another important limitation of the Act was that it applied only to parties in marriage or intimate partners who cohabitated.[50] Abuse among family members, same-sex partners and intimate partners who did not live together was excluded from the ambit of the Act. The Act also did not define domestic violence, which limited its application to women suffering from physical abuse alone. Further, the express purpose was to promote family unity, rather than protect women, which subordinated women's individual rights to her role as wife, mother and homemaker.[51] The Act failed to focus on the survivor of abuse, instead dealing with domestic violence as a nuisance that should not be allowed to clog the criminal justice system or undermine the family unit.

The practical application of the Act further limited women's access to justice. There was little instruction to the police and magistrates on how to use it and when to use their discretion to protect women.[52] This allowed police and magistrates to avoid intervention into domestic violence completely or to apply stereotypes and bias in deciding when domestic violence warranted legal protection.[53] More importantly, magistrates typically did not hear interdict applications over weekends and in the evenings, when most incidents of domestic violence occur.

(b) The Domestic Violence Act 116 of 1998

South Africa adopted the Domestic Violence Act 116 of 1998 (DVA) as a comprehensive legal remedy to domestic violence. One of the DVA's most important innovations is its broad definition of domestic violence. Section 1(viii) defines domestic violence to include physical abuse, sexual abuse, emotional, verbal and psychological abuse, economic abuse, intimidation, harassment, stalking, damage to property, entering the victim's home without permission and any other controlling or abusive behaviour intended to harm the victim. The DVA also protects persons in any domestic relationship, whether married, in a same-sex or heterosexual relationship, cohabitating (regardless of relationship) or parent-child.[54]

(i) Protection orders

Under the DVA, a victim of domestic violence may apply for a protection order to stop the abuse and to stop the abuser from entering the mutual home, the victim's residence, or the victim's place of employment.[55] The court may place other conditions on the order, including that the police seize any weapons or help the victim retrieve property from her home.[56] The court can evict the abuser from the home and force him to pay rent for and/or emergency maintenance to the victim.[57] The court also has the power to limit the abuser's custody rights to children.[58] If the court grants an interim or final protection order, it must issue a suspended warrant for the arrest of the abuser that will become active if the abuser violates the order.[59]

(aa) The application process

The victim of abuse (or applicant) must apply to a court for a protection order. Typically this is done during court hours unless the applicant can show she would suffer undue hardship if she were forced to wait for the court to open.[60] A woman may seek an interim protection order if she can show she would suffer undue hardship waiting for a hearing on a final protection order.[61] The DVA requires the court to hear these applications as soon as possible.[62] An interim or final protection order becomes effective only after it has been served on the abuser.[63]

A variety of problems arise from the application process. To begin with, the application forms are written in technical English and Afrikaans and are confusing and time-consuming.[64] Researchers report: "This form is difficult to complete, even for those who have received training on how the forms should be filled out. It is our finding that most of the forms examined in this study were filled in inaccurately and were incomplete."[65] Courts have few resources to assist applicants, and volunteers are not always available in the courts.[66] Because these forms serve as the basis for the court order, incomplete or inaccurate forms lead to ineffective orders – with obvious implications for the extent and effectiveness of protection offered to women.

Secondly, the attitudes of both police and court personnel may act as a deterrent to pursuing matters. The research study of Parenzee *et al* explained that both groups of personnel feel frustrated by the implementation of the DVA:

> "The frustration felt by these personnel can be attributed to a combination of a stressful, oftentimes unrewarding and unsupportive work environment as well as a lack of understanding of the dynamics present in domestic violence cases. These emotions are then directed towards complainants seeking assistance. An unexpected consequence of this was also revealed in our interviews with court and police personnel. Namely, the tendency to over-empathize with the respondent (the abuser). In both sectors there were an alarming number of interviewees who identified more closely with the circumstances of the respondent than with those of the complainant."[67]

This is consistent with a Human Rights Watch report, which concluded that South African magistrates and judges often use sexist and discriminatory assumptions to the detriment of the victims of abuse and that police are hostile towards them.[68]

Thirdly, it is often difficult to access the protection orders at night or on weekends. Police are reluctant to contact the court after hours, expecting the woman to wait until the court opens[69] – thus potentially risking women's safety.

Fourthly, this entire process costs money. Ultimately, victims of domestic violence pay for the sheriff to serve the interdict, the cost of transportation for at least two trips to the court, as well as in lost wages if they have to take time off from work. These are high and possibly insurmountable costs for impoverished women. While the state must bear the costs of service if a means test indicates that the applicant cannot afford the sheriff's fee, in practice it would seem there is little consistency around the criteria applied in conducting such tests. Thus at some courts, impoverished women will receive state aid while at others they will not benefit from this provision in the DVA.[70]

(bb) Court hearings and breaches of the protection order
Once a victim completes the application process for a protection order, she faces new impediments to accessing justice. Although the DVA requires a hearing as soon as possible, the court process suffers from long delays. Courts have limited resources to hear these cases.[71] The delayed process means that women seeking protection orders risk continued abuse during the waiting period. Even if the court grants an interim or final protection order, service of the order on the abuser, which is required before it can be enforced, may be delayed. In Cape Town, the standard time span for service was between one day and three weeks; in George it could be served up to three months later and, in Mitchells Plain, up to four months later.[72] For women terrified of abuse, this gives little security.

The imprecise language of certain sections of the DVA is equally problematic. Nowhere does the DVA define "undue hardship", which the victim of abuse must prove to receive a protection order, or "imminent harm", which must result from the abuser's breach of the protection order for him to be arrested without a warrant. Courts rely on affidavits taken by typically untrained clerks to determine whether the woman's complaint meets the standard of "undue hardship" or "imminent harm." Poor quality affidavits undermine women's access to justice: "If the information provided is vague and unspecific, magistrates do not feel equipped to make a finding of undue hardship or imminent harm."[73] Women remain vulnerable "due to impressionistic decisions being taken based upon their appearance or incomplete testimony."[74]

Magistrates also have wide latitude to interpret these terms. Without appropriate training regarding domestic violence, ill-informed attitudes towards victims or ignorance of what constitutes abuse could deny many women their legal remedies to violence. Women suffering from psychological, emotional or verbal abuse will have the most difficulty proving these terms. Although emotional abuse is the most commonly cited reason given by a woman reporting a breach of the order, little training is offered to magistrates as to what constitutes emotional violence and why it must be taken seriously.[75]

Another area of difficulty relates to the seizure of weapons. A study of protection orders under the DVA in Cape Town, Mitchell's Plain and George found that magistrates rarely ordered seizure of weapons in comparison with the number of times applicants referred in their applications to the use of weapons against them. It was also noted that applicants did not often request the seizure. The study also suggests that the lack of detail in the protection order forms around what constitutes a dangerous weapon may also make it difficult for police officers to confiscate weapons.[76]

The DVA allows for the eviction of abusers from the joint home if it is in the best interests of the complainant.[77] This provision recognizes that women have limited access to shelters and should not be forced into homelessness to avoid abuse. Despite the logic of the provision, researchers noted "that magistrates, untutored in the dynamics of domestic violence and unpoliticized in terms of gender politics, are reluctant to evict batterers from their home."[78] Rather than force the abuser to take responsibility for his actions, the victim has to leave to avoid abuse.

Perhaps most importantly, protection orders do little to protect the long-term safety of domestic violence victims. Except in instances of severe violence, a man who breaches a protection order is released or receives bail while he awaits trial, providing him with the opportunity to breach the order again.[79] Once convicted at trial, a study of sentencing found that first-time offenders on average received a three-month suspended sentence.[80] The maximum sentence a man received for a breach of a protection order was one year's imprisonment. The magistrates' approach seems to assume that arrest will be enough of a deterrent to stop the abuse, although a court order failed to do so.[81]

In seeking to obtain a protection order, abused women must negotiate unfamiliar and alien procedures, resort to complex forms in languages often foreign to them, and engage with police and court personnel who may be hostile and reliant upon stereotypes and gender bias to determine the victim's relief from violence. Possibly the most upsetting aspect is that once a woman completes the process successfully, men are allowed to breach protection orders with relative impunity, usually risking only a suspended sentence for doing so. Faced with each of these barriers to justice, women grow demoralized with the limited legal remedies available to them to stop abuse. This combination of difficulties may well be why at least one writer has asserted that a court order represents the woman's last hope.[82] Research provides some support for this claim. A national survey of one thousand women who had experienced abuse recorded that women were least likely to turn to legal mechanisms to stop the violence. Only 11% of women in this study sought legal advice around the most serious incident of abuse they experienced. Recourse to legal assistance was also dependent upon geographical location, with 6% of rural women, 13% of women living in townships and 28% of women living in suburban areas seeking such help.[83]

(c) Criminal charges

The DVA is a civil remedy, with the criminal prosecution arising from charges of contempt of court against an abuser who violates a civil order. Because the DVA does not create a separate criminal offence for the commission of domestic violence, women can lay a range of other criminal charges against their abusers. The police must advise women of this right to press charges and the Clerks of Court are obliged to advise women of this right when they seek protection orders.[84] But while the DVA recognizes a wide variety of behaviours as constituting abuse, not all of these behaviours can be prosecuted as a violation of criminal law. This means that abusers are unlikely to be prosecuted for emotional, verbal, psychological and economic abuse and even minor physical abuse although all of these are recognized as forms of domestic violence.

As with the protection order, attitudes of prosecutors, judges and magistrates to domestic violence also emerge as problems. Human Rights Watch reported that prosecutors drop domestic violence charges easily and, when they follow through on cases, treat them less seriously than other cases.[85] Many judges and magistrates were found to apply stereotypes and gender bias to their decisions in the cases.[86] All of this increases women's secondary victimization as well as their belief that the legal system cannot help them.

Finally, unless the abuser is locked away for the duration of the trial and then imprisoned (if convicted), laying criminal charges could be dangerous for the woman. If left at home, there is nothing to stop the abuser from hurting the woman, because she dared go to the police, or coercing her into dropping the charges.[87] Knowing this, victims often are reluctant to press charges against their abusers.

(i) The role of the police
The implementation of the Domestic Violence Act and the pursuit of criminal charges depend in large part on the police, who are typically the first step for an abuse victim who seeks a legal remedy. It is often thought that the police and the legal system can always protect an abuse victim, but, as is the case in other parts of the world, the police often cannot, or choose not to help abuse victims.[88]

When a woman approaches the police about an incident of violence, the police are obliged to inform her of her legal remedies. Importantly, the DVA obliges the police to help her locate shelters for abused women.[89] It also requires them to help the woman retrieve her property from her home, as well as assist her in finding medical treatment.[90] The police must "render such assistance to the complainant as may be required in the circumstances,"[91] which means police should no longer be able to ignore domestic violence.

For criminal cases or cases in which the abuser breaches a protection order, the police are responsible for taking statements from the victim and witnesses. They help the victim complete an affidavit regarding the abuse. They are responsible for opening a docket, investigating the victim's allegations and arresting the abuser. If the police believe the woman is in danger, they do not need a warrant before arresting him.[92] With regard to protection orders, the police are also responsible for serving a notice of a hearing and for serving the order on the abuser.[93]

(ii) Problems with implementation of that role
While in theory the police have the power to assist an abused woman effectively in her quest to stop the violence, in practice they often do not utilize these powers. One of the main reasons for this failure is lack of resources. Although the DVA places obligations on the police, the government does not allocate enough resources to ensure they can meet their responsibilities.[94] One of the more serious resource obstacles is lack of vehicles. When women cannot afford the sheriff's service fees, the police may be required to serve a protection order on the abuser before it will be activated. Any delay in service leaves the victim relatively unprotected. Research highlighted delays in this service that range from 1 day to 4 months.[95] The Independent Complaints Directorate (ICD) reported to Parliament in 2001 that protection orders were left to pile up in police stations waiting to be served. In fact, in the last six months of

2000, the ICD received 115 reports that the police did not fulfil their obligations under the DVA.[96]

Another major obstacle to women's access to justice is police attitudes towards domestic violence and its victims. As already described, police often do not take domestic violence claims seriously, which leads them to investigate abuse with little enthusiasm.[97] They prioritize calls based on what they view to be the seriousness of the violence: "If they tell us that there is a serious domestic violence incident where the woman is bleeding and thrown out of the house, that [would] be important to respond to… but if they (police dispatchers) simply say "domestic violence", that is not necessarily enough for us to prioritise [the call]."[98] This finding emphasizes that women who anticipate violence and wish to pre-empt it may well be ignored.

Many police hold sexist stereotypes of domestic violence. They empathize with the abuser, leaving them little sympathy for the victim. In fact, a high rate of domestic violence has been reported among the police.[99] Parenzee *et al* conclude that progressive legislation combined with unprogressive attitudes among law enforcement agents creates these negative attitudes.[100] Without resources to train police to deal with domestic violence, these negative attitudes remain unchallenged.

These problems are magnified in rural areas. Artz interviewed 196 abused women from 15 rural communities in the southern Cape. She documented that women who seek police assistance in these communities are subjected to inappropriate responses or not assisted at all. Women who approached the police were met with disbelieving attitudes and were discouraged from laying charges.[101] Sixty-seven per cent of the interviewees indicated that they had difficulty convincing the police they were in danger or in need of protection. Over 80% of the women reported having to wait for a lengthy period before being assisted; 34% were told to stop wasting police time; 26% were accused of provoking the violence; and 39% were accused of lying. Further, 43% were told they provided insufficient evidence to lay charges,[102] while 20% were told they could not bring charges unless they had an interdict to stop the abuse.[103] Bearing in mind that the police typically are women's first recourse to formal legal remedies, unsympathetic, obstructive and hostile attitudes may prevent women from continuing to seek help from the criminal justice system.

These negative views of the police have been entrenched for a long time. Excerpts from a South African Police Service Submission to the Police Board in 1994 highlight this:

- "It is a world-wide belief that the police should not interfere or become involved in household disputes. The rationale behind this relates to law enforcement as the primary function of the police – and law can only be enforced when someone lodges a criminal complaint with the police. Once involved in household disputes, the police are blamed for interfering in private matters.
- The priorities of policing are determined by the community. Figures of other serious crimes reported to the SAP confirm this fact. More attention has to be devoted to those serious crimes, which are more frequently reported."[104]

A 1999 study also showed that women feared asking police for assistance because they feared their partner's violent response and because they "knew" the police would not help them.[105] That women do not always resort to the police in cases of domestic violence has also been found by other studies. Fewer than half (46%) of the 1000 women interviewed for the national survey by Rasool *et al* reported the most serious incident of abuse they experienced to the police.[106] Unless and until police attitudes towards domestic violence and its victims change and police receive proper resources to implement the DVA, women will not consider the police a viable option for escaping abuse.

Finally, the historically racialized distribution of services also affects the nature and extent of help available to women living in violent circumstances. As a consequence of the Group Areas Act, in 1994 for instance, 74% of the country's police stations were located in white suburbs or business districts.[107]

(iii) Why women drop charges
Women drop criminal charges against their abusers for a variety of reasons. First, they may still care for their partners and be hopeful of their capacity for change. The prospect of arrest and prosecution often encourages much remorse in abusive men along with promises to change – if only given another chance. As was highlighted earlier, many members of South African society strongly encourage women to remain

in their relationships out of duty to their families. Secondly, women may be reluctant to utilize legal remedies that could result in their partner's imprisonment, particularly in those cases where the abuser is the sole breadwinner. Thirdly, if the process fails, complainants may be even more vulnerable to their vengeful partners. Rather than risk failure, they withdraw the charges. A fourth reason is that abusers intimidate or emotionally manipulate women into dropping the charges. Thus without the necessary support, the emotional and financial demands of the legal process often prove overwhelming and complainants withdraw their applications.[108]

(iv) Conclusion

A closer look at the implementation of the Domestic Violence Act by the police and courts and the prosecution of criminal charges for assault, or breach of a protection order, underscores that the South African legal system and law enforcement do little to help women stop abuse. This information explains that a woman who expects an attack but is not in the middle of one is not guaranteed police assistance. If the abuse is persistent, it is not guaranteed that she will obtain a protection order and have it properly implemented before the next incident of abuse. Confronted with prejudice and other obstacles, women are victimized again by a system that claims to help them. The Constitutional Court recognized these weaknesses when it wrote:

> "The ineffectiveness of the criminal justice system in addressing family violence intensifies the subordination and helplessness of the victims. This also sends an unmistakable message to the whole of society that the daily trauma of vast numbers of women counts for little. The terrorisation of individual victims is thus compounded by a sense that domestic violence is inevitable. Patterns of systemic sexist behaviour are normalised rather than combated. Yet it is precisely the function of constitutional protection to convert misfortune to be endured into injustice to be remedied."[109]

All this information helps to show why abused women reasonably believe the police or the legal system cannot effectively stop domestic violence. The realities of the process show that the assumption that the justice system can always help an abused woman is patently false.

(d) Health care workers

At a minimum, health care workers are obliged to treat abused women's injuries. But there are other equally important roles they could play in relation to domestic violence. These include identifying and asking about the abuse, providing information about legal remedies and other help and referring women to other service organizations.

Rasool *et al's* national survey suggests that women certainly do turn to health care workers, with 42% of the study sample having sought assistance from health care workers following the most serious incident of abuse experienced.[110] In this study factors which reduced the likelihood of women approaching health facilities included health care workers' lack of respect for women's privacy, unhelpful and blaming attitudes towards those experiencing abuse, as well as the complete absence of facilities – particularly in rural areas – compounded by lack of access to transport.[111]

Health care workers also do not always recognize, or ask, if their patients are being abused. Researchers reviewed 103 records for women they identified as abused at a Mitchell's Plain clinic in the Western Cape, finding that in more than 50% of the cases, the abuse was neither recognized nor documented.[112] A similar finding was made in an analysis of records at Alexandra Clinic, Gauteng. Out of 398 records of all women presenting with a history of assault, the assailant and cause of injury had been recorded in a scant 22% of cases, with 17% of assailants identified as husbands. The term "abused woman" appeared in only one set of records.[113]

Health workers can provide important care and support if they ask about and then address the issue of domestic violence. Their concern and knowledge could result in placing more women in contact with helping agencies, better record-keeping of women's attempts to seek help (which is often relevant in criminal and civil litigation involving domestic violence) and earlier intervention into the problem of domestic violence.

Women do not seem averse to being asked about the presence of domestic violence in their lives. Eighty-seven per cent of 412 women (both abused and non-abused) attending a primary health care clinic in Mitchell's Plain indicated that they would accept clinic staff asking if they were experiencing some form of abuse. Ninety-three per cent thought that social workers should also be investigating the presence of abuse in patients' lives.[114]

(e) Civil society organizations

Findings from the national survey by Rasool et al, referred to earlier, suggested that fewer then half (46%) of women sought counselling after the most serious incident of abuse they experienced. Women in rural areas were less likely to seek such support (38%) compared to women in suburban areas (61%).[115] At least one explanation for this difference once again lies in the lack of facilities available in rural areas, with a counsellor claiming that only 35 lay counsellors able to deal with domestic violence existed in the whole of Mpumalanga province at the time of the interview.[116] Generally, while the absence of services is most stark in rural areas, the number of organizations overall that deal specifically with domestic violence is small.[117]

Domestic violence organizations and shelters generally were first started by white women and were, as a consequence, also located within historically white areas, which effectively placed them out of the reach of the majority of women. With the political shifts initiated in the 1990s, this situation began changing as black women started setting up township-based organizations. However, many of these organizations remain disadvantaged by their struggle for funds and other resources.[118]

Government social workers do not necessarily fill the gap in counselling services either, with some studies suggesting that such social workers may see the administration of grants and pensions as their primary concern.[119] Further, social workers' interventions have traditionally concentrated on child abuse, viewing domestic violence as a peripheral concern.[120] These agencies have typically referred women to the police rather than providing direct assistance[121] (although this situation is starting to change).

There is also no guarantee that either government social workers or civil society organizations will be any better informed about domestic violence than the criminal justice system. These forms of assistance may also hold women responsible for the violence: "They are told by professionals, family, friends and the batterer that alcohol or drugs causes battering. They are told that they are codependent or enable his behavior – if they would change, then their assailants would."[122] Each of these responses further isolates abused women and potentially reinforces the belief that others cannot be relied upon for help.

Another important service offered by civil society is shelters to which abused women and children can flee to escape the violence. Shelter services range from providing material necessities to counselling, legal advice, skills development and employment programmes. Shelters typically house women for between one and six months.

Despite the importance of this mechanism for the protection of abuse victims, civil society rather than government provides most of this type of assistance.[123] Shelters are a relatively new phenomenon in South Africa, the majority of which were built after 1990.[124] They are typically clustered in urban areas, making them inaccessible to women in rural areas. In 2000 there were a scant 25 shelters countrywide with only two shelters located in rural areas.[125] The longer-term shelters, which house women for 3–6 months, have long waiting lists and limited capacity.

The Domestic Violence Act obligates police to help an abuse victim locate a shelter. The dearth of shelters however, makes it difficult for the police to comply with this obligation to ensure women's safety. A recent study quoted a police officer expressing frustration with the shelter system:

> "In May we had a domestic violence case and the complainant was taken to a shelter. But they can only stay at the shelter for three months. It is four months since we helped the complainant and her case is still not dealt with by the courts. It is not finalized. This woman is out of the shelter and has moved into the home where the respondent is because she has nowhere else to go."[126]

In the absence of long-term housing and financial assistance, shelters are at best a short-term solution that in the end may result in the woman returning to her abuser.

3. Personal networks: Communities, friends and families

According to the Rasool *et al* survey referred to earlier, the most important personal network for victims of domestic violence is their families, with 60% of women approaching their families for assistance after the most serious abusive incident experienced.[127] Friends were approached for assistance in 43% of cases, and religious leaders on 20% of occasions.[128]

People who have been victimized are very vulnerable to the opinions and judgments of others. While a supportive response may do much to mitigate the impact of the abuse, a blaming or negative response also has the power to compound the original harm.[129] Regrettably, personal networks do not always provide effective support to women or alternatives to escape abuse. Families, friends and community members may simply not know how to help, or may see it as culturally inappropriate to intervene in the abuse. They may also not have the financial means to assist an abused woman and may not be able to provide her with shelter. Concern over whether or not friends will gossip about the abuse may also deter women from speaking to their friends.[130]

Research conducted in South African rural communities highlighted many of these difficulties. In families guided by customary law, the parents of the husband were expected to intervene to stop the violence, as the husband and his family become responsible for the woman upon marriage. Unfortunately, if the in-laws did not view the violence as a problem, they did not intervene.[131] Further, the in-laws often blamed the woman for the violence, stopping her from seeking help again.[132] Women neighbours in the rural communities were unwilling to intervene for fear of reprisals from own husbands or from the abusive man.[133] Men were equally unwilling to intervene, typically because they had little respect for women.[134]

4. Access to economic and tangible resources

The precarious nature of some women's economic circumstances places them in positions where finding and remaining with a male partner may be as much a matter of economic necessity as it is of romantic choice. Consequently, one of the main reasons women provide to explain why they do not leave their abusers is that they do not have the economic means to do so. Without the monetary support of their abusers, even when it is limited through economic abuse, women may find themselves homeless, single parents – often without child care. These challenges are further compounded when women are unemployed or employed in low-paying work. UNICEF has described this relationship as follows:

> "The link between violence and lack of economic resources and dependence is circular. On the one hand, the threat and fear of violence keeps women from seeking employment, or, at best, compels them to accept low-paid, home-based, exploitive labour. And on the other hand, without economic independence, women have no power to escape from an abusive relationship.

The reverse of this argument also holds true in some countries; that is women's increasing economic activity and independence is viewed as a threat which leads to increased male violence."[135]

Women in South Africa experience high rates of unemployment and poverty.[136] The box below provides some statistical data regarding poverty in South Africa generally, as well as specific data about women. What it points out, in addition to women's greater risk of poverty, is the legacy of apartheid. Black women are the majority of South Africa's poor, with most living in rural areas that have limited access to social and economic opportunities.

- Approximately 65% of all South Africans live below the poverty datum line. Almost all are black. Of these poor, 19 million, or 46% of the total population, live on less than R353 a month.[137]
- Over 60% of households living in rural areas live below the poverty datum line.[138]
- Female-headed households are the most likely to suffer from poverty. This is in large part because these households are more concentrated in rural areas and because of gender discrimination in wage levels.[139] As of 1999, 42% of African households were headed by women.[140]
- 59,3% of employed women earn less than R1600 a month, while 39,94% earn less than R800 per month.[141]
- As of March 2004, South Africa's unemployment rate was 27,8%.[142] Under an expanded definition of unemployment, the rate is 41,2%. The official rate of unemployment of women breaks down as follows: 38,2% of black women are unemployed; 19,6% of coloured women; 21,3% of Indian/Asian women and 6,4% of white women.[143]
- Between 1996 and 2001, the number of unemployed women increased by more than 1 million.[144]

African women's entrapment may be further exacerbated by South African customary law, which also protects men's control over wealth and property, often to the detriment of women. Typically, a woman married under customary law can access property and wealth only through her husband.[145] Other than her personal clothing, customary law treats all marital property as the property of the husband.[146] Customary law expects the husband to protect his family and use this wealth for their benefit. In fact until the Recognition of Customary Marriages Act (No 120 of 1998) was passed, African women were treated as legal minors under customary law (see s 6 of the Act). In cases of domestic violence, it is unlikely that an abusive husband will give his wife resources so she can leave him. A woman who chooses to divorce her husband and was married after the date the Recognition of Customary Marriages Act went into effect (November 2001) will have the marital property fall under community of property. Marriages completed prior to the date of the Act, however, continue to be governed by customary law, which effectively turns over all marital property to the husband.[147]

Despite ample evidence of the link between domestic violence and poverty, South Africa does not provide direct financial assistance to poor and/or abused women. Because many women are unemployed, they cannot benefit from unemployment insurance. (All employed women do not benefit either; only recently has unemployment insurance been extended to domestic workers.) Women's status as poor does not directly qualify them for non-contributory welfare aid. Instead, they receive it as "primary caregivers" of young children, or because they are disabled or because they are elderly.[148] Although these grants are helpful, they draw attention to the bias that favours gender roles – women receive welfare assistance because of their status as mothers and caregivers, while men receive benefits primarily because they are employed and have 'earned' them. Poor women without children or who do not care for elderly relatives are almost completely excluded from financial assistance.

Women who live in remote areas and qualify for the grants often are not informed of them or have trouble accessing them.[149] Until April 2005 when the age was increased to 14, child support grants lasted only until the child turned 7, which further limited women's access to financial aid. Poor women are at heightened risk of economic dependence on the perpetrators of abuse and therefore are more likely to become trapped in the relationship.

It should be noted that some victims of domestic violence work outside the home. Some are educated and/or are financially independent of their abusive partners. Economic independence alone does not mean an abused woman can successfully leave the relationship, as all the other reasons why women do not leave continue to apply to them. It is a myth to believe that because a woman is educated and/or financially independent that she can always leave her abuser.[150]

(a) Private maintenance: Direct relief from the abuser
Some degree of financial assistance could be provided to victims of domestic violence by the abuser. This section details the options for assistance and any limitations to assistance that the abuser could be forced to provide. As this section will show, forcing the abuser to pay some form of maintenance to his victim requires going to court, which involves a potentially lengthy court process and assumes the abuser has the means to support the victim.

(i) Emergency financial assistance under the DVA
The DVA allows courts to compel the abuser to financially support the victim and her children as part of the protection order. This provision is particularly important for women's short-term interests. Unfortunately, police and the judiciary often misunderstand this provision, assuming instead that women must apply for maintenance under the Maintenance Act.[151] Magistrates also are reluctant to grant monetary relief without a full hearing on the means and expenses of the parties, which again leads them to push women towards seeking a maintenance order rather than relief under the DVA.[152] Finally, this measure works only if the abuser has the financial capability to pay the support.

(ii) Maintenance order under the Maintenance Act
In addition to emergency monetary relief provided for by the DVA, a woman may apply for a maintenance order under the Maintenance Act 99 of 1998 when an abuser has a legal duty to support her.[153] The legal duty of support between spouses and between parents and children arises under the common law.[154] The Maintenance Act does not create a legal duty of support between domestic partners or intimate partners who are not cohabitating, because the common law does not.[155] This means that an order can only be granted if the following conditions are met: abuser and victim are spouses or in a parental relationship and the abuser has the means to provide financial assistance.

A woman applies to a magistrate's court for a maintenance order. Once an application is made, a maintenance officer investigates the claim and summons the abuser to court.[156] After a hearing, the magistrate may issue the maintenance order requiring the abuser to pay periodic amounts of support, including additional amounts for child support.[157] If the abuser refuses, the woman may apply for a garnishee order, a warrant of execution against property (only in certain circumstances), or an order for the attachment of the abuser's debt.[158] The abuser also may be charged criminally for violating the order and, if convicted, could be fined or imprisoned.[159]

As with the protection order, women encounter many practical difficulties in utilising this option, such as long waits in court, uncooperative and inadequately trained clerks, difficulty obtaining the abuser's income statement and/or tracing an abuser who has absconded.[160] Research also suggests that some courts may well be awarding women amounts primarily based on what men are willing to pay, rather than on what they or their children need.[161]

Further, given that maintenance payments provide abusive men with yet another avenue for control (by failing to pay regularly, or not paying at all), some women choose not to seek maintenance in order to prevent further violence from their abusive partners.[162]

(iii) Maintenance order under the Divorce Act
A court may order one spouse to pay the other maintenance following a divorce or as an interim measure until the divorce and property distribution are finalized. Under the Divorce Act 70 of 1979, a court may determine the amount of maintenance owed based in part on the conduct of the spouses that led to divorce; presumably this means that domestic violence could be a relevant factor for a court to consider when ordering maintenance.[163] This option suffers from the same practical difficulties as maintenance orders outside of divorce.

5. Conclusion

This chapter has identified a range of factors forming the context in which battered women make decisions. It suggests that the ideal or optimal set of conditions necessary for assisting women to either stop the violence or successfully leave their partners include: a social milieu that condemns abuse; an effective, functioning criminal justice system which can be relied upon promptly to protect battered women's safety; service providers who enquire about the source of battered women's injuries or emotional distress; easy access to a wide range of readily available services – particularly in emergency situations; ready access to alternative accommodation and long-term housing; independent means and economic resources or, where these do not exist, government social security schemes; supportive family, friends and work colleagues; and service providers always intolerant of abusive conduct. As this chapter shows, the happy coincidence of all these factors in individual women's lives is anything but guaranteed.

While important efforts have been made by both government departments and non-governmental organizations to combat domestic violence, these remedies have met with mixed success in their implementation. Sometimes this is the consequence of having laws implemented by people who adhere to socio-cultural values and beliefs that blame women for abuse; at other times it may be the result of having too few, under-resourced, ill-trained and overworked personnel trying to do too much. Too few services, requiring rural women in particular to travel great physical distances, present yet another obstacle to women's help-seeking.

The effect of these barriers alone is considerable, before one has even begun to take into account how abusers respond to women's help-seeking, and the effects of battering upon women.

* * *

TO LEAVE, TO STAY, OR SEEK ASSISTANCE: THE STORY OF ANNE RIBERTS

The events of Anne Riberts' life over nearly two decades within an abusive relationship clearly depict the complexities surrounding decisions to leave, to stay, to return or to seek assistance. She did all of these throughout her three stormy marriages to the same man, who systematically abused her, psychologically, emotionally and physically. Her story also highlights the importance of access to support services. Because she was able to access support services, her abusive relationship had a very different outcome from that of women who kill their abusive partners. However, it also shows the difficulties women have in obtaining assistance from police, the courts and other social services.

Anne Riberts married Keith Bennett three times, in December 1976, December 1985 and June 1992. Three children were born of these marriages. She returned to him over and over again, "for the sake of the children."

Her relationship with her husband was always violent, but began seriously to disintegrate in mid-1995. In June 1996, he raped her repeatedly throughout one night. She laid a charge of rape against him but, when she went to the South

African Police Services (SAPS) Peace Office for an interdict against him, she was refused one. "I was told that I could not have an interdict because we were still living in the same house. The police informed him of this charge and he became violent against me. I moved out of my house the same day," she says.

In November 1996 he was acquitted on the rape charge. This was what Riberts had come to expect. Over the nearly two decades she was with him, she had laid many charges against him and he was always acquitted by the courts. In fact the only time the courts found him guilty was when he stabbed her and her sister with a carving knife: for this he was given a suspended sentence.

Fortunately Riberts had knowledge of shelters and found accommodation at the Nisaa Institute for Women's Development in Lenasia, Johannesburg. From there she moved into a flat. However, Bennett found out where it was and began to harass her and the children. He would come to the flat at any time, night and day, threaten her, demand money and assault her. During this time, he once hit her with a fist on the head, inflicting a wound that required stitches. He cut up her clothing, burnt her possessions and once poured acid over her belongings. He stalked her all the time and, if he could manage, would take her to a deserted place and "kick the living daylights out of me." The assaults were so severe that, according to Riberts, the only thing that went through her mind at that time was the wish to die.

The final and most violent incident occurred one Sunday evening as Riberts ironed the children's clothing for school. Bennett grabbed the iron and burned her on the arm. He raped her four times, then forced her to take an overdose of tablets at knifepoint. He then drove around with her in the boot of his car. Following that, he emptied a 25 litre can of petrol in her house. When he went to the shop to buy matches, Riberts' brothers arrived and found the house doused with petrol and their sister locked in the boot of the car, where she had been half comatose for a full day. She was unable to walk, from being hit with a piece of iron, and needed physiotherapy.

The first interdict she ever got against her husband was in 1997, after nearly twenty years of physical and psychological abuse and numerous court cases. However, even with the interdict, the abuse and harassment did not stop. In January 1999, he broke into her flat, assaulted her with a firearm and raped her. Her youngest son Isidore was in the flat at the time. Again, Bennett was acquitted. Finally, in February 2001 he went to her home and assaulted her, injuring her very badly, and shot her friend. For this he was charged with attempted murder, assault with grievous bodily harm (GBH), and possession of an unlicensed firearm and ammunition.

The Nisaa Institute took up the case and lobbied and mobilised on her behalf, bringing the case into the public domain. Other women's organisations joined the campaign to challenge the judicial system and it grew bigger and bigger, with letters of complaint being written to various government departments and a petition drawn up and circulated to enlist support. The case went onto national television.

As a result of the campaign, Riberts finally got justice. Bennett received a prison sentence, which he is currently serving.

According to Riberts, it was receiving support that enabled her finally to leave and gave her the courage to agree to go public through the campaign, thus highlighting the plight of women in her situation, and ensuring that her abuser would be sentenced. "Nisaa has always assisted me with the problems I had with Keith. When I was in the shelter the social worker would counsel me after hours when I was depressed. I was very suicidal and tried to commit suicide on many occasions. They provided protection when I had to go to court, because he is very violent and wants to assault me whenever he sees me, no matter where and when," she said.

Reference: Adapted from the story told by Anne Riberts to the Nisaa Institute for Women's Development, Lenasia

* * *

CHAPTER 2

Psycho-social explanations for the impact of abuse

Contents	Page
Suffer the little children: The story of Thembi	50
A. UNDERSTANDING THE BEHAVIOUR OF ABUSIVE MEN	53
1. Typologies	54
2. Leaving or ending relationships	58
B. DOMESTIC VIOLENCE AND ITS EFFECTS UPON WOMEN	60
1. Battered Women's Syndrome (BWS) and The cycle of violence	62
2. Coercive Control	67
(a) Methods and techniques of coercive control	68
(b) The process of Stockholm Syndrome/Traumatic bonding	73
3. Post-Traumatic Stress Disorder (PTSD) and Complex PTSD	75
4. Conclusion	77
No way out: The story of Anieta Ferreira	78
Annexure: Biderman's Chart of Coercion	79

SUFFER THE LITTLE CHILDREN:
THE STORY OF THEMBI

Thembi's story highlights the sad reality for children in cases where the mother is convicted and imprisoned for the murder of the father. Children often experience far-reaching psychological effects from this tragedy, as well as the trauma inflicted by the abuse they have experienced or observed.

Pule, a police officer, started assaulting Thembi's mother Tshidi regularly when Thembi was just four years old. He had already stopped Tshidi from working outside the home, discouraged her from visiting other people or from having friends. Pule had many extra-marital affairs, which did not bother Tshidi at first. But when he began bringing his mistresses home, using the spare bedroom, it did. Once she came home to find Pule in bed with his mistress. When she confronted him with it, he assaulted her. Pule did not confine his abuse to his wife. Thembi and her brothers received regular doses of physical and emotional abuse too.

The children witnessed their father threatening to shoot their mother with his service revolver. He once hit her so hard with the butt of his gun, on her head and across her face, that she needed stitches. She reported the violence to Pule's station commander. He would talk to Pule and sometimes confiscate his service pistol. Pule would then beg Tshidi to tell the station commander that he was behaving and it was safe to return his pistol to him. Then the abusive behaviour began all over again.

There were times when Thembi's mother had to flee her home for safety, often taking her children with her because they were also in danger. All the abuse and humiliation left Thembi's mother emotionally devastated. She was treated with a range of anti-depressants and other medications and was not always able to be the mother that her children needed. While still barely a teenager, Thembi was propelled into adult responsibilities. She managed the entire household, including cooking and cleaning, as well as doing her father's laundry and ironing when her mother could not.

Thembi felt powerless to help her mother when the beatings began. She and her brothers would scream in distress, often bringing neighbours to their assistance. When she was thirteen Thembi began having seizures that left her unconscious whenever she witnessed the domestic abuse or experienced stress. She too received both medical and traditional care. A doctor diagnosed her with epilepsy. The beatings she received were also severe. On one occasion Thembi's father assaulted her so badly she was hospitalised and missed her exams. Not surprisingly, her school performance declined, causing concern on the part of the teachers. At the age of fifteen Thembi was diagnosed with depression and somatisation. Her young and traumatic journey through life was made harder because she did not have many friends.

When Thembi was sixteen, the violence towards her mother became worse. Thembi's father shot at her mother and started threatening to sell their home and send them all to his parents in the rural area so that he could start a new life with another woman. Thembi's mother was not willing to go. It would mean further financial hardship and abuse. Pule's family had already assaulted Tshidi once. Tshidi's parents said she and her children were her in-law's responsibility. Tshidi had nowhere to go. She approached a man to help her kill her husband. Pule was shot that weekend; Tshidi was arrested later that week and remains in prison.

On Tshidi's imprisonment, life for Thembi and her brothers fell apart further. Her paternal relatives took her brothers away to live in a rural area. Thembi did not see them for three years: when she did, she was distressed at their deprived condition. Her paternal relatives blamed her for helping her mother to murder her father and refused to have anything to do with her. Her maternal relatives did the same. Thembi, at sixteen years old, feeling insecure and totally isolated, was left to fend for herself. Her paternal relatives took all the family's belongings. She was left homeless, without a support system and separated from her siblings.

Since her mother's imprisonment, Thembi has not had a fixed place to stay, but has been living with friends, acquaintances and her maternal uncle. Having no money to offer towards her upkeep, she has had to keep moving on – in the three years since her mother's imprisonment she has had to change her living arrangements at least ten times. Thembi was at the mercy of other people for accommodation and as a result she was sexually abused by different people with whom she lived, who used her inability to pay for her lodging as an excuse. Having no stable home severely disrupted her schooling. On top of that her peers teased her because she had no place to stay and was an "orphan" whose mother had killed her father.

Her paternal relatives squandered the maintenance due to her from her father's estate. When she was older and enquired about the money, they threatened to kill her. She had to leave school, as she could not afford all its costs. Feeling cheated in life, Thembi talks bitterly about how deprived and envious she felt of other girls her age.

Like Tshidi, Thembi became a teenage mother. Now 21 years old, she lives with the stresses of being young, single, unemployed and without support of any kind. Her baby's father has absconded. She worries about her brothers. She misses her mother and wishes Tshidi could be released so they could be a family again, no matter how difficult it would be. Visits to the prison don't occur often and are hard. They cost money and, despite the happiness of seeing her mother, leave Thembi very depressed.

Living with deep insecurity and deprivation in all facets of her life, Thembi is severely depressed, has poor self-esteem and often thinks of committing suicide. She has tried twice, once by hanging and the other time by overdosing on pills.

Reference: "Now we have Nothing" Exploring the impact of material imprisonment on children whose mothers killed an abusive partner. By Kailash Bhana and Tessa Hochfeld, the Centre for the Study of Violence and Reconciliation.

* * *

Living in an abusive relationship is an extraordinary experience. Not only must battered women seek ways of coping in a context in which the person who supposedly loves them most is also the person who harms them the most but they must also take the blame both for causing such injury to themselves and for failing to stop it. They may be stigmatized for airing private problems, yet condemned for staying silent. They are expected to leave at the first sign of abuse, but also to keep their families together and stand by their men. These paradoxes must also be resolved within a context in which they are often literally helpless – in the sense of being bereft of help – and confronted with the indifference and judgments of others.

This chapter sets out the variety of coping strategies that women employ in their endeavours to make sense of the profoundly abnormal experience of domestic violence, and also describes the psychological consequences of living with such mistreatment. It begins by explaining something of the mindset of abusers before setting out the dominant psycho-social theories explaining women's responses to abuse. It starts with what is probably the best-known theory – Battered Women's Syndrome – before outlining coercive control theories and Post-Traumatic Stress Disorder. Most of these theories show that battered women do not suffer from bizarre and unique psychological disorders.

They illustrate instead how much the coping behaviours they rely on have in common with the coping strategies of those who have been traumatized generally.

This chapter is particularly important because it answers many common questions, including why women do not leave their abusers. It also explains why women reasonably fear their abusers and why they can predict their abuser's behaviour, including the next incident of violence. All of these explanations inform the elements of criminal defences and sentence mitigation on behalf of abused women who kill, which will be described in Part 2 of the book.

A. UNDERSTANDING THE BEHAVIOUR OF ABUSIVE MEN

The next stage in understanding domestic violence, and one typically missing from trials of women who kill their abusers, is an explanation of why men abuse. Once practitioners understand the goals of abuse, they can better understand women's reactions to it. The most important point to extract from this section is violent men's need to control, psychologically and physically, their victims' use of space and time – indeed "to annihilate their wives' self-esteem, to enslave them psychologically."[164] This information begins to show why many abusers are unable to accept their partners' leaving and go to great lengths to ensure they remain in the relationship (unless, of course, the abuser has decided the woman should leave).

The unequal nature of power in relationships between men and women plays an important role in laying the groundwork for abuse. Violence often begins when men perceive that their wives are challenging the authority expected in traditional male gender roles.[165] Thus research with South African men who admit to treating their partners abusively shows that many of these conflicts arise through men's attempts to control their women and their sexuality, as well as the household.[166] Sixty-nine per cent of men in one study said conflicts began when the woman "sat" on his head,[167] 63% when she answered him back and 71% when he drank alcohol. Her suspicion that he was having affairs was the source of 63% of violent episodes, while conflicts over children initiated 68% of conflicts.[168]

Some men learn these gender roles from their own family experiences. Abusive men often grow up in traditional models of the family, where the father is the breadwinner and the mother responsible for the home and the children.[169] One study that researched men's perception of their violence recorded the impact of their family upbringing, noting: "Traditionally gendered roles are not surprising, but in the context of men's domestic violence they become the structural bedrock from which boys develop a sense of their own entitlement in relation to women as partners and mothers."[170] Thus in the hands of abusive men, traditional gender roles are distorted or used as an excuse to justify abuse.

Further, 75% of the men who participated in the study had been abused during the course of punishment as a child.[171] The most violent of these men were the ones who both witnessed parental violence and suffered from child abuse.[172] Through family socialization, some men learn to use violence as a method of dealing with conflict. Thus in some instances, the seeds of violent conduct are sown long before any violent confrontation between husband and wife.

Traditional views of masculinity also seem to influence some men's socialization towards domestic violence. In one study, men described how difficult it was for them to express vulnerability, sadness and fear, while it was acceptable and easy for them to express anger.[173] The researchers concluded: "It is evident . . . that many of these men as boys were thrust into a hierarchical, competitive and physical culture which significantly impacted on their views of women, their own roles as husbands and fathers and which nurtured their propensity to resort to violence in certain circumstances."[174]

1. Typologies

There is no one type or "profile" of abuser. Depending on their theoretical orientation, different studies categorize abusers differently. Nonetheless, there is a good deal of overlap between their various typologies.

Based on the degree of violence they perpetrate, researcher Edward Gondolf has distinguished four basic types of abuser:

- Type I batterers are rare (comprising 5% of Gondolf's survey) and described as "sociopathic." They inflict the most severe injuries, may also sexually abuse both their wives and children, seriously abuse drugs and/or alcohol and also have a long arrest record.

- Type II batterers were described as "antisocial" and made up 32% of Gondolf's study. While also severely violent, they did not inflict as vicious a level of violence, but were also most likely to use weapons.
- Type III batterers, making up 30% of the sample, were designated "chronic batterers." They subjected their victims to significant amounts of abuse (although not to the same degree of injury) and were less likely to have used weapons during their assaults.
- Type IV's (33% of the study) battered their partners sporadically. They engaged in the least severe physical and verbal abuse and also did so least frequently. According to Gondolf, the victims of such abusers were the most likely to return as well as the least likely to resort to the police.[175]

Dutton's typology of abusive men shares some similarities with Gondolf's. Dutton proposes three different groupings of abusers: the over-controlled-dependent, the instrumental-antisocial (he includes men described as psychopaths within this group) and impulsive-borderline abusers.[176] Over-controlled-dependent men experience chronic frustration and resentment but deny their rage. They attempt to avoid conflict until the accumulation of unexpressed emotions erupts into violence. Because of the rigid control this group maintains, violence tends to be less frequent.[177]

The remaining two categories of abusive men act out their feelings frequently.

The impulsive-borderline category of abusers responds spontaneously to building inner tension that they cannot express, exploding into sudden and violent rages. Impulsive abusers typically are violent in domestic relationships only. Dutton describes some of their typical behavioural and emotional traits as: "withdrawn, asocial, moody, hypersensitive to perceived slights, volatile and over-reactive, calm and controlled one moment and extremely angry and oppressive the next - a type of "Jekyll and Hyde" personality."[178] Another aspect of their "Jekyll and Hyde" conduct is the charming and pleasant facade they present in public which disguises the violence and abuse they exhibit towards their partners in private – often making it difficult for outsiders to believe the abuse.[179] It is this category of men who go through battering cycles, which include a period of tension build-up, sudden violence, followed by reconciliation with the victim. This research comports with Lenore Walker's description of the cycle of violence described later.[180]

This category of men also suffers from severe rejection anxiety. They are irrationally jealous and fear their partners will abandon them. Although highly dependent upon their intimate partners, they are unwilling to admit their dependency, expressing it instead through controlling actions designed to ensure the woman's constant availability. Further, perceiving their dependency as weakness, they also harbour strong feelings of resentment and anger towards their partner due to her perceived power over them.

In contrast, the instrumental-antisocial abusers use violence coldly, as a means to an end. This category is known for "narcissistic entitlement and psychopathic manipulativeness,"[181] meaning that they threaten or act violently towards anyone who does not fulfil their demands.[182] They are less likely to bond with their intimate partner, instead treating relationships as expendable.[183] They report more frequent and severe violence than the impulsive group.[184]

Based on how abusers describe their violence, researchers in Australia categorize abusers into two different groups – tyrannical and exploder. Tyrannical abusers use violence as a method of control, giving them the means to ensure that they get what they want: "In describing their violence, there was a sense that these men knew what they were doing and they intended to frighten, intimidate and punish. They saw their violence as a justified or understandable response to frustration and anger."[185] For this group, violence is one of many tactics they use for control.

Attempts to respond to tyrants place women in a no-win situation. If they behave submissively and "walk on eggshells" to avoid conflict, they ultimately reinforce the abuser's behaviour, teaching him that he can control his intimate partner through violence and other techniques.[186] Once this type of relationship is established, the abuser need not resort to violence to control his partner, the threatened possibility of violence is enough to control her.[187] But should women attempt to stand up to the control tactics, the men then explode violently.[188]

Exploders act impulsively when they mentally and physically abuse their intimate partners. They typically explode in response to perceptions that they are being criticised, or that their authority is being challenged.[189] They use violence to stop what they experience as unpleasant situations, explaining that they explode when their partners ignored their warnings to "back off".[190] Despite the descriptions of the abuse as impulsive, researchers believe that this violence "is something that can be explored, understood and predicted."[191] Relationships with an exploder are "characterized by high levels of conflict, partner violence, alcohol abuse by either or both partners and symmetrical escalation."[192]

Precisely because of the fear it instils in the minds of its victims, the "uncontrollable" rage abusers exhibit is an effective tool for controlling others. Thomas Schelling, writing about conflict generally, describes such outbursts as the "paradox of irrationality", pointing to how strategic displays of irrationality can influence others to behave in ways they would otherwise resist.[193]

In a study in which researchers witnessed the arguments of their subjects, researchers concluded that although they could not predict when violence in battering relationships would occur, they were able to identify warning signs. The warning signs involved the abuser's belligerence and contempt for his partner combined with efforts to control or dominate her.[194] Importantly this research substantiates the point that women can anticipate violence through warning signs peculiar to their abusers.

Jacobson and Gottman categorize abusers as either pit bulls or cobras. Pit bulls suffer from a slow burn of anger which builds into a violent explosion. They have contempt for their partners but generally depend on them; they are torn between scorn and neediness.[195] As their name suggests, they are unable to let go, display high levels of jealousy and are tenacious in their attempts to keep their partners by their side. Further, a pit bull's anger is characterized by control:

> "Through this scrutiny and these constant demands, Pit Bulls establish control. Control is important to these men because they genuinely feel that they will be abandoned if they do not maintain constant vigilance over their wives."[196]

Cobras, in contrast to pit bulls, are far calmer and in control of their violence. Although they escalate to violence rapidly, the escalation is a dominance and intimidation technique to gain control quickly.[197] The vast majority of cobras examined in the research suffered from antisocial personality disorder.[198] Violence appears to have a calming effect on some of this group, who are violent in non-domestic relationships as well.[199]

Regardless of how abusive men are categorized, however, they generally underestimate the severity of their violence, as well as its frequency.[200] On their accounts violence is "a mystery that just happens,"[201] which is either "forgotten", or treated as a minor event, usually justified by something she did. Explanations for the violence are manipulated in such a way as to present the men as moral enforcers, merely acting to ensure that their female partners toe the line and behave like "proper", "good" women.[202]

Abusive men in general are often unable to express their physical, sexual and emotional needs (being aware only of sensations of unease or unhappiness), but nonetheless expect their partners to anticipate, identify and satisfy that which they themselves are unable to articulate. Punishment for failing to anticipate, interpret and fulfil these needs then follows.[203]

The psychological process of projection offers a useful means of understanding how abusers come to see their partners as deserving of abuse. Projection is a way to disown or rid one's self of unacceptable feelings and impulses by denying such thoughts in oneself and identifying them in, or projecting them onto another. (One simple example of this process at work is the abusive man who regularly has sex outside his relationship but is pre-occupied with imagining that it is actually his partner who is unfaithful and untrustworthy.) In this way, abusers rid themselves of feeling of weakness, fear and self-contempt, by seeing them in the victim who can now be despised and condemned for being such a pitiful and inadequate character.[204] Feelings of inadequacy and helplessness are masked and a sense of omnipotence created in their stead. This, however, becomes yet another source of abusive men's dependency on their partners. Without her, upon whom else can they project feelings of vulnerability, weakness and helplessness? Who is there to magnify or reflect back to the abuser his omnipotence and control? As Motz puts it, "he must see himself through her eyes and his sense of manhood and power is derived from her devotion to and fear of him."[205]

Ultimately, the one on the receiving end of such projections becomes the equivalent of a sponge absorbing her partner's inadequacies and self-contempt. Her sense of self eroded through ongoing intimidation, threats and abuse, she may ultimately be impelled to feel inadequate and helpless and behave accordingly.[206] When the victim takes on the abuser's projections, this is termed projective identification.

2. Leaving or ending relationships

Given what is at stake – masculine identity, personal privilege and material benefits – the loss of their female partners presents abusive men with something of a crisis. To pre-empt this state of affairs from ever arising, abusive men, particularly those who fear abandonment or who seek total control over their victims, often threaten their victims with further violence or death if they leave. Objectively, these are not empty threats. Research on femicide highlights that "the link between separation and murder is more than incidental: Homicidal husbands are often noted to have threatened to do exactly what they did, should their wives ever leave them and they often explain their homicides as responses to the intolerable stimulus of the wife's departure."[207] US and Canadian studies of men who kill their intimate partners have shown that the predominant reason for killing was that their partner left them or intended to leave.[208] Most of the killings occurred within the first year after separation.[209]

South African data also highlights how dangerous leaving may be for some women. One study, which analysed 941 police, court and mortuary records for the period 1990–1999 in the province of Gauteng, found leaving to be the second most-common reason why women were killed by their intimate partners. The most common context in which women were murdered involved struggles over women's sexual choices and behaviours (which typically revolved around men's jealous suspicions that their partners were being unfaithful).[210]

Certain factors increase the risk that an abuser will kill his intimate partner, including:

- If the abuser has threatened to kill himself, his partner, children, or her relatives.
- If the abuser has fantasies of homicide or suicide.
- Whether the abuser owns weapons, has threatened to use them or has used them.
- If the abuser believes he owns his victim: "A batterer who believes he is absolutely entitled to his female partner, her services, her obedience and her loyalty, no matter what, is likely to be life-endangering."
- If the abuser is dependent on the victim, having made her central to his life.[211]

Evidence that any of these factors existed could bolster a woman's claim that she feared her abuser would kill her.

In addition to death, women have good reason to fear harassment, stalking or further emotional or physical abuse if they try to leave:

"Many domestic violence victims who do leave their abusive partners spend the rest of their lives 'trying to avoid men fanatically dedicated to pursuing them or even killing them.' It is estimated that at least half of the woman who leave their abusive partners are followed or harassed as a result."[212]

The Canadian Department of Justice found that just over half of the criminal harassment charges in Canada were filed by an intimate or ex-intimate partner of the perpetrator.[213] Criminal harassment includes repetitive, unwanted telephone contact, stalking, threats of violence and actual physical violence. The risk of harassment is so great that some experts on domestic violence suggest that stalking and harassment of ex-partners should be considered the fourth step of Walker's cycle of violence, described in the section on Battered Women's Syndrome.[214]

In conclusion, these descriptions of abusers have several themes in common. The first is the importance of control in domestic violence. Some abusers dominate in order to control their building insecurities or other tensions, others use control as a means of getting what they want. Women then come to fear their abusers, often submitting to their control tactics to avoid conflict. When men threaten their partners with violence if they leave, this is another method of control. It is particularly effective since many men who kill do so because their partners have left them. Leaving is therefore not synonymous with safety and does not necessarily end the violence.

The second important theme that emerges from these descriptions of the psychology of abusers is how little the woman's behaviour has to do with their men's violence. The origins or sources of the failures and disappointments for which women are punished often have their roots in situations that occurred long before the couple met.

Thirdly, violent men generally elevate their personal requirements above those of others and are inflexible with regard to them.[215]

B. DOMESTIC VIOLENCE AND ITS EFFECTS UPON WOMEN

Given the nature of domestic violence, there is no single, defining, psychological "profile" of an abused woman. Instead, as the growing body of scientific literature in this field makes clear, there are many diverse "profiles". Abused women will, therefore, not respond identically to abusive circumstances, nor will abusive circumstances have exactly the same effects on all women.

The next section sets out the major theories put forward to explain the nature and effects of domestic abuse. These are:

- Battered Women's Syndrome and the cycle of violence
- Coercive control, including traumatic bonding and Stockholm Syndrome
- Post-traumatic stress disorder (PTSD) and complex post-traumatic stress disorder

Each can be used to explain why some women kill their abusers, although some theories are more useful than others. They are not necessarily mutually exclusive, with some placing their emphasis on methods and techniques employed by abusers and others focusing on the psychological outcomes of trauma. Some of the psycho-social theories apply beyond the battering context and regardless of the victim's gender. These theories highlight how the experience of being at the mercy of another person with the power to enforce his/her will produces a relatively consistent set of behavioural, cognitive and emotional responses. These theories explain that abuse victims are just that – victims – whose primary goal is survival.

Before examining each of these theories, some general points need to be made. First, to understand the psychological impact of domestic violence, it is important to look at the overall pattern of coercive control present in the relationship, rather than specific instances of violence. As Stark puts it:

> "Work with battered women outside the medical complex suggests that physical violence may not be the most significant factor about most battering relationships. In all probability, the clinical profile revealed by battered women reflects the fact that they have been subjected to an ongoing strategy of intimidation, isolation and control that extends to all areas of a woman's life, including sexuality; material necessities; relations with family; children and friends; and work. Sporadic, even severe violence makes this strategy of control effective. But the unique profile of 'the battered

woman' arises as much from the deprivation of liberty implied by coercion and control as it does from violence-induced trauma."[216]

Secondly, the impact of psychological and emotional abuse on women should also not be underestimated. For example, Bollen *et al* reported that 63% of women in their study identify emotional abuse – either by itself or in combination with other types of abuse – as the worst form of abuse they had experienced.[217]

Additionally, while domestic violence does result in serious psychological costs to its victims, this does not mean that abused women are unreasonable, irrational or even "crazy." Indeed, precisely because they live in circumstances where danger and threat are ever-present, this may well encourage the development of "situational reason" or "survivor" logic; their decisions are rational within the context of highly unreasonable behaviour and demands. Under these circumstances it is essential to abused women's survival that they develop a heightened capacity to assess incipient violence, based on their prior experience and increasing familiarity with their partner's "warning" signs and tactics.[218]

Terms such as "syndrome" and "disorder" should also be applied cautiously to abused women. This is the language of pathology, which can serve to make women's responses to domestic violence appear deviant and inexplicable – as if the bizarreness of domestic violence is normal and women's responses to it abnormal. This sort of paradigm keeps practitioners and lay persons from understanding that abused women's responses typically are survival tactics rather than psychological weaknesses. Further, fear of one's partner does not translate into a global inability to assert one's self in all circumstances.[219] Nor does self-esteem diminished within the context of the relationship necessarily translate into a global sense of incompetence. For some women, performing well at work may be an important coping strategy, enabling them to maintain at least some positive beliefs about themselves in the face of the abuser's denigration.

1. Battered Women's Syndrome and the cycle of violence
Battered Women's Syndrome (BWS), identified by psychologist Lenore Walker, is probably the best-known theory put forward to explain the effects of domestic violence.

The cycle of violence identified by Dr Walker concludes that violent relationships are cyclical in nature and consist of three-stages:[220] the tension-building phase (minor abuse); followed by an explosion or a major abusive episode; followed by a "honeymoon" or contrition phase.

The first stage – tension-building – is the period in which the relationship becomes strained and difficult and minor abuse begins. To avoid it, the woman tries to pacify her abuser, showering him with love. The woman grows complaisant to the violence, a complaisance the abuser does not trust. This only increases the tension.

The tension alleviates only after the abuser explodes into violence. In his mind, he either lost control or believed that he was teaching his partner a lesson. He justifies his violence by blaming the victim. In some instances, the abused woman may have precipitated the violence simply to control when the inevitable would happen.

In most cases, following a battering incident, abusers become extremely sorry and apologetic, promising never to repeat their violent behaviour again. They shower their female partners with gifts and attention in order to demonstrate their contrition. This is the honeymoon stage and is often prompted by the woman's attempts to leave or lay charges.

It is within this context of post-violence contrition that the abused woman renews her faith in the basic goodness of the abuser. Consequently, the potential for redemption allows the woman to deny the negative feelings that the abuser arouses in her. Denial is a necessary means of suppressing a counter-productive reaction to something experienced as overwhelming. It also allows the abused woman to be more receptive to the abuser's intermittent expressions of kindness and fuels her hope that the abuser ultimately will change his behaviour. However, it is only a matter of time before the honeymoon stage comes to an end and tension once again begins to escalate.

Walker noted that within this cycle, over time, the battering becomes more severe as the honeymoon period becomes shorter and the tension-building and violent incidents longer.

The effect of this cycle upon women is described as "learned helplessness", a concept derived from behavioural psychologist Martin Seligman's experiments upon dogs. Seligman locked dogs in cages from which they could not escape and administered electric shocks to them. The dogs initially attempted to evade the shocks but once they realised they could not escape, gave up trying to do so – even when the cage doors were opened. Only after the animals were repeatedly dragged to the doors of their cages did they "unlearn" this response.

In the battered woman, "learned helplessness" is used to explain a condition of passivity caused by her recognition that she has no power to stop or escape from her partner's violence.[221] She begins to believe that her violent partner is omnipotent and will thwart her escape efforts. Instead of focusing on changing her circumstances, the victim learns to cope with each incident of abuse separately.[222] She learns to anticipate the abuse and, in so doing becomes hyper-sensitized to her abuser's behaviour. The apathy and helplessness engendered by the abuse makes it difficult and, sometimes impossible, for women to leave their abusers.

Legal practitioners defending abused women who kill have used BWS effectively to explain the following:

- The woman's hyper-sensitivity to her abuser's mood and behaviour allows her to predict accurately when an attack is imminent.[223]
- Abuse can result in a slow-burn of emotions, so that a person acting in provocation may not react suddenly.[224]
- The reasonableness of the abused women's behaviour in killing in a non-confrontational situation.[225]
- Why the abuse victim does not leave her abuser.[226]
- Why the abuse victim does not seek help from the police. [227]
- Why a woman's psychological response is reasonable in the context of abuse.[228]
- That so-called common-sense views of battering are myths.[229] These myths, which the theory has been used to dispel, include:
  - a woman must be a masochist if she stayed in the relationship;[230]
  - the woman provoked the violence and therefore deserved it;[231]
  - if the violence was so severe, the victim would have left her partner, so the abuse must be exaggerated and the accused must lack credibility;[232]
  - reasonable people would not allow themselves to be abused;[233]
  - spousal abuse occurs only among lower socio-economic groups and to women of colour.[234]

Battered Women's Syndrome has, increasingly, come under fire for being anti-feminist, unscientific, and unnecessarily exclusionary. Legal practitioners and women's advocates argue that BWS replaces one set of myths about abuse victims with another. Instead of looking at women's responses to abuse as a normal response to an abnormal situation, the theory treats these women as though they suffer from a psychological disturbance. Rather than treating these women as survivors employing survival skills, they are treated as psychologically disabled. It stereotypes women as passive, emotional, excitable in a minor crisis, dependent, weak, fearful, irrational and gentle.[235] As justices of the Canadian Supreme Court explained:

> "By emphasizing a woman's 'learned helplessness', her dependence, her victimization and her low self-esteem, in order to establish that she suffers from 'battered woman syndrome', the legal debate shifts from the objective rationality of her actions to preserve her own life to those personal inadequacies which apparently explain her failure to flee from her abuser. Such an emphasis comports too well with society's stereotypes about women."[236]

Further, BWS creates the impression that there is only one type of response to domestic violence that all "real" battered women will manifest. Women who do not fit these stereotypes are excluded from BWS, as are women who cannot fit into the narrow definition of learned helplessness.[237] The Wyoming Supreme Court upheld the conviction of a battered woman who killed her abusive husband while he was sleeping, noting:

> "Appellant hardly qualifies for what the literature describes as a battered wife. She was not afraid to contact the police, having done so on five prior occasions. Each time the police came to their residence, there was an argument between the parties over who had done what, who was at fault; and in each instance appellant was enormously drunk."[238]

In effect, "this means that if a woman does not fit into this pattern of violence outlined by Walker, she may not be considered a battered woman, despite her experiences."[239]

In the US both lesbian and African-American women have had the most difficulty using the theory, because they must first counter stereotypes that define them as aggressive before they can prove learned helplessness.[240] In fact, critics argue that BWS was developed based on the experiences of middle-class white women to the exclusion of women of colour and poor women.[241] Learned helplessness also excludes women who resist their abusers and women who are financially independent.[242]

Even more problematic is the belief that lethal self-defence contradicts learned helplessness, which destroys the accused's credibility.[243] However, Browne explains that there is no inconsistency between learned helplessness and a battered woman who kills.[244] Instead of passivity, she engages in lethal violence when she endures an act of abuse that is significantly above what she considers "normal" and thinks it is impossible to survive the next episode of abuse.

BWS also relies on a model of recurring episodes of severe violence,[245] which does not account for ongoing minor acts or other controlling behaviour. Nor does it account for violent responses from abused women who suffer non-physical forms of abuse, even though, in South Africa, these forms of abuse have been accorded legislative recognition as domestic violence. Further, the three-stage cycle of violence described by Walker is certainly not present in all abusive relationships, with South African research suggesting that many men in this study demonstrated neither contrition nor remorse after their abusive behaviour. This study found that only a quarter of women in their sample reported their partners as being apologetic following an incident of violence. Men who were physically abusive were the most likely to respond remorsefully.[246]

The last area of criticism is that BWS is no longer good science and does not respond to new research critical of it. As the Australian High Court said:

> "Critics of the scientific foundation of BWS have described it as having 'no medical legitimacy', as failing to meet established criteria for 'scientific reliability', as being an 'unsubstantial concept' increasingly doubted in United States courts where it originated and likely soon to 'pass from the American legal scene'."[247]

In conclusion, as a description of the trajectory of some violent relationships, Walker's cycle of violence does have use and value. Whether it results in the specific syndrome she describes is more contentious. Indeed, others have suggested that what results from this cycle is not "learned helplessness" but "learned hopefulness" – the belief that the abusive partner will change his personality and behaviour.[248] Finally, as pointed out in the *1998 Manual*:[249]

> "'Learned helplessness' is misinterpreted when it is defined as a mental defect or character flaw. The whole point of learned helplessness as a psychological theory is to remove the stigma of mental defect from the battered woman by emphasizing that the behaviours associated with it developed as an adaptive survival mechanism in response to abuse."

2. Coercive control

The theory of coercive control does not portray battered women as helpless or predisposed to helplessness or docility. Instead it explains that part of the process of coercive control involves destroying, often brutally, her resistance and support mechanisms. It also acknowledges the power of fear in producing behavioural and psychological change.

The origins of coercive control theory lie in the experiences of people who have lived in situations of captivity (such as Holocaust survivors, prisoners of war and political prisoners[250]) or who have been taken hostage and display symptoms of "Stockholm Syndrome"[251] or "traumatic bonding." According to Herman, captivity "brings the victim into prolonged contact with the perpetrator, [and] creates a special type of relationship, one of coercive control."[252] The purposes of such behaviour appear to be twofold: complete control of the victim; and making the victim appear to acquiesce in her domination – for when victims can be made to seem complicit in their subjugation, then abusive behaviour can be justified and its harmful nature disguised.[253] Further, since to outsiders the victim appears accepting of the mistreatment, it may well reduce the likelihood of external assistance being offered.

Situations of coercive control may also produce in the victim what psychoanalyst Anna Freud described as "identification with the aggressor." This term refers to the way those in life-threatening situations come to identify with the person who holds power over them; in effect, trying to see the world through the aggressor's eyes in an attempt to anticipate and ward off danger.

One key difference between abused women and prisoners is that unlike captives, women do not need to be captured or detained within the relationship; they are initially there out of love for their abusive partner. Consequently they may initially be less inclined to resist than other captives because of their commitment to the relationship.[254] However, by the time affection has dwindled, women may have been made captive through economic dependence, physical force and social, psychological and legal subordination.[255] Sometimes they are also literally imprisoned or locked up.[256] Further, it is also likely that physical, sexual and verbal maltreatment by a husband or lover may take on greater significance than when performed by a stranger.[257] Unlike strangers, male partners have the power to be both the most dangerous and the most rewarding person in the woman's life.[258]

(a) Methods and techniques of coercive control
While a variety of methods are used to accomplish control, Herman notes that there is "remarkable consistency" in the methods used by human beings to suppress and control one another.[259] So consistent, in fact, that in 1973, Amnesty International was able to compile a "chart of coercion" describing these methods in detail (see Annexure at the end of this chapter).[260] These behaviours violate victims' fundamental human rights, including their rights to dignity, physical and psychological security and autonomy.[261]

Through the systematic, repetitive infliction of psychological trauma coupled with violence, terror and helplessness are inculcated in the victim and her sense of self in relation to others is destroyed.[262] These techniques may erode the victim's personality to the extent that a new self-image and identity must be reconstructed.[263]

While violence is certainly a feature of coercive control, it need not recur constantly nor to the same brutal degree on every occasion. An abuser can take coercive control by using violence only when necessary and to the extent necessary to instil fear and obedience in the victim. Thereafter the mere threat of violence alone may be sufficient to frighten women into compliance.[264] Abusers also use violence to reinforce the futility of the victim's escape or cries for help.

Violence may also sap victims of their strength and break down their will. Physical exhaustion and assault create the kind of emotional depletion that facilitates the breakdown of people's identities. Other means of inducing debility and exhaustion include:

- depriving the abused woman of sleep by waking her up for late night arguments and interrogations, or causing anxiety-induced insomnia – typically by threatening to hurt or kill the woman in her sleep.[265]

Threats are also used to enforce the expectation that the battered woman should be awake when the batterer returns home, regardless of the time or the fact that she receives no warning of his return;
- inadequate provision of basic necessities such as food, shelter, heating and medical care (this may also affect the children).[266] It is not unknown for women or their children to beg food from their neighbours because their partners withhold household support;[267]
- chasing the woman (and sometimes the children too) out of the home late at night or in cold weather.[268] If this occurs late at night then the woman may well be inadequately clothed. In this way she is subjected to physical suffering as well as emotional humiliation.[269]

Threats to kill and injure not only the woman but also the children and/or her family, as well as threats of suicide[270] also result in fear, anxiety and despair. When these threats are not acted upon this has the paradoxical effect of making the victim feel grateful to the abuser for his restraint and, ultimately (if the threats are repeated often enough) for allowing her to live.[271] The presence of occasional kindnesses, or expressions of empathy or affection, encourage the woman to hope that the abuser will stop terrorising her and permit her to survive. As long as the victim perceives hope and kindness, she can deny her anger or rage towards the abuser. By suppressing these negative feelings and focusing on the positive, the victim enlarges the abuser's perceived kindness, enabling her to see the abuser as someone who cares too much about her to continue harming her.

To understand what will keep the abuser happy and so reduce the likelihood of his harming her, the victim attempts to get inside his head. Under these circumstances she becomes highly sensitive to the captor's moods and whims, as well as submissive to his demands and desires. Yet in trying to think and feel as the abuser does, the victim in effect adopts the abuser's outlook and perspective, including that she both causes and deserves the abuse. This is "identification with the aggressor." Over time her very identity will come to be constituted or defined by the abuser, replacing any former sense of self.[272] This loss of identity further exacerbates the woman's difficulty in leaving her abusive partner. Having become defined by him, the victim grows unsure of who she is without him.

Undermining the victim's self-image, identity, integrity and inviolability is another way of reshaping her thoughts, values and identity. This may take various forms, including humiliating, reviling and verbally abusing her.[273] Humiliating women in front of others is especially destructive, as such conduct is also likely to result in isolating women from others.[274] Severe emotional and psychological abuse breaks down the victim's personality and ultimately convinces her that such belittlement and denigration accurately describes who she is. Epithets, insults and contempt come to form the basis of the new image the victim internalizes of herself. The new identity, beliefs and values inculcated in this way contribute to the victim's beliefs that she deserves the physical and emotional abuse and that she cannot escape it.[275] Indeed, some women may come to believe that they will never cope on their own, or that they are so flawed and unlovable that no one else, apart from their partner, could ever find them attractive. Thus some women may prefer life with an abusive partner to the prospect of indefinite loneliness or isolation.[276]

Another means of making women feel responsible for the abuse is through the extraction of "confessions." One form this may take is forcing women to admit falsely to transgressions, so enabling the abuser to justify his assaults. More often than not this involves coercing the woman into owning up to nonexistent sexual relationships with others. A second form of coerced confession occurs when the abused woman agrees that she is to blame for the abuse.[277] These admissions of guilt further contribute to the breakdown of the victim's identity and self-worth as she is increasingly made to feel deserving of the abuse or instigating the punishment she has "provoked."[278]

If these false confessions are witnessed by a third person, they may damage the credibility of the abused woman. They can be used to discredit, among other things, her character, her mothering skills and her mental stability in divorce and custody suits. Her support networks may come to ostracize her, especially when she confesses to sexual infidelity. The undermining of an abused woman's reputation which results from false confessions may further alienate her from support systems.[279]

Forced confessions are often accompanied by other techniques designed to instil pseudo-guilt in the victim, once again making her appear deserving of the abuse. These include:[280]

- Guilt by association: The battered woman, for example, would be accused of wrongdoing if she associated with people disliked by the batterer (such as her family and friends).

- Guilt by intention: The victim is held culpable for having motives that could lead to actions seen as harmful to the controller. For example, having hotline or shelter numbers would denote the woman's guilt since it shows her intention to leave the marriage, as well as her disloyalty to her partner.
- Guilt for negative attitudes about the controller or for doubting his/her decisions: The coercive controller calls for blind obedience.
- Guilt for having knowledge that could be incriminating to the controller: The potential for this type of guilt is high for abuse victims since the incidents of battering could in themselves be harmful to the batterer's social reputation.
- Guilt for taking action harmful to the controller's interests: here the victim is accused of culpability, regardless of whether harm was intended or not. One example is the woman being delayed on her way home and consequently being unable to prepare her husband's meal on time. The abuser uses the delayed meal, which is contrary to his interests, to justify the beating.
- Guilt for failing to support the coercive controller's interests: in abusive relationships, a woman is expected to stand up for her partner regardless of the nature of his actions. Failure to do so is tantamount to a punishable offence. Battered women who are sometimes hostile to police may in fact be acting out of self-preservation, since they know that failure to support their partners will intensify the severity of their punishment once the police leave.
- Guilt for personal faults: the controller justifies the abuse by blaming the victim for real or manufactured personal faults. In women abuse situations, laziness, nagging and mental illness are listed as some of the faults deemed worthy of punishment;
- Guilt for having dangerous social origins: dangerous origins may be decided on the basis of race, class, religion, gender and family history.

The perpetrator also seeks to destroy the victim's sense of autonomy through monitoring and controlling her body and bodily functions. The sexual abuse present in some abusive relationships serves not only to demonstrate control over the victim's body[281] but also constitutes a form of degradation. The effect of such degrading treatment may ultimately lead women to submit to unwanted sex because the cost of resistance is more damaging to their self-esteem than capitulation.[282]

The abusive partner may also supervise what she eats, when she sleeps and what she wears.[283] Looking attractive may call forth jealous diatribes and demands to name the man for whom she is dressing.[284] Other forms of monitoring and surveillance may include phoning or arriving at the woman's place of employment to check that she is indeed at work, or checking her cellphone to see who has called her.[285] This jealous and possessive conduct is typically offered as proof of the abuser's overwhelming love for and need of the woman.[286] Children may also be asked to monitor and report on their mother's phone calls, visitors and activities.[287] Coupled with this may be the enforcement of trivial demands such as ironing clothing in a particular way.[288] The insistence upon petty rules further develops the habit of compliance.[289]

Because the perpetrator's power is limited when the victim maintains outside connections with others, he does his best to isolate her and sever her relationships with others. He may censor information the victim receives and isolate her from friends, family and other support systems that provide alternative views to explain her plight. Her contact with others may be limited to those who reaffirm the batterer's perspective, validating her culpability and invalidating her experiences. Friends and family often inadvertently become the batterer's co-conspirators, especially when they keep the abuser's secrets. They sometimes repudiate the abused women's claims or respond in shock or disbelief, which further isolates her. These reactions frequently are grounded in the exemplary public behaviour of the batterer.[290] Ultimately, the abuser may demand the sacrifice of relationships with friends and family as proof of her loyalty and obedience.[291]

Isolation has other damaging effects. In the aftermath of an abusive or traumatic incident, the victim needs comfort, support and nurturance. If she has been isolated from others then there is little chance she will receive this from outsiders. The victim is left with little choice but to seek support from her abuser. To leave him may mean leaving what she believes to be the only source of love, company and support she has.

Ultimately an omnipotent and omnipresent aura may come to surround the abusive partner, the quality of which is well captured in this description:

> "The repeated experience of terror and reprieve, especially within the isolated context of a love relationship, may result in a feeling

of intense, almost worshipful dependence upon an all-powerful, godlike authority. The victim may live in terror of his wrath, but she may also view him as the source of strength, guidance and life itself. The relationship may take on an extraordinary quality of specialness. Some battered women speak of entering a kind of exclusive, almost delusional world, embracing the grandiose belief system of their mates and voluntarily suppressing their own doubts as proof of loyalty and submission. Similar experiences are regularly reported by people who have been induced into totalitarian religious cults."[292]

Herman suggests that the final step in achieving complete control occurs when the victim "is forced to violate her own moral principles and betray her basic human attachments. Psychologically, this is the most destructive of all coercive techniques, for the victim who succumbs loathes herself. It is at this point, when the victim, under duress, participates in the sacrifice of others, that she is truly 'broken'." [293] In some abusive relationships, it is the children who will be sacrificed. While some women will defend their children – even kill the abuser rather than permit their child's harm[294] – others are too subjugated to intervene.[295]

Two stages may be discerned in this process of "breaking." The first is reached when the victim relinquishes inner autonomy, world view, moral principles or connections with others for the sake of survival. There is a shutting down of feelings, thoughts, initiative and judgment, resulting in what psychiatrist Henry Krystal has described as "robotisation."[296] Once the victim is reduced to a goal of simple survival, psychological constriction becomes an essential form of adaptation to her circumstances. This narrowing applies to every aspect of life – to relationships, activities, thoughts, memories emotions and even sensations. Thoughts of the future become unbearable as life is reduced to an endless present. This disrupts individuals' sense of continuity in time.[297]

The second stage is achieved when the victim gives up the will to live.

(b) The process of Stockholm Syndrome/Traumatic bonding
Two other features of abusive relationships produce powerful emotional attachments between the victim and the abuser: power imbalances within the relationship, coupled with intermittent good-bad treatment.[298]

Chapter 1 has already outlined the socio-cultural beliefs that create inequality within intimate relationships. Violence and abuse further deepen this imbalance. As the power imbalance magnifies, the self-esteem of the victim weakens, making her dependence on the aggressor more pronounced. Concomitantly, the person in control becomes dependent on the victim to sustain his inflated sense of power.[299] This ensures a two-way bond; the abuser is as dependent upon the victim as she is on him. (This explanation has much in common with the processes of projection and projective identification described earlier).

Abusers also alternate their violence and other mistreatment with occasional indulgences in the form of apologies, small favours, permission to visit family and friends, or gifts. The capricious granting of such rewards also encourages compliance.[300] The effect of this intermittently pleasant behaviour is to reduce and minimize the abuse and transform the abuser temporarily into the loved, hoped-for husband.[301]

The creation of this traumatic bond is not immediate but develops over time. The first abusive incident typically occurs when the relationship is still new and feelings of hope and optimism predominate. Because there has been no prior evidence of violence in the relationship, the woman may, once the first shock and hurt has worn off, accept her partner's remorseful apologies and promises that it will never happen again.[302] Women may still harbour strong positive feelings towards their partners at this stage in the relationship. Thinking of their partners as cruel and hurtful may be a total contradiction of feelings of love and commitment. As the violence continues and worsens, women then make numerous attempts to change their behaviour, thinking themselves the cause of the abuse.

However, by the time women come to see that the abuse is inescapable, the emotional bond produced by the trauma of domestic violence is fairly strong.[303] The effects of this bond can be discerned when women who have left suddenly decide to return, a process which Dutton and Painter liken to the force of an elastic band "snapping" women back into the relationship. They suggest that once the immediate trauma or crisis that precipitated the woman's departure subsides, her immediate fears begin to abate and her attachment to the abuser begins to express itself. At this point she is emotionally drained and vulnerable and in need of support and comfort, care which would previously have been provided by the abusive partner. As the couple's time apart increases, positive memories may increase and memories of the severity of the abuse diminish.[304] In this state of emotional deprivation (almost always combined with harsh economic and legal conditions), the woman returns to her abuser.[305]

Coercive control theory explains many features of abusive relationships that puzzle people – such as the woman's loyalty and attachment to her partner in the face of her great fear of him. It illustrates how these features exist not only in situations of domestic violence but also in other circumstances where people are held captive. Like others who have been prisoners of war, political prisoners, hostages, or cult survivors, battered women have been subjected to ongoing processes of intimidation and abuse that systematically degrade their sense of self over time and isolate them from others.

3. Post-Traumatic Stress Disorder (PTSD) and Complex PTSD

Being the victim of or even witnessing a traumatic event may result in shock, disorientation, bewilderment, anxieties, difficulty in concentrating, passivity and incapacity. When these responses are manifested over an extended period of time (usually for a month a more), the resulting condition is described as post-traumatic stress disorder (PTSD).[306] PTSD is a recognized anxiety disorder that typically arises following exposure to an uncommon, highly stressful event (such as military combat, rape, assault or a natural disaster). It is characterized by three different sets of responses, all of which must be present in an individual in order to qualify for a diagnosis of PTSD. These symptoms include:

- re-experiencing the trauma through painful, intrusive memories or recurrent dreams;
- Hyper-vigilance, exaggerated startle responses, disturbed sleep, difficulties in concentrating or remembering, avoidance of people, activities and places that act as reminders of the trauma;
- Numbing or diminished responsiveness, including a loss of interest in life and feelings of detachment and estrangement from others.

Because PTSD describes in clinical terms the result or outcome of abuse, rather than the processes constituting abuse, it is compatible with any of the psycho-social theories previously described.

Research with women who have experienced domestic violence reveals that a substantial proportion (ranging from 31% to as high as 84% in one study) exhibit PTSD symptoms.[307] Further, women need not experience severe violence in order to display symptoms of PTSD, while psychological abuse may be as damaging as physical violence.[308] At least one study of eighteen women, convicted of killing their abusive partners, found that almost all reported symptom patterns commensurate with a diagnosis of PTSD prior to killing their abusive partners.[309]

There is however, at least one important difference between battered women and others exposed to trauma. In the case of battered women, the stressors causing trauma (such as assault and rape) are not uncommon but the everyday facts of their lives. To acknowledge the cumulative impact of such repeated abuse, Herman proposes the following criteria for the diagnosis of Complex Post-Traumatic Stress Disorder: [310]

- A history of subjugation to totalitarian control over a prolonged period of months/years.
- Alterations in controlling how one feels and behaves, including suicidal thoughts, self-injury, explosive or severely inhibited anger, and/or compulsive or inhibited sexuality.
- Alterations in consciousness including amnesia, dissociation, flashbacks.
- Alterations in self-perception, including a sense of helplessness, paralysis, self-blame, guilt, aloneness.
- Alterations in perceptions of the perpetrator, especially a preoccupation with the perpetrator that can include obsessive desire for revenge, belief in the perpetrator's omniscience, idealisation, gratitude, or belief that the perpetrator has supernatural powers.
- Alterations in relations with others including isolation or withdrawal, disruption of intimate relationships, desire for rescue, failure to protect the self.
- Alteration in systems of meaning such as a loss of faith or a sense of despair.

In addition to these various symptoms, other forms of emotional distress may accompany post-traumatic stress in abused women. These include depression, suicidal ideation, drug and alcohol dependence, sleep disorders, phobias, anxiety disorders, somatisation and cognitive difficulties.[311]

Importantly, the understanding that some battered women suffer from PTSD as a result of abuse helps to explain that a victim's reaction to violence is a normal response to an abnormal situation. It helps society understand that violence is violence, regardless of who perpetrates it.[312]

4. Conclusion

The psycho-social research surrounding domestic violence develops much of the basis for placing abuse victims' experiences within the elements of the criminal defences to murder and/or providing reasons justifying sentence mitigation. It highlights that domestic violence needs to be seen as a continuous process influenced by socialization toward gender roles, cultural beliefs/practices, law and politics. As important is an understanding of the psychology of the abuser, which helps practitioners understand abusive men's conduct as the source of women's psychological distress – rather than seeing women's behaviour as the cause of violent men's conduct.

The psychological theories take the next step and explain women's reaction to abuse. Each theory takes a different approach. Battered Women's Syndrome explains domestic violence as a three-stage cycle that ultimately renders the abuse victim passive and hopeless in the face of violence. This theory has been employed successfully on behalf of women who kill their abusers, but currently is strongly criticized in academic and legal circles. Coercive control theory likens the experience of domestic violence to one of captivity. It highlights how interrogators, torturers, hostage-takers and cult leaders have made an art of the methods stumbled upon by violent men to control their female partners. Traumatic bonding, or Stockholm Syndrome, describes how an abuser successfully uses violence to warp and solidify his initial bond with his victim. He uses violence and isolation techniques to convince her to fear him and that he is her only source of love and support, which effectively traps her in the relationship. The theory of PTSD and complex PTSD highlights that many of the psychological symptoms experienced by battered women are similar to those who have been traumatised generally and that these responses are normal in the context of an abnormal situation.

Each of these theories dispels common myths about abuse victims, including that they provoke or enjoy abuse, that they must not want help because they refuse it, as well as that they can always leave their abusers. They also explain women's heightened sensitivity to their abusers and their resultant ability to sense incipient abuse. Perhaps most importantly, each theory explains how it is that abuse victims come to believe they cannot escape the violence and why that belief is rational.

* * *

NO WAY OUT!
THE STORY OF ANIETA FERREIRA

For ten years Anieta Ferreira was subjected to extreme physical, psychological, economic and sexual abuse. Isolated from others and with very limited social support, she became so entrapped in the relationship that, in her mind, the murder of the abuser was the only way of escaping him and getting her life back.

Rejected at birth by her mother, Anieta was raised by her maternal grandmother until she was five years old. This led to a sense of abandonment and lack of attachment to her nuclear family.

When she started school, she was suddenly separated from her grandmother, the only close relationship she had known, and returned to the home of her mother, who treated her with ruthless cruelty. She accused Anieta, then aged six, of "whoring" with her own father. Anieta was prevented from forming any meaningful relationship with her father, of whom she was very fond. Her mother always made her feel inferior to her siblings. She was forced to work in the house, whereas they were not expected to do so. They were driven to school while she had to walk. She received old clothing when her sister was bought new clothing. Anieta did not express any anger towards her mother. She suppressed her feelings and simply took the bad treatment meted out to her, but she was left with a sense of worthlessness.

Anieta's mother forced her to leave school at 16 with a standard eight pass. It was while working at the post office in Nelspruit, Mpumalanga, that she met and married her husband, with whom she had four children. This marriage was abusive, with the husband not providing for her at all. Having left the post office job during the marriage, Anieta was dependent on welfare grants to support herself and her four children. Eventually, she left her husband and put her children into foster care, in order to find work. She first found a job with an elderly couple in Parys in the Free State in exchange for board and lodging.

Annexure: Biderman's Chart of Coercion[313]

General Methods	Effects (Purposes)	Variants
Isolation	Deprives victim of all social support of his ability to resist; develops an intense concern with self; makes victim dependent upon interrogator	Complete solitary confinement; complete isolation; semi-isolation; group isolation
Monopolization of perception	Fixes attention upon immediate predicament; fosters introspection; eliminates stimuli competing with those controlled by the captor; frustrates all actions not consistent with compliance	Physical isolation; darkness or bright light; barren environment; restricted movement; monotonous food
Induced debility; exhaustion	Weakens mental and physical ability to resist	Semi-starvation; exposure; exploitation of wounds; induced illness; sleep deprivation; prolonged constraint; prolonged interrogation; forced writing; overexertion
Threats	Cultivates anxiety and despair	Threats of death; threats of non-return; threats of endless interrogation and isolation; threats against family; vague threats; mysterious changes of treatment
Occasional indulgences	Provides positive motivation for compliance; hinders adjustment to deprivation	Occasional favours; fluctuations of interrogators' attitudes; promises; rewards for partial compliance; tantalising
Demonstrating "omnipotence"	Suggests futility of resistance	Confrontation; pretending co-operation taken for granted; demonstrating complete control over victim's fate.
Degradation	Makes cost of resistance appear more damaging to self-esteem than capitulation; reduces prisoner to "animal level" concerns	Personal hygiene prevented; filthy infested surroundings; demeaning punishments; insults and taunts; denial of privacy
Enforcing trivial demands	Develops habit of compliance	Forced writing; enforcement of minute rules

Some time later she was employed as a housekeeper by Cyril Parkman on his small farm outside Rustenburg in North West province.

In the beginning Parkman was polite and Anieta felt happy. However, he soon started shouting at her if she did not complete her tasks. As she had done so effectively with her mother, she suppressed her anger, and tried to avoid confrontation. Parkman never paid her what he had initially offered but she felt reasonably content, as she had a cottage on the property and was given food by him.

After she had been at the smallholding for three months, Parkman asked Anieta to move into the main house with him. Although the relationship developed into a sexual one, it was more like that of parent and child. He was twenty years older than she, and insisted that she only ever call him Mr Parkman. He punished her for not performing her duties properly in ways that resembled a father disciplining a child.

The first physical abuse came when he slapped her for making a telephone call to her children, which had been forbidden. Parkman had refused to allow her to speak to her children, as he claimed that during a visitation one of her daughters was "dressed like a prostitute". He would also check the monthly telephone bills to see whom she had called. This was the beginning of a process of isolating her from the outside world, which included forbidding her to speak to the neighbours, lest she tell them about the abuse.

Parkman would draw up a lengthy daily work schedule for Anieta. If she did not complete all these tasks, he would punish her by locking her into a room for anything from three days to two weeks at a time without food. During these times, one of the farm workers would smuggle food to her. Neighbours remember watching Anieta regularly carrying out strenuous manual labour while Mr Parkman drank beer and ordered her about. He was a heavy drinker who often came home drunk late at night. He would wake Anieta in the early hours of the morning to make him a meal. She never knew when Parkman would throw her out of the house. He frequently dropped her off in the nearby town and told her not to come home. On one occasion, he even asked a friend of his to drop her off in Johannesburg and tell her not to come back.

The physical violence escalated over time. Parkman broke Anieta's finger and her nose and regularly threatened her with a knife and a gun. There were times when the neighbours had to come to her rescue. Parkman would also routinely strangle her, which necessitated her having an operation on her throat, as it became so badly damaged that she was unable to swallow.

Parkman constantly criticised and verbally abused Anieta by calling her a "useless whore," amongst other things. He would embarrass and humiliate her by insulting her in the presence of other people. He was also very jealous and would accuse her of wanting to have sex with other men. Even when they were walking in town, he would accuse her of looking at other men. As a result she took to looking down and never lifting her head while walking, so that he could not accuse her of this.

Apart from this physical and emotional abuse, there was severe sexual abuse.

She called the police a few times but stopped after Parkman cut the telephone wires and threatened to make sure she never saw her children again.

Anieta tried to leave, but never really had the means, as Parkman did not allow her to handle any money. He would pay cash for everything. Even if she went to the hairdresser he would go with her in order to pay. Any attempts she made to become financially self-sufficient failed as soon as he found out about them. On one occasion she got a job, but on her first day at work, Parkman went to the office and accused the owner of having sex with her. She lost the job the same day.

Anieta made several attempts to leave him, but he always found her within a week or so. On these occasions he would be contrite and full of promises to change. He would give her gifts and beg her to come back to him – even crying and crawling on his knees on occasion to gain her sympathy. This always made her feel sufficiently sorry for him to return.

Anieta had no family support. She also lived in a rural farming community that had no shelters or services for women in her position. Her isolation from others and lack of contact with the outside world meant that the only voice Anieta ever heard was that of Parkman, telling her how inadequate she was as a woman and as a human being. Her self-confidence plummeted and she began to think she deserved the beatings. Because of the control he exercised over her and the fact that he always found her when she left, Parkman seemed almost omnipotent in her eyes. In fact, she did not, according to her own account, realise that she was in an abusive situation. For her, life was not very different from the way it had always been.

The lack of support structures in her life, and Parkman's cutting her off from all contact with her family and friends, also meant that she literally had nowhere to go. She also began to believe that it was pointless to continue trying to leave as he would always find her.

The turning point for Anieta came two weeks before the murder. Parkman called her out of the house to where he had assembled about 15 of the farm workers and told Anieta to show them her genitals. Humiliated, she refused and walked back into the house. Parkman shouted abuse at her, saying "you are so *useless that not even blacks want [to have sex with] you." She muttered that she did not want to sleep with anyone. Parkman heard the comment and later that night, repeated it to her, saying he would "show her." He then raped her and told her that he was going to arrange for black men to rape her. She became very fearful of black men, thinking every time she saw a black man that he had been sent by Parkman to rape her. She became hyper-vigilant and slept only fitfully.*

A few days after this one of the farm workers suggested to Anieta that she approach a sangoma to mix a potion that would make Parkman less aggressive. She tried this for a week, but it did not work. This led her to believe that the situation was now desperate, with no way out. Given that Parkman had always acted on his threats in the past, she truly believed that he would have her raped. She did not believe it possible to leave him, her many unsuccessful attempts reinforcing her belief that he would never let her go. She killed him with the assistance of two men, believing it to be the only way to protect herself.

CHAPTER 3

When abused women kill

Contents	Page
A. DOMESTIC VIOLENCE AS A PROCESS	84
B. THE EVOLUTION OF CRISES	88
C. SOCIAL JUDGMENT THEORY	89
D. WOMEN WHO KILL: THE RESEARCH FINDINGS	91
E. CONCLUSION: THE ROLE OF THE EXPERT WITNESS	93

SOUTH AFRICA'S COURTS have stated that "the crucial question" in relation to women who kill their abusive partners is "why she decided on murder rather than to leave the deceased."[314] The previous two chapters addressed this question by examining the social and psychological barriers imprisoning women in abusive relationships. Chapter 1 outlined a framework for understanding the context in which abused women make decisions – to leave, to stay, to return, to seek assistance. It also outlined the barriers women encounter in seeking help. Chapter 2 then focused on describing the psychological dynamics of abusive relationships, highlighting how particular kinds of behaviour produce a complex cocktail of fear, immobility, anger, despair and hope in abused women which fundamentally alters their sense of self.

This chapter pulls these various constituents of women's experiences together and looks at how their interaction over time produces the spiral of entrapment that culminates in some women killing their abusers. It sets out the processes involved in entering, remaining and leaving abusive relationships, highlighting the way in which, if support is not forthcoming, the woman's entrapment within the relationship then results. The next section explores the factors that lead women to kill their abusive partners. It outlines the stages leading to an acute crisis and describes social judgment theory to explain how some women reach the point where they are no longer able to tolerate the abuse. It concludes with some empirical information around battered women who kill their abusive partners.

A. DOMESTIC VIOLENCE AS A PROCESS

Domestic violence is dynamic, with the nature, type and severity of the abuse changing over time, as do the responses employed by women to cope with the violence in the relationship. Five stages of change that women go through as they deal with the abuse have been identified: entering the relationship; managing violence; experiencing a loss of self; re-evaluating the relationship; and restructuring the self.[315] Another writer identifies a four-phase process of entrapment and recovery comprising binding, enduring, disengaging and recovery.[316]

During these early stages of entering the relationship and becoming bound to the abuser, the onset of abuse is gradual and subtle, with the first violent episode typically treated as both exceptional and aberrant rather than an indication that a violent relationship has begun. At this point it may be less painful to receive a beating than to abandon the hopes, expectations and feelings upon which the relationship is based.[317]

Yet as women discover over time, domestic violence and its threat continues unabated, even in times of relative calm. Defining the periods immediately preceding or succeeding a single incident of abuse as the start and end of an episode of violence becomes difficult, as "… the cessation of one episode of violence may constitute the beginning of another, even though the next attack may not occur until considerably later."[318] There are times of non-violence but these are not necessarily safe times. This has led one writer to observe: "As long as courts view domestic violence as an 'event' or as a story divided into instances of brutality, they cannot understand battering as a deliberate course of criminal conduct, as a narrative of female subordination or as a lived political reality."[319] Within this context battered women learn to anticipate punishment and become vigilant to its signs – yelling, clenched fists, changes in the tone and speed of speech.[320]

As women struggle to endure or manage the violence, they may develop and employ different kinds of rationalizations to cope with what is happening to them.[321] These include:[322]

- denial of injury, in which the woman downplays or dismisses how her partner has hurt her, especially if no physical marks result. This may be reinforced by others who may also suggest that "only" bruises have been the result or that the woman is lucky no bones have been broken;
- denial of the victimizer, which places blame for the abuse on external forces beyond either the man or the woman's control. Alcohol or unemployment are two examples of these external causes;
- denial of options, which comprises two elements – the practical and the emotional. Practical options typically refer to women's access to alternative housing, an income, childcare – those resources required to enable her to survive without the male partner's income. The idea of emotional options refers to women's beliefs about whether they can survive without their partners or not.

Women may also attempt different strategies to end the abuse. These include thinking about how to change their behaviour, how to take care of their children and maintain their households, how to obtain and save money and who to approach for help and advice. Sometimes they actively defend themselves but these attempts usually diminish with time, as women learn that striking back results in worse beatings or other negative consequences.[323] These defensive attempts to protect themselves may be what give the impression that both partners are violent. The women's actions must, however, be seen within the overall context of the violent relationship, rather than abstracted from it.

But as these various tactics prove themselves ineffective, women may begin re-evaluating the relationship and start disengaging from it. Thoughts of leaving may increasingly enter their thinking, a process which Wuest and Merritt-Gray[324] describe as "reclaiming self." Reclaiming self includes the stages of counteracting abuse, breaking free, not going back and moving on. "Counteracting abuse" includes the various tactics women engage in to resist the abuse, while "breaking free" refers to the gradual process of disengaging from the abusive relationship. Disengagement, an "eclectic, repetitive and tortuous" process, involves women starting to test out their options and the responses of others, taking risks (for which they may not be entirely ready), stepping outside of the relationship and then often pulling back and returning to the familiar. This process begins to give women a sense of how leaving will affect them personally, as well as in relation to their friends, family, the abuser and the community. Once women manage to break free, they focus on "not going back". Requirements for a successful transition to this stage include feeling at least some degree of safety, wanting to take more control, having somewhere semi-permanent to live and being able to access help.

At least some women may not make the transition to this stage. Chapter 1 outlined the many obstacles women encounter in seeking social support that effectively stack the odds against abused women. Inasmuch as they are trying to learn how to access the criminal justice system, so is their abusive partner also learning to use the system and exploit its loopholes[325] (by evading efforts to serve divorce summons on them, or obtaining counter-protection orders against their partners, for example).[326] Those who assume that leaving is an immediate, once-off decision, rather than a process of breaking free, may also frustrate women's attempts to leave. If they do not understand how tenuous and exploratory women's efforts are at this point, they may well label women who return as lacking in credibility, not serious about leaving and thus undeserving of help on an on-going basis. If this is the attitude adopted by family, friends and service providers, it may well stifle and discourage women.

Thus instead of "not going back" women may "give up" on trying to leave.[327] Indifferent and ineffective assistance, difficulty in obtaining financial assistance and a safe place to stay, as well as unsuitable counselling interventions, all contribute to revictimizing women, who then return to the relationship. At this point, their field of initiative and activity becomes increasingly circumscribed; they no longer think of how to escape from the relationship but focus instead on how to make their circumstances bearable.[328] A sense of entrapment within the relationship may come to dominate their thinking: "Emphasizing entrapment as the model experience in battering shifts attention to the woman's increasingly constrained strategic choices ('control in the context of no control') and their experiential correlates."[329] To outsiders, women's decisions may appear weak or counter-productive – but this is because they are unaware of how forcibly restricted women's choices have become.[330] This sense of entrapment may also produce a kind of "funnelling" of women's vision.[331] This arises as they try various options over time to end the abuse, but these ultimately prove unsuccessful. Each failed attempt at seeking help narrows the range of possible actions available to women and contributes to the belief that no one else can be relied upon or trusted to assist them. As the likelihood of leading a life free from violence, threat and fear becomes less and less possible, the grimmer women's choices become. Within such a claustrophobic and trapped context, killing the abuser may appear to be the only means of self-preservation open to them (and their children in some instances).

Over the course of an abusive relationship, a number of different crisis points may have been reached and many of the options outlined earlier will have been attempted. By the time some battered women start thinking this way, they are living in a state of chronic trauma and stress, which requires only a final crisis to precipitate the killing. It is the cumulative failure or ineffective resolution of these crises that may, in this final crisis, push women to take such drastic action.

B. THE EVOLUTION OF CRISES

A crisis may be defined as an acute emotional upset in which one's usual problem-solving abilities fail.[332] While acute crises may temporarily distort an individual's cognitive functioning (such as memory and decision-making) due to interference by intense emotion at that point in time, they do not affect overall mental competence.

Two kinds of response are typically required to deal with crises: natural crisis management (referring to individual responses to traumatic life events); and formal crisis management, which involves assistance from sources outside the individual and her immediate family. Applying individual strategies alone to social problems like domestic violence is unlikely to be effective as a combination of personal coping strategies and social support is required to resolve crises around battering.

The evolution of circumstances into full-blown crises follows particular phases:[333]

1. *Traumatic event causes an initial rise in anxiety level* – the woman's partner strikes her. She is shocked and wonders why, and worries about what she can do to prevent it from happening again. If he expresses contrition, or if no other abusive incident follows soon after this event, the effects of this particular trauma may be contained and confined to this particular incident alone. But if this not the case, then the next stage in the development of a crisis may be reached.
2. *Failure of usual coping strategy or problem-solving technique* – she tries to talk to him, he refuses to talk, she attempts to placate him and he either ignores her or hits her again.
3. *Anxiety levels rise even further, following failure of coping strategy* – in response, new and alternative coping devices are tried, such as seeking help from a relative or calling the police. If these are effective and assist the woman to manage her anxiety, then there may be no further progression towards a crisis.
4. *State of active crisis* – as social support and personal coping strategies fail, the problem continues, culminating in a breaking point. At this point, the woman's intense fear, despair or anxiety may become unbearable and a suicide or homicide attempt is made.

This final, active crisis is likely to be precipitated when women feel the abusers' actions fall outside the range of what they can accept and their survival instincts erupt, leading them to take action to protect themselves (or their children).[334] Social judgment theory provides an explanation for how the shift from victim to perpetrator occurs.

C. SOCIAL JUDGMENT THEORY

Sherif and Hovland suggest that people order their experiences or perceptions along a continuum that ranges from acceptable to unacceptable.[335] The range of possibilities to which people are willing to adapt is termed the "latitude of acceptance". Those stimuli falling outside of this range fall into either the latitude of non-commitment – stimuli that people are neutral about, neither accepting nor non-accepting – or the latitude of rejection.

End-points or anchors define the extremes (or cut-off points) of the latitude of acceptance. These end-points are determined both by internal factors (such as people's psychological and genetic make-up) as well as by external factors such as societal values and beliefs. Previous experiences will also affect how acceptable or unacceptable people may judge stimuli to be. In the absence of outside influences, a person's internal anchors will play a more significant role in how she or he evaluates a situation.

In terms of this model, events falling at the ends of the continuum, or even slightly outside of its end-points, will remain acceptable as the continuum expands to include them in a process called assimilation. But if the stimulus falls too far outside of the latitude of acceptance, the person will reject the experience, bringing a contrast effect into play.

Applying this approach to abused women, the latitude of acceptance refers to those aspects of the abuser's behaviour to which the woman is able to adapt. Where women locate the end-points of this latitude will be influenced by the degree to which they have been socialised to adjust to, or accept, a partner's behaviour. They determine the endpoints based on prior exposure to similar experiences, such as abuse within the childhood home, and the degree to which they feel trapped within the situation and feel they must adjust to their partner's abuse.

As chapter 1 showed, South African society (like many others around the world) has been slow to react critically to domestic violence. Abusive behaviour continues to be excused and minimized, while limited societal resources exist to challenge domestic violence and support abused women. In the absence of strong external condemnation of domestic violence, many abused women will be more dependent on their internal anchors or resources to determine the latitude of behaviours they will accept. Common variables that affect how women respond to domestic violence and where they place their end points include:

- her fear of her partner's threats to retaliate against her, her children and/or others important to her;
- her hope that her abuser will change;
- the results of her attempts to seek help from the criminal justice system, religious leaders, health workers, family and friends;
- her economic dependence on her partner;
- her shame and embarrassment associated with reporting the abuse.[336]

As abusive behaviour falls closer to the end-points of the range, so abused women adjust their latitude of acceptance in order to incorporate these changes. Thus living in abusive circumstances involves women in a constant process of assimilation and readjustment as they attempt to find ways of coexisting with the abuser.

The contrast effect of social judgment theory arises when either an abusive incident is so much more brutal or degrading than usual that women doubt they will survive the next assault, or the act falls significantly outside the range of what they are prepared to assimilate. According to Browne, the discovery of physical or sexual abuse of a child often pushes women beyond what they are willing to assimilate.[337] At this point, final hope for change is removed; the woman believes she cannot escape the abusive situation and cannot survive within the relationship as it exists.[338]

The Canadian Supreme Court accepted the social judgment theory as a basis for understanding why abused women kill. It wrote:

> "Repeated instances of violence enable battered women to develop a continuum along which they can 'rate' the tolerability or survivability of episodes of their partner's violence. Thus, signs of

unusual violence are detected. For battered women, this response to the ongoing violence of their situations is a survival skill. Research shows that battered women who kill experience remarkably severe and frequent violence relative to battered women who do not kill. They know what sorts of danger are familiar and which are novel. They have a myriad of opportunities to develop and hone their perceptions of their partner's violence. And, importantly, they can say what made the final episode of violence different from the others: they can name the feature of the last battering that enabled them to know that this episode would result in life-threatening action by the abuser."[339]

It is important to bear in mind, however, that the concept of funnelling, the process of crises and social judgement theory is most appropriately applied to women who do not kill under circumstances of classic self-defence as it is traditionally understood. As the research findings presented in the next section show, many killings occur within the context of an immediate and life-threatening attack upon the woman by her abusive partner, requiring her to take immediate action to defend her life.

D. WOMEN WHO KILL: THE RESEARCH FINDINGS

Maguigan's review of 223 cases in the United States involving abused women who killed their partners found that these killings occurred most often in the course of an attack upon the woman, with 75% of the deaths studied having occurred during a confrontation.[340] A further one in five of her sample (20%) killed their abusers when they were asleep, drunk or otherwise vulnerable, or hired a third party to perform the killing, when no imminent danger seemed apparent.[341]

Research undertaken at three Gauteng courts found a similar local pattern. This study analysed conviction and sentencing patterns in all 164 cases of spousal murder heard between 1994 and 1998 at Witwatersrand Local Division High Court, Transvaal Provincial High Court and one regional court, the Johannesburg magistrate's court. In this sample of cases, men who killed their female partners outnumbered their female counterparts by over three to one (125 cases involved men and 39 involved women). The majority of women in this study (22, or 56%) killed their partners under circumstances in which they were being abused.[342] While most of the 22 abused women in this study killed during the course of a direct attack upon them, six used either third parties or killed the man while he was asleep or otherwise vulnerable.[343]

Browne's study in the United States identifies the following as risk factors associated with abused women killing their partners:[344]

- frequency of incidents of assault;
- severity of injury;
- frequency of alcohol intoxication or other substance abuse by the man;
- forced or threatened sexual assaults on the woman;
- the man's threats to kill;
- suicide ideation by the woman.

While the identification of these factors in individual women's circumstances may indicate high-risk situations, their presence will not always result in a killing. In some instances all six factors may be present but no killing will occur, while in other circumstances only some of these factors will be present yet a death will result. Thus the presence of even some of these factors in a relationship suggests risk that the victim will kill her abuser.[345]

Ewing describes the situation in which a woman kills her abuser as involving rapidly escalating, serious sexual and physical abuse, as well as abuse of her children.[346] She has, typically, been threatened with death and weapons. She also is more likely to have fewer social alternatives for escaping the abuse.

Further support for the thesis that abused women kill under circumstances of great desperation, when they perceive no other options available to them, emerges from an analysis of US homicide data covering two different periods, 1976 to 1984 and 1980 to 1995. During the first period, the number of women killing male partners declined by more than 25%. Statistical analysis of these figures indicated that the number of women perpetrating such killings was lower in those states where resources such as shelters, crisis lines and domestic violence legislation existed.[347] This downward trend continued during 1980 to 1995,[348] leading the researchers to conclude that legal and extralegal resources for battered women had provided women facing violence and threats with a greater variety of alternatives, thus preventing them from resorting to lethal defensive action.[349]

E. CONCLUSION: THE ROLE OF THE EXPERT WITNESS

The context in which some battered women resort to killing their abusive partners, as described and explained above, is crucial to helping courts understand the multi-layered circumstances trapping women within violent relationships. It is the role of the expert witness to take this information and apply it to their particular client's circumstances so that the court may come to a proper understanding of the woman's actions.

The expert witness will need as much information as possible about the woman's socio-cultural milieu, the relationship and her decision to kill, as well as the extent and types of abuse she suffered and what, if any, help she sought and why (presumably) such help failed or was not forthcoming. The expert must also enquire into the reason(s) why the abused woman did not leave the relationship, focusing particularly on why she felt she could not escape the abuse. Both the statistical data and generalized information about why women do not leave should support the subjective reasons the client supplies for why she did not leave, or why her attempts to obtain help proved fruitless.

Once the expert compiles this information, she or he must explain the woman's individual experiences with violence and her reasons for killing, then situate these explanations within the experiences of domestic violence victims as a group. This serves the purpose of placing the circumstances in which the woman found herself before the court as well as explaining why her response to those circumstances is normal in the context of abuse. Importantly, the expert testimony should explain the woman's lack of options to end the abuse. Appropriate expert testimony further should debunk myths and stereotypes of domestic violence and its victims that could lead to an unfair trial.

As the Canadian Supreme Court has said, expert testimony can go a long way towards accomplishing this:

"Expert evidence on the psychological effect of battering on wives and common law partners must ... be both relevant and necessary in the context of the present case. How can the mental state of the appellant be appreciated without it? The average member of the public (or the jury) can be forgiven for asking: why would a woman put up with this kind of treatment? Why would she continue to live with such a man? How could she love a partner who beat her to the point of requiring hospitalization? We would expect the woman to pack her bags and go. Where is her self respect? Why does she not cut loose and make a new life for herself? Such is the reaction of the average person confronted with the so-called 'battered wife syndrome'. We need help to understand it and help is available from trained professionals.'[350]

Chapter 4 provides a fuller description of the types of expert testimony required for the defence of a battered woman who has killed her abusive partner.

PART II

Legal defences and mitigation of sentence for abused women who kill

CHAPTER 4
Defences for women protecting their lives

Contents	Page
A. CONSTITUTIONAL FRAMEWORK	99
B. SELF-DEFENCE	103
1. Legal theory of self-defence	104
2. Elements of self-defence under South African law	105
(a) Elements of the attack	105
(i) Unlawful attack	105
(ii) Upon protected interests	108
(iii) Imminence	109
(b) Defensive action	120
(i) Defensive act must be directed at the attacker	120
(ii) Defensive act must be necessary to protect the accused	120
(aa) Options to avoid abuse	120
(bb) Distinguishing the Engelbrecht case	127
(iii) Reasonable relationship between defensive act and unlawful attack (proportionality)	133
(c) Reasonableness test for self-defence	138
3. General defence of reasonableness	144
4. Self-defence for abused women who hire contract killers	144
5. Conclusion	146
C. PUTATIVE SELF-DEFENCE	147
1. Elements	148
(a) Honest belief	148
(b) Mistake of fact	151
(c) Exceeded bounds of self-defence	152
2. Conclusion	153

A. CONSTITUTIONAL FRAMEWORK

South Africa's Constitution provides an important framework within which to view domestic violence and the treatment of women who kill their abusers, particularly those who kill in non-confrontational situations. The rights and duties described in the Constitution set the minimum standards by which a person should expect to live as well as what she or he can expect the state to provide, protect and/or enforce. It is within the framework of constitutional rights and duties that advocates can most cogently argue for the reconstruction of criminal defence law to include women's experiences with violence.

Domestic violence infringes on a variety of women's fundamental rights. The most obvious is the right to psychological and physical integrity, explicitly contained in the right to security of the person.[351] Importantly, the effects of psychological abuse should not be overlooked or minimized when considering cases of domestic violence, since women often feel most harmed by psychological abuse.[352] Closely linked to the right to freedom and security of the person is the right to have one's dignity respected.[353] Domestic violence, in any of its forms, shreds women's dignity.

Domestic violence also violates women's equality rights through the process of gender subordination.[354] As described in Chapter 2, violence against women typically is about control, whether the abuser uses violence to get what he wants or to assure his psychological well-being. For many abusers the entitlement to control over women derives from distortions of traditional family roles, particularly of the woman's role as wife. As the Constitutional Court in *S v Baloyi* concluded: "To the extent that it is systemic, pervasive and overwhelmingly gender-specific, domestic violence both reflects and reinforces patriarchal domination and does so in a particularly brutal form."[355]

Because of the abusers' often successful attempts to control their victims, domestic violence also needs to be viewed as a violation of women's autonomy rights.[356] This point grows more obvious in the face of the statistics that show the elevated risk of stalking, harassment, violence and death to women who assert their autonomy and leave an abusive relationship.[357] Practitioners need to canvass each of these rights violations when arguing a defence or mitigation of sentence. This approach is consistent with the Supreme Court of Appeal decision in

Ferreira v S, which specifically requires courts to examine women's decisions to kill in light of the abuser's violations of their rights.[358]

The next step in viewing domestic violence within a constitutional framework requires looking at the duty the Constitution places on the State to protect these rights and, even more specifically, protect women from domestic violence. The general duty of the State derives from section 7(2) of the Constitution, which commands the state to "respect, promote and fulfil" constitutional rights. According to the Constitutional Court, the duty to protect against domestic violence derives from reading s 7(2) with s 12(1), which provides for the security of the person:

> "Indeed, the State is under a series of constitutional mandates which include the obligation to deal with domestic violence: to protect both the rights of everyone to enjoy freedom and security of the person and to bodily and psychological integrity, and the right to have their dignity respected and protected, as well as defensive rights of everyone not to be subjected to torture in any way and not to be treated or punished in a cruel, inhuman or degrading way."[359]

The duties of the State are positive in that it is required to act to protect and promote rights, and negative to the extent that it is required to refrain from actively violating rights.

When the police and courts fail to protect women from domestic violence, they violate their obligations under the Constitution and increase women's traumatisation. Accordingly, the Constitutional Court in *Baloyi* explained:[360]

> "The ineffectiveness of the criminal justice system in addressing family violence intensifies the subordination and helplessness of the victims. This also sends an unmistakable message to the whole of society that the daily trauma of vast numbers of women counts for little. The terrorisation of individual victims is thus compounded by a sense that domestic violence is inevitable. Patterns of systemic behaviour are normalised rather than combated. Yet it is precisely the function of constitutional protection to convert misfortune to be endured into injustice to be remedied."[361]

A breach of the State's duty influences women's decision to kill. As Chapter 1 describes, the ineffectiveness of the State responses to domestic violence works to convince women that they cannot escape the violence they face. It leads some women to stop seeking State help, viewing it as hopeless and, in many instances, likely to lead to a violent response from the abuser.

The violation of women's fundamental rights continues through the prosecution stage for women charged with the murder of their abusive partners, particularly those who kill in non-confrontational situations. South Africa's women infrequently have been able to benefit from criminal defence law as a result of gender bias. Only rarely have defence counsel argued any criminal defences for women who kill their abusers in non-confrontational situations and, even then, the arguments typically have been limited to non-pathological criminal incapacity. [362]

The predominant reason for this failure seems to be that defence counsel cannot see how non-confrontational killings fit within the traditionally narrow interpretations of the elements of the defences. The narrow interpretations in turn result from the gender bias in the development of criminal defence law that for the most part reflects only men's experiences with violence.[363] Laurie Taylor provides two reasons for the bias favouring men's experiences: "first, the great majority of criminal defendants have been male; second, criminal law has been developed by male common-law judges, codified by male legislators, enforced by male police officers and interpreted by male judges and juries."[364]

One of the easier examples of the bias is reflected in self-defence law. Self-defence was developed based on the idea of a single, unusual and sudden attack by a stranger of roughly equal size that forces the typically male victim to respond immediately, such as during a barroom brawl. In contrast to men, women most often kill members of the opposite sex and the victims are usually their intimate partners.[365] Many of these women kill men who abused them and a significant minority kills in non-confrontational situations rather than the heat of the moment. Self-defence law does not account for situations of abuse where the violence is frequent, typical and predictable and situations in which an immediate response in self-defence is likely to be ineffective and lead to severe repercussions.

Convincing defence counsel to argue self-defence and putative self-defence in addition to non-pathological criminal incapacity for women who kill in non-confrontational situations is only the first hurdle. The second hurdle is ensuring that women have equal access to a trial free of gender bias and have the equal opportunity to present a defence.[366] For example, while the only decision directly addressing self-defence for these women initially creates a strong legal framework for their access to the defence, the application of the law to the facts showed that the real barriers to such access remain in place.[367] The explanation for the barriers seems to be that legal practitioners cannot accept that the police and courts fail in their duty to protect abused women from domestic violence. The need to maintain the utmost faith in the criminal justice system seems to blind them to the reality of women's experiences with domestic violence.

Part II of this book argues for the infusion of women's experiences into the elements of the defences to end the effective exclusion of women from the defences. This requires provision of the social context evidence described in Part I, along with an explanation of how the evidence meets the requirements of each element of the defences, broadening the interpretations of the elements, while fulfilling the purposes of the defences.

The main argument for reconstructing criminal defence law to ensure women's access to the defences and a fair trial lies in the obligation of equal treatment under the law contained in section 9 of the Constitution. Equal protection of the law does not require courts to treat all criminally accused the same, but instead requires "treating an abused woman accused with due regard for gender difference in order to achieve equality of judicial treatment."[368] Instead of applying the gender-biased standards for the criminal defences equally to men and women, s 9 of the Constitution requires having both men's and women's experiences equally inform the elements of the defences.[369] Failure to do this treats women's experiences and responses to violence as deviant simply because they are not the same as men's.[370] This approach and this book are not advocating for a special defence for women who kill their abusers but rather seek to correct the existing gender bias in criminal defence law.

Importantly, the Constitution takes the next step and mandates that the judiciary take proactive measures to correct existing gender bias in criminal law. Section 39(2) reads: "when interpreting any legislation, and when developing the common law ... every court, tribunal or forum must promote the spirit, purport and objects of the Bill of Rights." The Constitutional Court in *Carmichele v Minister of Safety and Security* interpreted this provision as placing a positive duty on the courts to ask whether the common law requires development in accordance with s 39(2) and, if so, then to consider how to develop it.[371] This applies to both civil and criminal law,[372] as well as to statutory law. Advocates for abused women who kill should rely on these provisions to justify restructuring and/or reinterpreting the defences.

In a partial success, such advocacy resulted in at least one South African court acknowledging the inherent gender bias in criminal law and attempting to correct the bias by infusing women's experiences into the elements of self-defence. The Witwatersrand Local Division of the High Court agreed that "the development of the elements of the recognised defences has largely ignored women's lives and their experience of violence."[373] The court highlighted that self-defence needs to be developed to meet its obligation of equal treatment of women within the defence and broadened many of the elements to meet this requirement. Unfortunately, as will be described below, the finders of fact in the *Engelbrecht* decision erased many of these gains.

Over and over again, women victims of domestic violence suffer severe violations of their rights; first at the hands of their abusers, then at the hands of the State that protects them inadequately. For women who kill their abusers, particularly those who kill in non-confrontational situations, these constitutional rights violations continue through the prosecution stage. At the final stage, one of the few ways the legal system can rectify this situation is to provide women with equal access to criminal defences to murder and to a fair trial.

B. SELF-DEFENCE

The first and perhaps most controversial of the defences that should be accessible to abused women who kill in non-confrontational situations is self-defence. In South Africa, self-defence is usually referred to as private defence, thus the terms self-defence and private defence will be used interchangeably. Although it is generally accepted that a woman may justifiably kill her abuser in the midst of a violent attack, the question here is how a woman can claim self-defence if she kills her abuser while he is sleeping or even by contracting a killer. In the highly publicized *Engelbrecht* case, the Witwatersrand Local Division explicitly accepted that an abused woman who kills her abuser in a non-confrontational situation may qualify for private defence, although ultimately the accused was convicted of murder.[374] This section of the chapter explains why a woman who kills in a non-confrontational situation should be able to rely on self-defence, as well as how to advocate this defence on her behalf.

1. Legal theory of self-defence

The purpose of self-defence is to allow a person to protect him/herself from a violent attack when there are no other options available to avoid it.[375] In many situations, a person can call the police, or even leave, to stop an assailant. Where there are safe alternatives to defending oneself, the law expects the person to use them. Only when a person has no reasonable alternative can she or he use self-defence. The law recognizes self-defence as a criminal defence to assault or murder charges, refusing to punish a person for taking necessary steps to protect him/herself.

A superficial glance at cases in which women kill their abusers when they are sleeping, or by using a hired killer, suggests that self-defence law does not apply to them. Common sense tells us that an abused woman who is not being beaten at the moment she acts has other alternatives to killing her abuser. After all, if the abuse was so bad, she would simply leave.

As described in Part I of this book, abusive situations do not fall within the realm of a layperson's common sense. Research shows that it is not as easy for a woman to leave as it seems and, in fact, may be dangerous for her; Chapter 2 summarizes these difficulties. Chapter 1 describes how government responses to domestic violence shut down several other alternatives to self-defence. The police frequently refuse to intervene in domestic violence situations, sometimes ignoring protection orders. Courts do little to punish abusers and there are insufficient shelters for abused women. Informal networks such as family and friends similarly fail these women. In the context of abuse victims' lives as a whole, many and sometimes all of the alternatives to self-defence fall away.

An examination of the elements of self-defence within the context of domestic violence shows that South African criminal law is broad enough to include some women who kill their abusers in non-confrontational situations within the boundaries of the defence. After a look at the elements, the chapter explains how to apply self-defence to these cases, further explaining how to distinguish future cases from the decision in *Engelbrecht*. These arguments are punctuated with references to foreign examples in which abused women have succeeded with the defence.

2. Elements of self-defence under South African law

The elements of self-defence are as follows:

- An accused used force to repel an unlawful attack
- upon a protected interest;
- the attack must have commenced, or must be imminently threatened;
- the defensive action must have been taken against the attacker;
- the defender must have reasonably believed the act was necessary to protect against the attack;
- the response must be reasonable in light of the unlawful attack (proportionality).[376]

The accused must set out the foundation for each element sufficiently to show that "there is a reasonable possibility that he acted in self-defence."[377] To defeat the defence, the prosecutor must refute the possibility beyond a reasonable doubt.

(a) Elements of the attack
(i) Unlawful attack

An accused may argue self-defence if she or he was responding to an unlawful attack or a threat of an unlawful attack when she or he killed. This requirement separates self-defence from another criminal law defence – necessity, which allows an accused to defend against a lawful act. The unlawful attack may be an omission and does not have to be intentional.[378] The attack also may be aimed at another person, rather than at the accused.[379]

This element sets up the first potential hurdle to a woman's access to self-defence when she kills her abuser in a non-confrontational situation. Many South African criminal law experts, as well as many of their foreign counterparts, cannot locate an unlawful attack when the woman kills an abuser who is sleeping or otherwise not engaged in a fight.[380] They are looking for an overt act to which the woman is responding. Any break in violence is interpreted as an end to the unlawful attack and, therefore, the woman's need to defend herself.

In cases of abused women who kill their batterers in non-confrontational situations, the overt act is actually a threat of violence. The unlawful attack is not the last incident of violence, which suggests that the woman acted out of revenge. Rather, the last attack along with evidence of the history of abuse in the relationship explains the ongoing threat, which is the unlawful conduct against which the woman was defending.

For example, every day for a week, a man comes home from work and beats his wife. On the morning of day 8, the woman shoots her husband while he is sleeping. A court could infer from the pattern of abuse that she was responding to a threat of abuse from her husband although she did not expect it to happen for hours. As the Wyoming Supreme Court concluded: "The confrontational nature of an incident where a battered woman kills her abuser might only become apparent when viewed in the context of a pattern of violent behaviour rather than as an isolated incident."[381]

The main criticism of allowing the history of abuse to evidence an unlawful attack is that without an overt threat, the unlawful attack is merely speculative. These criticisms relate to the question of imminence, not whether the unlawful attack exists, and will be discussed separately below.

In the only decision on point in South Africa, the Witwatersrand Local Division accepted that a threat of violence could serve as the unlawful attack element of self-defence. The court took a particularly broad view of this element, finding:

> "That the unlawful 'attack' against which she defends herself or others may be one individual incident of abuse, a series of violations or an ongoing cycle of maltreatment… The attack may, but need not necessarily, be physical in nature and may include psychological and emotional abuse, degradation of life, diminution of dignity and threats to commit any such acts."[382]

In *S v Engelbrecht*, a woman suffocated her husband in his sleep after years of suffering physical, sexual, mental and economic abuse at his hands. Throughout their relationship, the husband would push, slap, beat and strangle the accused. On many occasions he would watch pornographic videos and force her to act out the scenes with him. He would scream at her, call her names, accuse her of adultery and harass and stalk her, among other forms of psychological violence. The accused tried to leave her husband on numerous occasions; she filed for divorce three times, attempted to press criminal charges several times and sought a protection order three times. In many instances, her efforts to stop the abuse were thwarted by the very powers charged with protecting her – the police and courts. She ultimately reconciled with her husband after more than a year of seeking help, feeling that she could not escape him and that financially she needed him.

The accused killed her husband six months after their final reconciliation. On the day of his death, the husband ordered her to pick up pornographic videos for him at a local sex shop. While she was there, she bought a pair of thumb cuffs. When the accused returned home, her husband, who had been drinking, began watching the video while their young daughter walked around the apartment. After watching a man shave a woman's pubic area on the video, the husband demanded that he do the same to the accused. She refused, tried to bargain with him and then was forced to submit. The daughter walked in on the forced shaving and appeared frightened; the husband then chased her from the room.

Later that day, while watching TV the daughter bumped the husband; he responded by yelling at her and then grabbing her and smacking her several times on her buttocks. When the accused tried to stop him, her husband started kicking her. He then pushed and shoved their daughter into her room and threatened to kill the accused if she tried to intervene. She told him that he could kill her but she was going to protect her child. The accused's husband continued to drink through the day. He may have taken sleeping pills at night as well. While the husband was asleep, the accused alleges that he began thrashing in the bed. She cuffed his thumbs and tied a plastic bag around his head, suffocating him.

The court ultimately concluded that the accused was responding to an unlawful attack based on the systematic abuse and attempts at controlling her, which included

> "… bodily manhandling and beating, verbal insults and threats, sexual violation and ridicule, attempts to isolate her from others, electronic monitoring and physical surveillance, sleep deprivation, enforcement of trivial demands, economic restrictions, physical, psychological and emotional humiliation and degradation both

publicly and privately, destruction of property, ever present control and domination."[383]

Essentially, the court accepted that the abuse did not consist of isolated incidents but created a pattern that would not stop without interference. It also accepted that the efforts at control, which are a large part of domestic violence, continue even when the violence does not.[384] As a result, the accused was always under a threat of violence. The court further believed that the accused felt that the threat included her daughter.[385]

Courts and legislatures in the United States, Australia and Canada also have accepted that a woman may be responding to an unlawful attack when she kills her abuser in a non-confrontational situation.[386] In fact, the American state of Arkansas has a statute that allows a pattern of domestic violence to serve as the unlawful attack against which the accused was defending. Accordingly, a person may argue self-defence when she or he responded to "the continuation of a pattern of domestic violence."[387] Two other states' statutes, in Maryland and Louisiana, allow an accused to admit evidence supporting a self-defence claim even if there is no apparent overt attack or threat to which the accused was responding.[388] They permit the accused to use a pattern of abuse to explain why she needed to defend herself.

(ii) Upon protected interests

An accused may argue self-defence when she or he was protecting "an interest which legally deserves to be protected."[389] South Africa takes a generous approach when determining which interests may be protected.[390] According to J M Burchell, "... our courts treat private defence casuistically and the tendency seems to be to expand rather than to limit the legal interests which a person is permitted to protect by force."[391]

Domestic violence violates a variety of women's constitutional rights, which South Africa's courts have recognized.[392] These rights, fully described above, are legally protected interests that should be discussed as part of a self-defence case.[393] Importantly, freedom from violence should include all forms of domestic violence described in the Domestic Violence Act.[394] The *Engelbrecht* decision followed the inclination toward expanding the types of legally protected interests, concluding:

> "It follows that the interests which are attacked and which an abused woman may protect include her life, bodily integrity, dignity, quality of life, her home, her emotional and psychological wellbeing, her freedom as well as those interests of her children. In short, she defends her status as a human being and/or mother."[395]

The interests that an abused woman is protecting when she acts in self-defence become important again when assessing the element of proportionality.

(iii) Attack imminent
The next element of self-defence is the imminence requirement. An accused must provide some evidence that the unlawful attack she or he feared had begun or was imminently threatened at the time she or he defended him/herself. A person cannot defend against an attack that will happen at some unknown point in the future, because at that stage the attack is merely speculative.[396] Instead, the person is expected to take protective measures only.[397] Nor can a person defend against an unlawful attack that has already concluded because that would be revenge.[398] South African courts historically construed the imminence requirement narrowly in cases involving abused women, concluding that the moment the physical abuse stopped the confrontation ended even if the abuser continued to verbally abuse or threaten the accused.[399] In a recent development, the *Engelbrecht* decision expanded the interpretation of imminence in these cases to include situations where the unlawful attack is inevitable.

In an effort to fulfil the constitutional requirement to eradicate gender bias in the common law, the Witwatersrand Local Division of the High Court reinterpreted the imminence element to allow for the inclusion of abused women's experiences within self-defence. The court determined that, "where abuse is frequent and regular such that it can be termed a 'pattern' or a 'cycle' of abuse then it would seem that the requirement of 'imminence' should extend to encompass abuse which is 'inevitable'."[400] Essentially, the court concluded that if the attack will happen unless someone or something unusual intervenes, it is imminent even if it is unclear when the violence will occur. Expecting the woman to wait for the unlawful attack to occur before she can respond would serve no purpose and place her in danger.[401]

The theory behind including inevitability within the interpretation of imminence stems from understanding that the imminence requirement serves as a proxy for proving that the defensive action was necessary.[402] If there is an imminent attack, such as with an upraised knife, it is assumed that a person could not flee the threat of harm or call the police for assistance, which makes self-defence necessary.[403] While imminence may be the easiest way to prove that defensive measures were necessary, it is not the only one.[404] Where an attack is inevitable, it requires intervention to prevent it, which means it is no longer speculative.[405] Whether an abused woman is justified in using self-defence then will depend on whether she can show that there was no other reasonable way to stop the threatened violence.

While the change in the interpretation of the imminence requirement provides women with new access to an old defence, it does so without changing the theoretical basis of private defence. The purpose of the defence remains the same, which is to allow a person to defend against an unlawful attack when the state cannot help her, but the elements of the defence are expanded to accommodate the experiences of abuse victims. Allowing an abused woman to present evidence that an attack is inevitable, rather than temporally imminent, and that she had no other way to protect herself, places the accused on the same footing as other self-defence claimants – she protected herself when the threat arose and she had no other way to stop it. The theoretical underpinnings of the defence remain unchanged even without evidence of strict temporal imminence.

The court in *Engelbrecht* relied in part on the decision *Ex parte Minister van Justisie: In re S v Van Wyk*[406] as precedent for allowing self-defence against an inevitable attack.[407] In *Van Wyk*, the accused owned a store that was broken into repeatedly. The accused notified the police, set up anti-theft measures and even employed guards. All of these actions failed to stop the burglaries. The accused then set up a shotgun to shoot at the legs of an intruder. He posted notices warning of the shotgun and notified the police of his actions. An intruder was killed when he entered the store. Two members of the bench explained how these facts fit within classic private defence:

> "The stated case differs from ordinary cases only in that in the defence, that is the placing of the gun, there was no immediately threatening danger that could be resisted by a defender who was present ... there was however, actually threatening harm by intruders which Van Wyk could expect with reasonable certainty and which he could not reasonably prevent except *in absentia.*"[408]

The court accepted the pattern of theft as evidence of an imminently threatened attack, although at the time the accused rigged the shotgun, there was no thief in the store.

When arguing the inevitability of the unlawful attack on behalf of a woman who killed her abuser in a non-confrontational situation, defence counsel must address two points. The first is that the threat of violence persists unabated in abusive relationships regardless of whether the couple is currently fighting. As described in Chapters 2 and 3, domestic violence is a process and a lull in the violence is one step in that process. Rather than looking at each incident of violence individually, courts have to understand the cumulative fear that builds in abusive relationships and the abusers' continual need to reinforce their control through violence. Expert testimony can bring home these points.[409]

The second point relates specifically to the relationship between the accused and her abuser – the defence must provide evidence of why the abuse was inevitable within their particular relationship. The accused can rely on a pattern of abuse in the relationship to make this point. Consider again the example where, every day for a week, a man comes home from work and beats his wife. A court could infer from the pattern of abuse that on the morning of day 8, when the woman killed her sleeping husband, that she was responding to an imminent or inevitable threat of abuse.

Defence counsel in *Engelbrecht* successfully combined testimony of the pattern of abuse in the accused's relationship with a general explanation of the continuous nature of the threat of violence in all abusive relationships to meet the inevitability requirement established by the court. The court explained:

> "We are all of the view that, by contrast (to the sleeping Mr. Engelbrecht), Mrs Engelbrecht could not be and was not at rest. There is no respite for the abused victim who awaits the next indication of mood or behaviour from the abuser. We agree that, in the pattern of violence and the cycle of abuse which comprised the Engelbrecht relationship, the interludes between violent or cruel episodes may be as stressful as the actual assaults… The threat of violence or psychological or emotional cruelty endures beyond the immediate proximity of Mr and Mrs Engelbrecht. It reached past each one of their separations since Mr Engelbrecht was adept

at finding Mrs Engelbrecht at work, in the shops, asleep in her flat, socialising with her friends, at her new residence and at her proposed employment in another town. Each time he did so another act of domestic violence was perpetrated by him.

* * *

It was always possible, and always present in her mind, that this man would repeat his domestic violence and accordingly, Mr Engelbrecht only needed to enact relatively minor acts of reinforcement to reinforce the anxiety and fear of further abuse."[410]

The court in *Engelbrecht* was convinced that the next act of abuse was, based on the pattern of abuse in the accused's relationship, just around the corner.

In addition to evidence of a pattern of abuse and closely related to it, defence counsel can also explain that a woman's experience with her abuser allows her to predict when she is being threatened with actual and inevitable violence, even if others could not. As explained in Chapter 2, women attempt to cope with abuse by identifying signals of future abuse, such as facial expressions, verbal cues and other behaviour that typically precedes the violence. Experts explain that abused women develop a heightened sensitivity to their abuser's behaviour, which gives them the predicative capability.[411] Essentially, a "woman may be aware of pre-assault symbols, such as heavy drinking, that would not signify imminent danger to outsiders."[412]

For example, consider the woman who is severely beaten each time her boyfriend wakes up with a hangover. On the night he is killed, the boyfriend comes home drunk and passes out on the couch. The woman kills him while he is sleeping. A court could locate an imminent attack from evidence that the husband was drunk. Another example is the woman who kills her husband after he accuses her of cheating on him. From past experience, the woman has learned that when her husband acts with jealousy, it is a prelude to abuse. For some, a facial expression alone can signal abuse. Although an outsider would not see the threats in these behaviours, the women have learned to predict their abusers' violence as part of their survival skills.

Evidence that supports a pattern of abuse and the woman's ability to predict her abuser's violence based on "pre-assault symbols" could also support classic definitions of imminence. In some instances, the pattern of abuse both makes the threat evident and tells the woman when she reasonably can expect the next incident of abuse, such as in the example of a woman who is beaten by her husband after work every day for a week. Evidence of symbolic behaviour works the same way. The woman's experience with her abuser explains that unless someone or something unusual intervenes, a lull in violence will not eliminate the threat.

Although not referenced by the court in *Engelbrecht*, there is South African precedent for the approach to the element of imminence in self-defence cases that a lull in violence does not end its threat, even if the assailant cannot carry out the attack immediately. It does this without relying on evidence that another attack was inevitable. In *S v Mogohlwane*, the accused had been robbed by the deceased and threatened with an axe on a street near his home.[413] The accused went home and attempted to get help from his parents to recover the stolen goods. When that failed, he grabbed a knife and returned to the street where the deceased had remained. The accused demanded his property, which the deceased refused. When the deceased again threatened the accused with the axe, the accused killed him. The accused claimed self-defence against a murder charge.

According to the court in *Mogohlwane*, "the decisive question is thus whether the deceased's assault on the accused must really be regarded as having been completed and ended when the accused approached him with a knife and tried to remove the bag from his possession or control."[414] If the accused protected himself during the course of the robbery, then he could argue self-defence; otherwise, he would be convicted of murder.

The court concluded that the accused had acted during the course of the robbery, although he had walked into his home and away from the street and the deceased prior to killing him. The court based its conclusion on the following facts: (1) at the time the deceased took the accused's property, the deceased had overpowered the accused; (2) the accused believed there was no meaningful interruption in time between the taking of the property and the deceased's death; (3) at the time of the accused's action, the deceased's "thieving intention" continued; and (4) overall, the events occurred in a relatively close period of time. Ultimately, the court acquitted the accused on the basis of self-defence.

For purposes of women who kill their abusers, the important facts are the same. At the time of the attacks, the abused women are overpowered by their abusers; the continuing threat of violence in domestic violence situations leads women to believe that there is no interruption in violence; and the abuser maintains his abusive intentions as part of his control techniques. The act of abuse and the woman's defensive action should also be treated as close in time when the unlawful attack consists of an ongoing and continuous threat.

While both the pattern of abuse and symbolic behaviour should be able to support a finding of temporal imminence in some cases, the *Engelbrecht* decision highlights the importance of the court's ruling that broadened the definitional requirements of imminence. In the finding of facts, the judge and two assessors found imminence because of evidence of inevitability. Satchwell J explained at some length her basis for concluding the abuse was inevitable:

> "Mr Engelbrecht would have hit or beaten or otherwise abused Mrs Engelbrecht again if he had not died. The events of the 29th June were no more than pointers to what would happen again and again. Nothing had changed in Mr Engelbrecht's psyche or in his tongue or his fists and so nothing would change in the cycle of abuse. Further domestic violence was therefore both foreseeable and inevitable… It is appropriate and reasonable in this case to find that domestic violence at the hands of Mr Engelbrecht towards Mrs Engelbrecht was indeed imminent, pending, hanging over her head, threatening, ready to befall her, foreseeable, and inevitable."[415]

Advocate Opperman, one of the assessors, stated expressly that the accused had failed to present sufficient evidence of temporal imminence, or "objective imminence," but had shown that the next attack was inevitable.[416] Had the court not adopted inevitability as an alternative requirement to or an additional definition of imminence, at least one of the assessors, and possibly both, would have found that the unlawful attack was not imminent.[417]

As with the element of an unlawful attack, the main criticism of allowing a pattern of abuse and symbolic behaviour as evidence of an imminent or inevitable attack is that without an overt threat, the unlawful attack is merely speculative.[418] Essentially, critics argue that such evidence punishes past behaviour rather than defends against imminent harm. Ignoring the pattern of abuse and pre-assault symbols, however, disregards the reality of domestic violence and women's experiences, perpetuating gender bias in criminal defence law. The main justification for the court's new interpretation for imminence to include inevitability also addresses this criticism – forcing a woman to wait for the upraised knife or fist before she can act in self-defence serves no real purpose when an attack is inevitable, expected and foreseeable, and only places the woman at greater risk.[419]

Another important gain for abused women who kill in non-confrontational situations is that the *Engelbrecht* decision expressly states what is implied in the *Van Wyk* decision: premeditation of a defensive act is not inherently inconsistent with the concept of private defence.[420] This point is particularly important for women who kill their abusers in non-confrontational situations, particularly those who hire third parties to complete the killing. It accepts what should be obvious but has been treated by the law as deviant – a person may plan how to defend him/herself in anticipation of an inevitable attack.

The *Engelbrecht* decision referred to comparative law in support of its decision to reform the common-law requirement of imminence as applied to women who kill their abusers. The remainder of this section will describe the Canadian and American cases on which the *Engelbrecht* court relied, as well as other comparative law that offers examples of the approach to imminence advocated for and applied in South Africa.

Canada takes an aggressive approach toward including abused women's experiences into self-defence. Canadian self-defence law is governed by s 34 of their Criminal Code, which contains no imminence requirement.[421] Although initially the courts interpreted the statute to include one, recent Supreme Court of Canada rulings have eliminated it.

The decision *Lavallee v Queen* was the first to overrule the imminence requirement.[422] The case involved a woman in a severely abusive relationship. One evening, her boyfriend threatened to kill her after their guests left their home. The woman shot the boyfriend as he was leaving the room to return to the guests. The Court found that a woman's fear of an imminent attack "may have been reasonable in the context of the relationship."[423] It observed that:

> "Another aspect of the cyclical nature of the abuse is that that it begets a degree of predictability to the violence that is absent in an isolated violent encounter between two strangers. This also means that it may in fact be possible for a battered spouse to accurately predict the onset of violence before the first blow is struck, even if an outsider to the relationship cannot. Indeed, it has been suggested that a battered woman's knowledge of her partner's violence is so heightened that she is able to anticipate the nature and extent (though not the onset) of the violence by his conduct beforehand."[424]

The Canadian Supreme Court explained that imminence is not the only way to determine whether an abused woman had any other alternatives to defending against an unlawful attack. The judge writing the majority opinion recognized the role of imminence in this determination, but refused to adopt a *per se* rule that unless an accused was in the middle of a confrontation she or he could not prove defensive measures were necessary.[425] Instead, the court exchanged an imminence requirement for evidence that self-defence was necessary. It explained that as a result of women's "size, strength, socialization and lack of training", abused women are not likely to win a hand-to-hand battle with their abusers. Quoting the *Gallegos* decision described below, the majority opinion explained that expecting a woman to wait until she is in the middle of a confrontation to respond to a threat of violence "is tantamount to sentencing her to 'murder by instalment'."[426] Later Canadian decisions have upheld that a woman may access self-defence even when an imminent threat or attack is absent.[427]

Some jurisdictions in the United States retain the imminence requirement, but broaden the definition to include when a threat of harm is inevitable. Two American states statutorily allow the pattern of domestic violence to determine imminence. Kentucky enacted legislation that explains: "'Imminent' means impending danger and, in the context of domestic violence and abuse as defined by Kentucky Revised Statutes ... belief that danger is imminent can be inferred from a past pattern of repeated serious abuse."[428] In Utah, the pattern of violence is one factor used to determine imminence.[429]

One of the more instructive cases in which a court in the United States allowed a woman to prove imminence using a pattern of domestic violence arose in New Mexico. In *State v Gallegos*,[430] a woman shot her abusive husband who was lying on the couch and then stabbed him several times, ultimately killing him. The lower courts refused to allow the accused to argue self-defence because they could not locate an imminent threat or overt attack on the part of the deceased. The New Mexico Court of Appeals overturned the lower court rulings, concluding:

> "Incidents of domestic violence tend to follow predictable patterns. Recurring stimuli, such as drunkenness or jealousy, reliably incite brutal rages. Remarks or gestures which are merely offensive or perhaps even meaningless to the general public may be understood by the abused individual as an affirmation of impending physical abuse. To require the battered person to await a blatant, deadly assault before she can act in defense of herself would not only ignore unpleasant reality, but would amount to sentencing her to 'murder by instalment'."[431]

The New Mexico Court, however, cautioned that the fact that the woman had been abused is not enough to qualify her for self-defence. Rather, she must provide some evidence that she believed she was in imminent danger at the time she acted.[432]

Relying on both the pattern of abuse and an abuse victim's heightened capabilities to predict violence, the Supreme Court of Washington allowed a battered child who killed his abuser in a non-confrontational situation to argue self-defence. The court explained:

> "That the triggering behavior and the abusive episode are divided by time does not necessarily negate the reasonableness of the defendant's perception of imminent harm. Even an otherwise innocuous comment which occurred days before the homicide could be highly relevant when the evidence shows that such a comment inevitably signaled the beginning of an abusive episode."[433]

Finally, the Supreme Court of the Northern Territory of Australia accepted that domestic violence is a process and that a threat of violence continues as long as an abuser remains able to carry out his threat. In *R v Secretary*, a woman killed her husband while he was sleeping. Just prior to falling asleep, the deceased had threatened her. The Supreme Court concluded:

> "At the time the threat was uttered there was an ability (actual or apparent) to carry out the threat when the stipulated time came. On the facts, short of being disabled from effecting the threat, whether by pre-emptive strike or the accused's flight or otherwise, the deceased's ability to carry out the threat continued."[434]

With proper advocacy, many abused women who kill in non-confrontational situations either can provide sufficient evidence that they faced an imminent, continuing threat and/or that the attack was inevitable, meeting the imminence element of self-defence.

Excerpts from *Lavallee v Queen 55CCC3d97(SupC+Can.1990)*

> The sense in which "imminence" is used conjures up the image of "an up-lifted knife" or a pointed gun. The rationale for the imminence rule seems obvious. The law of self-defence is designed to ensure that the use of defensive force is really necessary. It justifies the act because the defender reasonably believed that he or she had no alternative but to take the attacker's life. If there is a significant time interval between the original unlawful assault and the accused's response, one tends to suspect that the accused was motivated by revenge rather than self-defence. In the paradigmatic case of a one-time bar-room brawl between two men of equal size and strength, this inference makes sense. How can one feel endangered to the point of firing a gun at an unarmed man who utters a death threat, then turns his back and walks out of the room? One cannot be certain of the gravity of the threat or his capacity to carry it out. Besides, one can always take the opportunity to flee or to call the police. If he comes back and raises his fist, one can respond in kind if need be. These are the tacit assumptions that underlie the imminence rule.

* * *

> The implication ... is that it is inherently unreasonable to apprehend death or grievous bodily harm unless and until the physical assault is actually in progress, at which point the victim can presumably gauge the requisite amount of force needed to repel the attack and act accordingly.

In my view, expert testimony can cast doubt on these assumptions as they are applied in the context of a battered wife's efforts to repel an attack.

* * *

Even accepting that a battered woman may be uniquely sensitized to danger from her batterer, it may yet be contended that the law ought to require her to wait until the knife is uplifted, the gun pointed or the fist clenched before her apprehension is deemed reasonable. This would allegedly reduce the risk that the woman is mistaken in her fear, although the law does not require her fear to be correct, only reasonable. In response to this contention, I need only point to the observation made by Huband JA that the evidence showed that when the appellant and Rust physically fought, the appellant "invariably got the worst of it". I do not think it is an unwarranted generalization to say that due to their size, strength, socialization and lack of training, women are typically no match for men in hand-to-hand combat. The requirement ... that a battered woman wait until the physical assault is "under way" before her apprehensions can be validated in law would, in the words of an American court, be tantamount to sentencing her to "murder by instalment": *State v Gallegos* 719 P 2d 1268 at 1271 (1986) (NM). I share the view expressed by M J Willoughby in "Rendering each woman her due: Can a battered woman claim self-defense when she kills her sleeping batterer" (1989) 38 *Kan L Rev* 169 at 184, that "society gains nothing, except perhaps the additional risk that the battered woman will herself be killed, because she must wait until her abusive husband instigates another battering episode before she can justifiably act".

Excerpt from *State v Nemeth* 82 Ohio St 3d 202 (Sup Ct Oh 1998)

> Non-confrontational killings do not fit the general pattern of self-defense. Without expert testimony, a trier of fact may not be able to understand that the defendant at the time of the killing could have had an honest belief that he was in imminent danger of death or great bodily harm. Further, it is difficult for the average person to understand the degree of helplessness an abused child may feel. Thus, expert testimony would also 'help dispel the ordinary lay person's perception that a person in a battering relationship is free

to leave at any time'." . . . In either instance, the expert testimony 'is aimed at an area where the purported common knowledge of the jury may be very much mistaken, an area where jurors' logic, drawn from their own experience, may lead to a wholly incorrect conclusion.'

(b) Defensive action
(i) Defensive act must be directed at the attacker
This element merely requires that the accused have acted against the attacker committing the unlawful attack.[435] If the accused killed a third person to protect him/herself from an unlawful attack, the appropriate defence would be necessity.

(ii) Defensive act must be necessary to protect the accused
The next element of the test for self-defence is that the defensive action must have been necessary to protect the accused. This element explicitly states what is implied in the imminence standard: the accused must have had no other alternatives to stop the attack at the time she or he acted.[436] Providing sufficient evidence of the necessity of self-defence typically requires explaining why a woman did not leave, go to the police, the courts or to friends and family rather than kill her abuser.[437]

(aa) Options for avoiding abuse
The *Engelbrecht* decision divides women's options for ending domestic violence into two categories – turning to law enforcement and fleeing the violence; turning to informal support networks falls into the latter option. Within the category of law enforcement, an abused woman could apply to the courts for a protection order or apply to the police to press criminal charges for assault and/or arrest the abuser for violating a protection order. While the courts and the police could help abuse victims end their violent relationships, the law enforcement options do not necessarily require the women to leave their homes. Under the Domestic Violence Act, courts can order the eviction of the abusers from their homes or their imprisonment for violations of a protection order. Under criminal law, courts can also sentence abusers to imprisonment upon conviction on a charge of assault.

The court in *Engelbrecht* attempted to set some rules for the consideration of whether defensive action was necessary for a woman who is charged with the murder of her abuser. Quoting C R Snyman, it explained that "the basic idea underlying private defence is that a person is allowed to 'take the law into her own hands', as it were, only if the ordinary legal remedies do not afford her effective protection."[438] Thus, a court must "critically examine" whether law enforcement effectively prevented or was willing to end the domestic violence against the accused.[439] Essentially, the court should assess whether the police or courts actually provided, or realistically would have provided, a long-term solution to the violence in the accused's circumstances.

Outside the realm of law enforcement, abused women could try to end the violence with help from informal support networks or by leaving their abusers. The court in *Engelbrecht* treats them both as the option of fleeing. The court explains that the formal channels of support through law enforcement and the informal channels of requesting help from friends, family, neighbours, clergy, battered women's shelters and other informal support networks "would assist the abused woman to extricate herself from abuse or to provide refuge at a time of attack."[440] Logically, help from informal channels of support is tantamount to seeking help to flee one's home. Informal support networks have no power to remove an abuser from his home or to stop him from abusing his victim. Because domestic violence is a continuous process, providing refuge from one attack will not offer a long-term solution, although it may stop an immediate attack.[441] A long-term solution from informal networks, therefore, requires the victim to leave her home.

To the extent that access to informal support networks is treated separately from the option of fleeing, the *Engelbrecht* decision further concluded that whether informal networks could have helped the accused is irrelevant because "one should not place the onus upon the abused victim to initiate, discover or develop support systems where the law has failed."[442] Whether they could have protected the accused or prevented the unlawful attack speaks to whether there were less drastic means the accused could have used to protect him/herself, which should be considered the elements of proportionality. Despite the court's statement that access to informal support networks is irrelevant to the consideration of whether defensive action was necessary, defence counsel should be prepared to explain why the informal networks also were not a reasonable option to stop the abuse.

For women living with their abusers, fleeing the violence usually means fleeing their homes. For women who are not cohabitating with their abusers, it could be as simple as ending their relationships; if the abusers continue to harass and stalk their victims, however, then it means fleeing their homes. The importance of the distinction between the options that require a woman to flee her home and those that do not appears in the next rule or boundary set by the *Engelbrecht* decision, which relates to whether an abuse victim has a duty to flee.

Cases in which abused women kill in non-confrontational situations raise two separate issues with regard to this duty. The first is whether the woman has a duty to flee her home instead of acting in self-defence. Historically, it has been unclear whether the duty to flee exists under South African law regardless of the relationship between the accused and the assailant. The second duty is applied only in cases involving abused women and requires the abused woman to flee the relationship before defensive action becomes necessary. In practice some South African courts have applied both duties to abused women.[443]

The court in *Engelbrecht* does not explicitly eradicate the requirement of a duty to flee one's home to avoid taking defensive measures, but suggests it should not exist: "I am cautious about requiring the abused woman (and her child(ren) to vacate her (their) home leaving the abusive spouse in full occupation."[444] The court bases its caution in part on Snyman, who argues that a duty to flee "is a negation of the whole essence of private defence. Private defence deals with the defence of the legal order, that is the upholding of justice. Fleeing is no defence, but a capitulation to injustice."[445] Snyman concludes that even if a general duty to flee exists, no one should be required to flee from his or her home.[446]

The court also quotes from the Canadian Supreme Court decision in *Lavallee* to support its point: "Traditional self-defence doctrine does not require a person to retreat from her home instead of defending herself: A man's home may be his castle but it is also the woman's home even if it seems to her more like a prison in the circumstances."[447] The court in *Lavallee* refused to apply a duty to retreat from their homes to abused women when it did not place the same duty on other victims of crime.[448]

Because the court in *Engelbrecht* did not state unequivocally that there is no duty to flee from one's home, advocates advancing self-defence on behalf of a woman who killed her abuser in a non-confrontational situation must specifically fight against the application of the duty. The arguments against such a duty explain that a duty to flee, rather than act in self-defence, places an unfair burden on victims of domestic violence – unfair both because it may not exist for other victims of crime and because it is excessively burdensome on them.

First, a comparison between the *Nape* and *Mogohlwane* decisions highlights a double standard in the law that currently (or until the *Engelbrecht* decision) treats abuse victims differently from other criminally accused. In *Nape v S*[449] a woman killed her husband after a long history of abuse. Although she did not plead self-defence, the lower court noted in its consideration of mitigation of sentence:

> "The accused had a wide range of options open to her at the time of the commission of the offence, such as removing the firearm from where it was placed, going away from the house together with the children, even if it was late. Nothing could be more risky than staying in a house where somebody was threatening to use a firearm against you."

In this instance, the court believed that the deceased threatened the accused with a firearm. It did not dispute that she faced great danger at the hands of her abuser. Despite that, it required her to take her children and run. Her failure to do so weighed against mitigation of sentence.

In contrast, the court in *Mogohlwane*,[450] which is described under the element of imminence, did not place a duty to flee on the accused although it is apparent he could have fled safely. As a reminder, in *Mogohlwane* the deceased stole property from the accused and threatened him with an axe. The accused left and then returned to the scene of the robbery armed with a knife. Nothing required the accused to return and the accused knew the deceased was armed. Despite the opportunity to flee (or stay away), the accused confronted the deceased. The deceased again threatened the accused with an axe and the accused killed him. The accused successfully defended against murder charges on the basis of self-defence. The court did not place a duty to flee on him, although the argument favouring the duty to flee in *Mogohlwane* was stronger than in *Nape* because the accused was not being required to flee from his home but from the street.

Even if a duty to flee one's home applies to all persons who argue self-defence, placing such a duty on abused women creates an onerous burden on them when compared with other claimants of self-defence. In most criminal situations, fleeing one's home would be a short-term solution to a short-term threat. A person who runs from his or her home because of a burglar knows that he or she can call the police, allowing him or her to reclaim the home. An abused woman would be expected to give up her home permanently.

A duty to flee the home also is unfairly onerous because it places abuse victims in danger. Courts that apply a duty to flee to abuse victims assume that as soon as the woman leaves, the threat to her disappears. Solutions to domestic violence typically are not that simple. As explained in Chapter 2, the most dangerous time for a woman in any relationship is when she tries to leave. Additionally, many of these women have been threatened that if they try, their abusers will find them and hurt or kill them.

The expectation that the woman could flee does not account for women's reasonable fears. In fact, the law places them in a "cruel dilemma" when it suspends or lowers the sentences of abusive men who kill their intimate partners because they left, while refusing to accept an argument for self-defence because the woman stayed: "If she leaves and is killed, the law may say that the very act of leaving provoked her killer's distress. But if she acts on her own fears and kills, the law may question her claim for compassion precisely because she did not leave."[451]

The assumption that underlies the belief that a woman can always flee appears to be that if the man is beating his intimate partner, he wants her to leave. As explained in Chapter 2, men use domestic violence as a way to control women often because they specifically want them to stay. These women cannot simply pack a bag and walk out. Potentially, to avoid being found, they would have to give up their jobs and even their relationships with friends and family, in addition to their homes. Advocates arguing against a duty to flee must explain why many women cannot safely leave their abusers as well as describe the additional burdens it places on them.

The third boundary the court in *Engelbrecht* created when considering whether self-defence was necessary relates to the second type of duty to flee. Experience in foreign jurisdictions shows that even when courts accept that a woman has no duty to flee her home, they often replace it with a requirement that she leave her relationship when it becomes abusive or surrender the right to self-defence. This requirement arises from the belief that if the abuse were as bad as the woman claims, she would have left the relationship.[452] It assumes that if the woman did not leave, there must not be sufficient abuse to justify lethal self-defence. The court in *Engelbrecht* expressly rejected the application of this duty in self-defence: "Judgment should not be passed on the fact that an accused battered woman stayed in the abusive relationship. Still less is the court entitled to conclude that she forfeited her right to self-defence for having so done."[453] The court relied on the point that a woman's decision to remain in the relationship at some earlier stage does not speak to whether she needed to act in self-defence at the moment she killed.[454]

A closer look at the *Engelbrecht* decision shows that the assessors to some extent ignored the court's statement of the law, essentially punishing the accused for having returned to her relationship. Professor Naude, whose positions were supported by Advocate Oppermann on this issue, explained that accessing the legal system remained an option for the accused to avoid self-defence. They justified this conclusion in part on the fact that the accused never completed a divorce and ultimately reconciled with the deceased:

> "She did not pursue the first divorce action she initiated because she instructed them to be halted. She made no objection when Mr Engelbrecht decided to halt the second divorce action. Although the third divorce action became mired in delay when the report from the office of the Family Advocate was not forthcoming, those proceedings fell away when they became reconciled in December 2001. It was Mrs Engelbrecht who took Mr Engelbrecht into her home."[455]

Despite the court's unequivocal statement that the law does not require an abused woman to flee her relationship before self-defence becomes necessary, defence counsel will need to defend against the application of such a duty to abused women. The main argument is that such a duty creates a burden on abused women that does not exist for other criminally accused. As one academic explained, "(w)e do not ask of the man in the barroom brawl that he leave the bar before the occurrence of an anticipated fight, but we do ask the battered woman threatened with abuse why she did not leave the relationship."[456] Ms Justice Satchwell, in her minority opinion on the facts in *Engelbrecht*, similarly explained: "Courts do not normally demand an accounting from nor penalise the victims of crime or abuse as to the steps they have taken to avoid being murdered, raped, robbed, assaulted, stolen from and so on."[457] To allow this burden to continue treats the women as though they are responsible for creating the dangerous situation, which blames the victim and removes all responsibility from the abuser.

In the face of ambiguous precedent, advocates on behalf of these women need to fight against the application of either a duty to flee one's home and/or a duty to flee the relationship before self-defence becomes necessary. While doing so, advocates building a defence must be prepared to explain why the woman did not employ these options, as well as options offered by law enforcement agencies and informal support networks, before killing her abuser. Advocates must seek an answer to these questions directly from the abused woman, supporting her responses with the information contained in Chapters 1 through 3. The advocate should engage expert witnesses to clarify the woman's explanations and relate them, where necessary, to the psychological impact of abuse on its victims as well as to her previous efforts to seek help.

For example, expert testimony can clarify how the abuse could be so intolerable, although the woman remained in the relationship, as well as clarify why the woman's decision to remain does not mean she did not act in self-defence. It could explain that it is common for abuse victims to believe they cannot escape the abuse and that this belief is reasonable in the context of abuse. The testimony could describe that in most situations, the abusers intentionally instil this belief in their victims to keep them from running away or turning to the police or courts. The abusers reinforce this belief with violence. Over time, the process of domestic violence ensures that women have few options to escape the violence, all of which is exacerbated by insufficient responses by police and the women's social networks to their cries for help. Without expert testimony on the spiral of entrapment, courts may find it difficult to fathom why self-defence was necessary when an abuser was sleeping or watching TV.

In conclusion, a careful reading of the *Engelbrecht* decision suggests that the inquiry into whether the abused woman had any other options to stop the violence should stop at the efficacy of legal solutions. It arguably eradicated the duty to flee one's home and unequivocally eradicated a duty to flee the relationship. It also refused to consider whether the informal support networks could have provided an alternative to escape the abuse, first because at best these networks can only help the woman flee and second because the duty to protect the woman lies with the state. While we hope that other courts will follow the rules established by the *Engelbrecht* court, defence counsel needs to be prepared to address every option that might possibly have been open to the accused to avoid lethal self-defence and needs to be ready to defend against the application of a duty to flee in these cases.

(bb) Distinguishing the Engelbrecht *case*

Meeting the element of necessity of defensive action will be very difficult after the *Engelbrecht* decision. While the judge sought to expand the elements of self-defence to include women's experiences with domestic violence within their interpretation, the assessors who were responsible for deciding the facts of the case (along with the judge) destroyed what gains the expansion of the law had made. They set the level of factual proof of this element impossibly high. Essentially, the assessors require abused women to exhaust every avenue available to them to escape the abuse (without regard for what is reasonable); and by 'exhaust', the assessors mean that these women should try the options repeatedly, regardless of the responses their cries for help receive.

The accused in *Engelbrecht* asked the police to help her between 6 and 9 times over a two-year period. The police arrested her husband only once and, even then, only at the insistence of hospital employees. The police failed to investigate the criminal charges, which resulted in two postponements of the criminal case. During this time, the deceased was released on bail and eventually the accused, with her husband standing behind her, dropped the charges. On a later occasion, when the accused called the police begging for help, they challenged her because she had dropped the charges previously; ultimately the police did not show up. This was not the only time they failed to respond.

When the accused came to the police station for help several times, they required her to meet with a person from a Victim Empowerment Centre before pressing charges. Each time she met with Mrs van Kerken. Mrs van Kerken testified that she did not believe the accused had been abused, finding her difficult and her husband charming:

> "Mrs van Kerken advised Mr Engelbrecht to lay a complaint against Mrs Engelbrecht; Mrs van Kerken criticised Mrs Engelbrecht to the court for not being grateful but demanding; Mrs van Kerken presumed to form an opinion on a complaint of criminal action without any investigation which, in any event, was not hers to conduct; on one occasion Mrs van Kerken would not even record a complaint."[458]

Only after going to more senior police officials was the accused finally able to press charges. The deceased was never arrested, although the accused called several times to check the progress of the arrest. Despite the accused's efforts to approach the police for help, the vast majority of which were ultimately ignored, the assessors concluded that the accused retained the option of turning to the police, denying that self-defence was necessary.

The accused in *Engelbrecht* approached the courts on seven separate occasions for help, three times seeking protection orders, once through a criminal prosecution and three times with a divorce application. After being abused, the accused first applied for a divorce in April or May 2000; she stopped the proceedings after reconciling with the deceased. The next time she went to the courts for help, in September 2000, she simultaneously sought a protection order and a divorce and pressed charges that resulted in a criminal prosecution for domestic violence. All three of these court processes failed at one stage or another.

With regard to the protection order, the accused was granted an interim order in early October 2000. It appears either that the accused never received notice for the final hearing or that she was unable to leave work, hence she did not appear. In fact, only an advocate representing the deceased appeared and the advocate falsely told the court that the accused had dropped the criminal charges against the deceased as well as the application for the divorce. The magistrate had a copy of the accused's sworn statement, which under the Domestic Violence Act is a sufficient basis for granting a final protection order.[459] Rather than grant the order, the magistrate dismissed the application.

The criminal prosecution fared no better, having been remanded on two occasions because of the police's failure to investigate the claim. In November 2000, long after the hearing on the final protection order, the accused dropped the charges with her husband standing behind her. As

Satchwell J notes in her minority opinion on the facts, this should have raised questions:

> "It is surprising that the SAPS even allowed this to take place in this manner. Mrs Engelbrecht was not heard in privacy independent of the presence of the accused. After all if an alleged robber sat with the victim of the alleged robbery in the charge office when the complaint was withdrawn the SAPS would surely question the victim as to the circumstances of such 'withdrawal'?"[460]

The accused also sought a divorce, but the deceased eluded the sheriff on the six different occasions he tried to serve notice of the divorce proceedings. In December, the accused and the deceased reconciled and the accused stopped the divorce proceedings.

In February 2001 the accused again sought a protection order from the court and started divorce proceedings. The deceased followed the advice of Mrs van Kerken from the Victim Empowerment Centre and applied for a protection order against the accused. When the parties appeared before the magistrate in relation to the protection order, the magistrate dismissed both requests. There appears to be no reasonable explanation for the dismissal.[461]

With regard to the divorce proceedings, the deceased's request for a report regarding custody of their child to be submitted by the Office of the Family Advocate stalled the divorce. The accused's divorce attorney wrote four letters in a five-month period to the Family Advocate, pushing for the report. In November 2001, during the course of the divorce process and after a violent episode, the accused sought another protection order. The magistrate struck the application off the roll because there was no evidence that the deceased had been served. There is no record that the magistrate ordered notice to be served and the Domestic Violence Act does not, in any case, require the attendance of the respondent when a protection order is requested. In December 2001, the accused again reconciled with the deceased and stopped the divorce proceedings.

Of the seven attempts the accused made to use the court system to end her relationship or end the violence, the state's omissions resulted in the dismissal of one or possibly two applications for protection orders, delayed indefinitely two separate divorce proceedings and resulted in the postponement of criminal charges which were eventually dropped under questionable circumstances. Again, despite the failure of the court system to address the accused's needs on the numerous occasions she approached it, the assessors concluded that the courts could have provided her with effective remedies to stop the domestic violence.

In addition to her efforts to use law enforcement bodies to end the domestic violence, the accused also left the deceased on at least three separate occasions. While separated, the accused suffered from stalking, harassment and violence from the deceased, who was angry and frustrated that she had left him.[462] As a result of the deceased's behaviour, the accused moved five separate times. Twice she allowed him to return to her. During one of their separations, the accused applied for employment that would have required her to move far from the deceased. When the deceased learned of this, he called the prospective employer and told the personnel department that the accused was no longer interested. Although described under the factual findings for the element of proportionality, which is discussed below, the assessors also concluded that the accused could have simply fled the deceased and her home to escape the violence.[463]

The accused repeatedly employed all three primary options to end the domestic violence (turning to the police, the courts or simply fleeing), yet none of these options ever succeeded at stopping the violence. The assessors' findings of fact, in reality, place the duty on the accused to assure that the courts meet their legal obligations to notify her of court dates.[464] They blame her for dropping the charges against the deceased although the case had been postponed twice because the police failed to investigate the charges. Neither assessor addressed the details of the protection orders, including that one application was dismissed on the merits, one was dismissed because the state failed to notify the deceased of the action and one was dismissed based on inaccurate information.

The assessors' findings of fact with regard to whether defensive action was necessary establish precedent that an abuse victim must try each and every option objectively available to her, seemingly until one of them works. At no point do their findings account for an abuse victim's growing frustration and her loss of faith when her cries for help go unanswered. They ignored a point the Constitutional Court openly acknowledged:

> "The ineffectiveness of the criminal justice system in addressing family violence intensifies the subordination and helplessness of the victims. This also sends an unmistakable message to the whole of society that the daily trauma of vast numbers of women counts for little. The terrorisation of individual victims is thus compounded by a sense that domestic violence is inevitable. Patterns of systemic behaviour are normalised rather than combated. Yet it is precisely the function of constitutional protection to convert misfortune to be endured into injustice to be remedied."[465]

The factual level of proof required by the assessors also leaves almost no room for the possibility that these solutions may never work. Women who kill their abusers in non-confrontational situations will find it exceedingly difficult to provide sufficient evidence to meet this element of self-defence if other courts follow the precedent set by the assessors.

There are three ways for advocates to approach the *Engelbrecht* decision. The first is to discuss the failure of the assessors to apply the appropriate legal standard of proof or legal test to the facts of the case. The element that defensive action must be necessary requires the accused to supply evidence that there were no reasonable alternatives to self-defence. Stated differently, the test is whether a person in the accused's circumstances would reasonably have believed that she had no other alternatives, not whether there were, objectively, other alternatives. A full discussion of the failure of the assessors to apply the appropriate reasonableness test as to whether the accused acted because defensive measures were necessary is described below under the test for reasonableness.

The second way to approach the negative precedent for this element of self-defence is to argue that the assessors simply got it wrong. In the statement of the law, the court clarifies when probing whether law enforcement remained an option to avoid self-help: "it is essential that the court critically examines the extent to which the 'ordinary law of the land' was effective in preventing the precipitating unlawful attacks and freeing the abused from the attacks and their impact."[466] The assessors' examination falls far short of being critical and allows law enforcement failures to deprive an abused woman of her right to act in self-defence.

Relying on the assessors' factual level of proof of the necessity of defensive measures, which contradicts the requirements set out by the court's statement of the law, is faulty. Or, as Satchwell J remarked, requiring an accused to continue to employ options that had failed repeatedly in the past "impose(s) an unequal and discriminatory burden upon someone who merely wishes to enjoy a peaceful life but is prevented by an unrestrainable aggressor."[467]

In addition, the assessors' application of the law to the facts creates a dangerous situation for abuse victims. Consider a woman who has been severely and repeatedly beaten by her husband. At the conclusion of the latest bout of violence, the husband threatens to harm her if she calls the police. Given the woman's experience with her husband, she may reasonably believe that she cannot go to the police. Now consider this situation in light of the general knowledge that the police protection of victims of domestic violence is inadequate.[468] This combination seems to make it impossible for this woman to seek police protection. This analysis applies also to instances where the abuser threatens the woman if she tries to leave him. Chapter 2 explains why neither of these threats is empty. Requiring an abused woman to exhaust all of her options may require her to risk her life to save the abuser's.

In only a few rare cases will defence counsel be able to distinguish their cases on the facts, which is the third option for handling the bad precedent the *Engelbrecht* decision creates. Many abused women grow discouraged long before the accused in *Engelbrecht* did, which means few women who kill will have taken more steps than she did to end the violence.

Excerpt from *Lavallee*

> I emphasize at this juncture that it is not for the jury to pass judgment on the fact that an accused battered woman stayed in the relationship. Still less is it entitled to conclude that she forfeited her right to self-defence for having done so. I would also point out that traditional self-defence doctrine does not require a person to retreat from her home instead of defending herself: R. v. Antley, (1964) 2 C.C.C. 142, (1964) 1 O.R. 545, 42 C.R. 384 (C.A.). A man's home may be his castle but it is also the woman's home even if it seems to her more like a prison in the circumstances.

* * *

The obvious question is, if the violence was so intolerable, why did the appellant not leave her abuser long ago? This question does not really consider whether she had an alternative to killing the deceased at the critical moment. Rather, it plays on the popular myth already referred to, that a woman who says she was battered yet stayed with her batterer was either not as badly beaten as she claimed or else she liked it. Nevertheless, to the extent that her failure to leave the abusive relationship earlier may be used in support of the proposition that she was free to leave at the final moment, expert testimony can provide useful insights.

(iii) Reasonable relationship between defensive act and unlawful attack (proportionality)

South African law does not apply a strict proportionality test between the expected unlawful attack and the defensive action taken by the accused.[469] Rather, it requires that there be a reasonable relationship between them. Snyman explains that when judging proportionality, "only if there is an extreme discrepancy" will the accused fail to meet this element of the defence.[470] Importantly, this means that the "weapons used by the attacker and the defendant need not be commensurate."[471] Typically, courts expect that a person who killed another must have been protecting him/herself against serious bodily harm or death in order to meet the standard of a reasonable relationship between the attack and the defensive act.[472] Surprisingly, there has been one case that allowed a person to justify lethal self-defence to protect his property interests.[473]

The *Engelbrecht* decision, which is the only one to deal directly with an abused women's claim of self-defence after she killed her abuser in a non-confrontational situation, sets out a standard test for the element of proportionality: "If she could have averted the attack by resorting to conduct which was less harmful than that actually employed by her, and if she inflicted injury or harm to the attacker which was unnecessary to overcome the threat, her conduct does not comply with this requirement for private defence."[474] The court, however, broadens the determination of proportionality to include consideration of a multitude of factors that may influence the abuse victim's choice of defensive measures. These factors include but are not limited to:

- the parties' respective ages;
- the parties' relative strengths;

- the parties' gender socialisation and experiences;
- the nature, duration and development of their relationship;
- the content of the relationship, including power relations on an economic, sexual, social, familial, employment and socio-religious level;
- the nature, extent, duration, persistence of the abuse;
- the purpose of and achievements of the abuser;
- the impact upon the body, mind, heart, spirit of the victim;
- the effect on others who are aware of or implicated in the abuse;
- the extent to which it is possible for state-legislated, formal institutional, informal personal bodies and individuals to intervene to terminate the abuse;[475]
- the extent to which it is possible for the abused victim to access and utilise any of the above channels in the event that they previously fail to intervene unilaterally to impose Constitutional protections.[476]

The point the court seems to be making is that the deliberation of proportionality goes far beyond objectively comparing the threat from the unlawful attack and the accused's response into whether in the particular circumstances the defensive action employed was appropriate. For instance, the fact that the assailant is physically stronger than his victim, or that he was using control techniques to convince his victim that he was inescapable, may be more relevant to proportionality than whether he uses solely his fists to beat her.

The benefit of the court's approach is that it includes women's experiences with violence in the determination of proportionality. Proportionality must be viewed from the woman's perspective. Included in this perspective is her size, strength, relative power in the relationship, her conditioning to avoid physical violence and her experience with her abuser.[477] Consideration of these factors draws a more complete picture of the attack against which the accused was defending. The woman's experience with her abuser, the purpose of the abuse, the tactics he used to achieve it and the effect of abuse, not only on her but on witnesses to the abuse (such as children), explain the scope of the unlawful attack.

The last two factors listed by the court in *Engelbrecht*, ie the availability and willingness of law enforcement and informal support networks to stop the violence, seem to speak to the element of necessity of the defensive action rather than proportionality. The court provides little guidance as to why they are relevant here. While unclear, the relationship between the support networks and proportionality could be that when deciding how much force is necessary, a court or finder of fact must consider that even if the abused woman did not fear death or serious injury at the hands of her abuser, a lifetime of abuse from which she cannot escape may warrant a lethal response. Essentially, the abused woman may be able to support lethal self-defence against harm short of death or serious injury if she can show that the domestic violence is inescapable and therefore never-ending.

Another explanation for the inclusion of informal support networks as an issue related to proportionality derives from the idea that a person is allowed to defend him- or herself when law enforcement cannot help him or her. Accessing informal support networks to protect the accused or prevent the attack then is a form of self-help that could be considered a less drastic measure to deflect the attack than lethal self-defence, which is an appropriate consideration for proportionality. In reality, however, as described under the element of whether defensive measures were necessary, turning to informal support networks to escape violence means fleeing one's home, which either is not or should not be required for an accused to prove self-defence.

The end result of the inclusion of the options to escape the violence offered by formal and informal support networks as factors relevant to proportionality is that the assessors placed a duty to flee on the accused. Advocate Naude justified his conclusion that the accused failed to show proportionality, by giving as his opinion that she could have left the deceased.[478] Advocate Opperman emphasized that the accused had friends she could have turned to in order to escape the violence.[479] Unfortunately, the factors listed for consideration under proportionality ultimately eradicated at least some of the gains the court's statement of law made for abused women under the element of necessity of defensive measures.

The proportionality element of the defence raises two additional hurdles for abused women's access to self-defence that should be addressed by the advocates, although they were not evident in *Engelbrecht*. While the standard for proportionality appears broad, South African criminal law experts argued that abused women who kill in non-confrontational situations could have difficulty justifying the use of lethal force against a passive attacker.[480] This is tantamount to suggesting that unless there is an uplifted knife, there is no attack – a point that relates to evidentiary requirements of an unlawful attack and of imminence described earlier.

Again, faced with this hurdle, advocates for these women can rely on expert evidence to explain the continuous threat of violence in domestic violence relationships and, as a result, that the abuser, though not active at the time of the killing, was not actually passive. The advocate also could argue that, based on the woman's experience with her abuser, she reasonably believed that using a weapon against her unarmed attacker was the only way to stop the threat and keep her from being overpowered.[481] Evidence of the pattern of abuse could support this conclusion.

The second possible hurdle to meeting this element relates to the general expectation that a person can justify killing an assailant only if she or he feared death or serious bodily harm. South African criminal law experts suggest that the only way an abused woman can prove she was protecting herself against death or serious bodily injury when there was no overt threat is to show that she had been threatened with this kind of harm in the past. Essentially, if the woman can rely on the pattern of violence to infer a threat of abuse, the prosecution can rely on the pattern to prove that her life was not at risk.[482]

To avoid this debate, the accused woman must explain what was different about this threatened abuse that led her to believe that she faced death or severe bodily harm. The argument can be bolstered by expert evidence that abused women typically have a heightened sensitivity to their abusers as well as with the social judgment theory described in Chapter 3. For example, in Canada, the *Lavallee* decision accepted that:

> "Perhaps the single most important idea conveyed by expert testimony in such a case pertains to the notion that a battered woman, because of her extensive experience with her abuser's violence, can detect changes or signs of novelty in the pattern of normal violence that connote increased danger."[483]

The Canadian Supreme Court adopted the following important caution to expert witnesses and the accused's legal advocates:

> "Support for this assertion must come from the woman herself, in her spontaneous, self-initiated description of the events that preceded her action against the abuse. Only then can testimony

from an expert offer scientific support for the idea that such a danger detection process can occur and can be accepted to be as accurate as the 'reasonable man' standard would imply."[484]

The Canadian court utilized the social judgment theory to support the explanation that abused women develop survival skills that tell them when they cannot survive the next bout of violence.[485]

The experience of the defence in *Engelbrecht* highlights an important difficulty an accused can confront when trying to argue what had changed and why that led the accused to believe she needed to act in lethal self-defence. The accused in *Engelbrecht* had purchased thumb cuffs that she used later that day to confine her husband while he was sleeping, during which time she killed him. The accused denied the purchase evidenced premeditation. She then asserted that events that occurred after the purchase, including sexual abuse, triggered her belief that she could no longer survive the abuse and that her child was at risk. The court ultimately concluded that she premeditated the killing based in part on the purchase of the thumb cuffs.[486] At least one assessor in the case rejected that accused's assessment of what triggered her need for self-defence because the alleged triggering event occurred after she began implementing her premeditated plan.[487]

Advocates also need to be careful to defend against attempts by the prosecution to point to the fact that prior incidents of abuse did not cause death or serious injury to the accused to justify concluding she was not in danger of such harm at the time she killed. It is irrelevant what level of danger the woman faced in the past; what is relevant is the level of danger at the time she killed. To allow the past pattern of abuse to refute the woman's belief that she faced serious harm or death at the time she killed her abuser would create an inequity in the legal treatment of abused women's cases. Unlike other accused arguing self-defence, the abused woman would not be allowed to guess correctly the first time whether she faces death or serious injury. This approach would force her to encounter death at her abuser's hand without being allowed to defend herself.

One question that arises under this element of self-defence is whether a woman who finds herself trapped in a psychologically abusive, or in a low-level but persistently abusive, relationship could argue self-defence if she kills her abuser. As discussed briefly earlier, the inclusion of whether formal and informal support networks could have helped the abused woman as a factor for consideration under proportionality may provide space for these victims of abuse to argue self-defence, despite the appearance that the defensive measures were disproportionate. Essentially, the court would be weighing a lifetime of violations of the accused's protected interests against the death of her assailant.

Taking a similar approach, some academics argue that when psychological abuse and lower but persistent levels of abuse result in the utter devaluation of a woman's quality of life, she must be allowed to protect herself from a "spiritual death".[488] Advocates will face great difficulty gaining acceptance for these arguments, particularly since many weigh the right to physical life, which the deceased would lose, more greatly than a right to quality of life or psychological integrity the accused would lose.

(c) Reasonableness test for self-defence

The next inquiry in a self-defence claim is the reasonableness test. An accused must reasonably have believed that self-help was necessary in order to justify taking defensive action. Importantly, the belief does not have to be correct, just reasonable.[489] The test applies to each element of self-defence, which means, for example, that courts enquire whether self-defence was "reasonably necessary" and whether the accused's belief that the attack was imminent was reasonable.[490]

South Africa applies a mixed objective-subjective reasonableness test in which the court examines whether the accused's belief that she or he faced an imminent, unlawful attack and whether the force she or he used to defend against it was reasonable in her or his circumstances.[491] The court asks "what 'the fictitious reasonable man, in the position of the accused and in the light of all the circumstances' would have done."[492] The reasoning behind the mixed test is that no one can be held to a higher standard than what would be expected of the "average person" in the circumstances in which the accused found him/herself.[493]

The subjective element of the reasonableness test calls for the accused to put forward all evidence relevant to understanding the circumstances of the killing.[494] The purpose is to ensure that courts do not use hindsight to unfairly conclude that the accused was not entitled to act in self-defence. South African case law cautions that judges "must be careful to avoid the role of the armchair critic wise after the event, weighing the matter in the secluded security of the courtroom, by putting themselves in the position of the accused at the time of the attack."[495]

The *Engelbrecht* decision described that the Constitution, particularly the equality clause contained in section 9, mandates that a court deliberating the reasonableness of the actions and beliefs of a woman who killed her abuser must consider those actions and beliefs based on her experiences with abuse and its effect on her.[496] Quoting the Supreme Court of Appeal decision in *Ferreira v S*,[497] which is fully described in Chapter 5, a court now must "place itself as far as it can in the position of the woman concerned, with a fully detailed account of the abusive relationship and the assistance of expert evidence… It means treating an abused woman accused with due regard for gender difference in order to achieve equality of judicial treatment."[498]

The objective element of the reasonableness test asks whether the circumstances in which the accused found him/herself justify his or her subjective belief or, stated differently, whether the legal convictions of the community would agree with the need for self-help in the accused's circumstances.[499] The objective element serves as a protective measure to keep self-defence from becoming a justification for killing someone based on nothing more than purely subjective beliefs.[500] The court in *Engelbrecht* explained that the legal convictions of the community are based on society's morals and values, which includes the values of equity and justice. Additionally, it concluded that the legal convictions of the community must be "informed by the foundational values of the Constitution, namely 'human dignity, equality and freedom'."[501]

Taking its reasoning a step further, the *Engelbrecht* court clarified that informing the legal convictions of the community with constitutional values means that the reasonable person test applied in self-defence now must include women's experiences within it. The court accepted that historically, self-defence law "largely ignored women's lives and their experience of violence."[502] It approved of the following quote from the Supreme Court of Canada in the *Lavallee* decision:

> "If it strains credulity to imagine what the 'ordinary man' would do in the position of a battered spouse, it is probably because men do not typically find themselves in that situation. Some women do, however. The definition of what is reasonable must be adapted

to the circumstances which are, by and large, foreign to the world inhabited by the hypothetical 'reasonable man'."[503]

The *Engelbrecht* court thus requires that the reasonable person standard account for gender differences that may affect how women respond to domestic violence; essentially it requires the standard to be infused with women's experiences.[504] This does not mean that it adopted a reasonable woman standard.[505] The court again approved of the approach of the Supreme Court of Canada, this time as described in its decision *R v Malott*:[506]

"The majority of the court in *Lavallee* also implicitly accepted that women's experiences and perspectives may be different from the experiences and perspectives of men. It accepted that a woman's perception of what is reasonable is influenced by her gender, as well as by her individual experience, and both are relevant to the legal enquiry. This legal development was significant because it demonstrated a willingness to look at the whole context of a woman's experience in order to inform the analysis of the particular events. But it is wrong to think of this development of the law as merely an example where an objective test – the requirement that an accused claiming self-defence must reasonably apprehend death or grievous bodily harm – has been modified to admit evidence of the subjective perceptions of a battered woman. More important, a majority of the Court accepted that the perspectives of women, which have historically been ignored, must now feature equally in the form of the 'objective' standard of the reasonable person in relation to self-defence."[507]

The *Engelbrecht* court concluded its discussion of the objective aspect of the reasonableness standard by explaining that the inclusion of women's experiences within the test for reasonableness may require expert testimony to understand how a reasonable person would react in an abusive relationship.[508]

Advocates defending a woman who killed her abusive intimate partner in a non-confrontational situation will need to depend heavily on expert testimony to meet the evidentiary burden of showing reasonableness. Expert testimony can help courts understand why men abuse, the women's experiences with their abusers, the effects of the abuse on them and their experiences in seeking help: "Such testimony explains how conduct which seems patently unreasonable in the experience of the judges of fact, can be reasonable in contexts they have never previously encountered."[509] Experts must describe the abused woman's situation individually, which explains her subjective circumstances, as well as place her experiences within the context of abused women generally, which explains how a reasonable person in the accused's circumstances would react.[510]

Much of the expert testimony already recommended throughout this book applies to the evidence requirement for the reasonableness standard. For example, understanding why the abused woman feared an imminent attack also can explain why her belief was reasonable. As the South Carolina Supreme Court explained in a case in which a woman killed her abusive intimate partner in a non-confrontational situation: "where torture appears interminable and escape impossible, the belief that only the death of the batterer can provide relief may be reasonable in the mind of a person of ordinary firmness."[511]

To the extent advocates rely on expert testimony about the psychological effects of abuse on the accused to explain any element of self-defence, they must explain carefully that these effects are a reasonable response to an abnormal situation. In other words, they need to explain why many people in the abused woman's shoes would react similarly to the accused. Failure to do this could lead the court to conclude that the woman's belief that she needed to act in self-defence developed solely from her abnormal psychology and is inherently unreasonable.

The decision in *Engelbrecht* highlights the importance of expert testimony explaining the accused abused's woman's circumstances and placing those circumstances within the context of abused women generally. The defence in *Engelbrecht* seemed to fail because the assessors did not appropriately apply the mixed objective-subjective test of reasonableness to their decision on the facts of the case.

The assessors in *Engelbrecht* seem to accept the description of the accused's circumstances – that she was suffering from prolonged psychological, physical, sexual and economic abuse; that the deceased was using violence systematically to take control of the accused; that he continually violated the accused's constitutional rights; and that she felt that the state had failed her.[512] What seems to have failed is the element of the reasonableness test that requires the assessors to consider whether a reasonable person in the accused's circumstances would have responded in the same way, particularly as it applied to the question of the necessity of self-help.

The question that dogged the accused's defence was whether she had any other options to avoid taking defensive measures into her own hands. It is at this stage that the assessors ignored the aspect of the reasonableness test that asks whether a reasonable person in the accused's circumstances also would have believed those options were not available or would have been ineffective. Satchwell J stated expressly that she used the expert testimony for "purposes of identifying the reasonable behaviour of the reasonable woman in this particular situation and assessing the behaviour of Mrs Engelbrecht against such a standard."[513] At no stage do the assessors appear to have done the same thing.

Advocate Opperman agreed with Professor Naude's justification that self-defence was not reasonably necessary on the basis that "the legal system, including the SAPS and the Domestic Violence Court, were prepared to assist Mrs Engelbrecht. However, she had lost interest in the various actions instituted by her."[514] At no point does he (or she) ask what was reasonable in the accused's circumstances. In contrast, Judge Satchwell, in her minority opinion on the facts, adopted the evidence of the experts that explained the effect of the failure of law enforcement to end the abuse on victims of domestic violence generally and then considered the accused's behaviour in light of that standard:

> "When evaluating Ms Vettens (sic) evidence that a person in an abusive relationship experiences a process of 'funnelling' during which the range of options available to her, having been tried, become narrower and more constricted until they perceive only a single option: the killing of the abuser, Judge Satchwell takes note that the evidence clearly shows that Mrs Engelbrecht did, over a period of time, attempt to access a range of options to free her of Mr Engelbrecht prior to resorting to the use of lethal force. I can only agree with the experts that 'Each of these options had proved unsuccessful and communicated to her mind the omnipresence and omnipotence of the deceased'."[515]

The assessors also had precedent from the Constitutional Court, which has been quoted repeatedly throughout this chapter. The Constitutional court acknowledged expressly the overall impact on abuse victims when law enforcement does not stop the violence:

> "The ineffectiveness of the criminal justice system in addressing family violence intensifies the subordination and helplessness of the victims. This also sends an unmistakable message to the whole of society that the daily trauma of vast numbers of women counts for little. The terrorisation of individual victims is thus compounded by a sense that domestic violence is inevitable."[516]

Moreover, the assessors failed to look at reasonableness in light of the constitutional duties placed on the law enforcement agencies to protect an abuse victim from domestic violence, which reflect the legal convictions of the community. As a reminder, the Constitution requires law enforcement agencies to take positive measures to protect women from domestic violence:

> "Indeed, the state is under a series of constitutional mandates which include the obligation to deal with domestic violence: to protect both the rights of everyone to enjoy freedom and security of the person and to bodily and psychological integrity, and the right to have their dignity respected and protected, as well as defensive rights of everyone not to be subjected to torture in any way and not to be treated or punished in a cruel, inhuman or degrading way."[517]

This positive duty means it is not solely the abuse victim's responsibility to ensure the violence ends, which means that at the point when she alerts the police and courts to the criminal abuse, they have a responsibility to act to stop it. The assessors in *Engelbrecht* ignored this duty and essentially removed the responsibility from the police and courts to take effective measures to protect the accused.

Another way to look at how the assessors dealt with reasonableness is to consider the similar facts in a different context. How would society respond if the police refused to respond on all but one occasion to the between 6 and 9 times a family called them because they were trapped inside their home as a violent criminal tried to break in? Would society effectively deny the family the right to act in self-defence on the possibility that the 10th phone call would spur the police into action?

Again, the assessors failed to consider how the average person would act in similar circumstances.

Looking at the self-defence argument as a whole, the legal statements of the elements of the defence are sufficiently broad to allow abused women who kill their batterers in non-confrontational situations to argue self-defence. Unfortunately, the recent decision in *S v Engelbrecht* presents some barriers to the general application of the defence because of the way in which the assessors in the case applied the law to the facts. Good advocacy and appropriate expert testimony will be needed to explain why the assessor's findings of facts did not comply with the judge's statement of the law and why reliance on any "standard" set by those findings is unfair.

3. General defence of reasonableness

The *amicus curiae* in the *Engelbrecht* case argued for the creation of a general justification defence of reasonableness to encompass the cases of abused women who kill in non-confrontational situations. The proposed defence simply asks whether a reasonable person in the accused's circumstances would have acted the same way. The *amicus* argued that, rather than trying to fit these women's circumstances within the rigid criteria of self-defence, the court should simply test whether the woman's defensive actions were reasonable in her circumstances.[518]

The suggestion finds some support in a statute in the State of Nevada in the United States that allows an accused to argue that their behaviour was lawful in "all other instances that stand upon the same footing of reason and justice as those (defences) enumerated."[519] The statute allows an accused who cannot meet the specific elements of self-defence, but whose reasons for killing rest on the same underlying rationale of self-defence, to argue that their behaviour was fully justified. An accused who succeeds at the general defence would be acquitted of murder.

The *Engelbrecht* court declined to adopt the new defence because it could not differentiate it sufficiently from self-defence. The court explained that it could not locate elements of a general reasonableness defence that would be different from those required by self-defence.[520]

4. Self-defence for abused women who hire contract killers

Arguing self-defence on behalf of abused women who kill in non-confrontational situations is difficult at best. For women who kill by hiring a contract killer, the hurdles to accessing the defence seem even more insurmountable. The act of hiring smacks of premeditation and cold-calculation and suggests that either the attack the abused woman feared was not imminent or that she had other options for avoiding it.

The issues of imminence and other options to avoid abuse are no different in principle for women who kill their abusers themselves and women who hire killers as long as the women feared an unlawful attack during the entire period between when they made the decision to hire a killer and when the abusers were killed. Unless something changed drastically, time does not increase the woman's options for escaping abuse once those options have become ineffective and/or unavailable. The means used to kill the abuser do not change the arguments. However, the longer the time span between the triggering event that leads the abused woman to fear an imminent or inevitable attack and the deceased being killed, the more speculative the threat will appear. Thus a woman who hires a killer over a three-month period will have more difficulty proving imminence than a woman who hires a killer who kills the deceased in the same day.

As to premeditation and cold calculation, South Africa historically has taken a harsh stance against contract killings. However, the cases in which contract killings typically arise are vastly different from the cases in which women hire third parties to kill their abusers. These women are not killing for financial gain, which is often the reason for contract killings, but to protect their lives. In a sense, the contract killer is no different from a gun or a knife to the abused woman.

Two recent decisions in South Africa could place women who hire third parties to kill their abusers on the same legal footing as other women who kill in non-confrontational situations. In *Ferreira v S*, a recent decision on mitigation of sentence for a woman convicted of murder for hiring men to kill her abuser, the Supreme Court of Appeal suggested in *obiter dicta* that a woman's moral blameworthiness does not depend on her decision to hire killers as long as she continued to perceive a threat of violence from the time she hired them until the deceased was killed.[521] The Court saw no difference between a woman who kills in a non-confrontational situation using a contract killer and one who does it herself when all other circumstances are the same.[522] This same reasoning applies to self-defence.

More directly in point, the *Engebrecht* decision explicitly adopts the approach that there is nothing inherently inconsistent between self-defence and premeditation.[523] The court reached this conclusion based on the broadening of imminence to include inevitability. Essentially, if an abused woman can show that the next attack is inevitable, she can meet the requirement of imminence for self-defence. When an attack is inevitable, she may have time to plan her defensive action, which is premeditation. As long as the abused woman had no other reasonable options to avoid self-help, then the premeditated defensive action was necessary. This approach by the court in *Engelbrecht* could go a long way toward opening up self-defence to women who hire third parties to kill their abusers.

5. Conclusion

Self-defence can be made applicable to abused women who kill in non-confrontational situations by infusing the elements of the defence with women's experiences. The knee-jerk reaction of the legal community that works to exclude these women from self-defence can be countered with expert testimony, appropriate legal advocacy and the broadening of the elements of the defence under *Engelbrecht*. This does not necessitate changing the purpose of the defence.

To summarize briefly, an abused woman who kills to protect her life, but kills in a non-confrontational situation, typically is responding to a threat of further violence. While the threat may not be obvious to an outsider, the pattern of abuse in the relationship and/or the woman's heightened sensitivity to her abuser's behaviour explains the existence of the threat as well as why that threat was imminent and/or inevitable. These arguments require expert testimony and can be bolstered with a discussion of domestic violence as a process as described in Chapters 2 and 3.

An abused woman can support that she had no other option to stop the abuse than to kill her abuser by detailing her personal experiences, employing those options with social-context evidence, described in Part I, about the general difficulties women have accessing the alternatives. The fact that there was time between when the woman expected the unlawful attack and when she killed does not mean she could escape the abuse. Time does not by itself create effective solutions to domestic violence. Nor does time negate a reasonable relationship between the woman's fears for her life and safety and her decision to kill her abuser. The fact that the abuser was apparently passive at the time he died does not change that he was threatening the woman with violence.

Finally, South Africa's reasonable test for self-defence provides ample opportunity for courts to consider the woman's experiences with violence. By placing the court in the woman's circumstances, South African law allows the woman to provide specific evidence regarding the history of the abusive relationship and the patterns of abuse to explain the reasonableness of her actions. Expert testimony then can place the woman's experiences within the context of domestic violence generally and explain that her response was reasonable given the abnormal situation in which she found herself. The contextual understanding of the woman's experiences and domestic violence generally should allow some abused women who kill in non-confrontational situations to succeed in an argument for self-defence.

C. PUTATIVE SELF-DEFENCE

The second defence for an abused woman who kills because she believes she is acting to save her life is putative self-defence. This involves an accused who believed mistakenly that she or he was acting lawfully in self-defence. This defence strikes at the intention element of murder that the prosecution must prove before the accused can be convicted. If the accused honestly believed that defensive action was necessary, she or he could not consciously have acted unlawfully, which is an essential element of the crime of murder. This defence recognizes that the law does not punish someone for murder when that person genuinely did not know that the lethal conduct was unlawful.

Although an accused who meets the test for putative self-defence cannot be convicted of murder, she or he could be convicted of culpable homicide. For culpable homicide, the prosecution must prove the accused believed negligently that she or he was acting in self-defence. The test is whether a reasonable person in the accused's circumstances would have believed she or he was acting in self-defence.[524] If the accused acted reasonably, she or he cannot be convicted of culpable homicide.

Advocates on behalf of women who kill their abusers can advance this defence in addition to self-defence. This means that the accused would contend that she acted in self-defence but, should the court conclude her belief was mistaken, it should find putative self-defence. These arguments are not inconsistent. Essentially, the accused would maintain that she acted in self-defence. Unless this defence is rebutted beyond reasonable doubt by the prosecution, an acquittal must follow. In the alternative it can be contended that even if, objectively, it was not self defence, the accused believed that she was acting in self-defence when she killed her abuser. If this is not disproved by the prosecution, a finding of putative self-defence will follow and the question of the reasonableness of the belief arises. Should the court decide her belief was unreasonable, the woman would be convicted of culpable homicide. Otherwise she must be found not guilty. The advocates would use the same types of factual and expert evidence and arguments for putative self-defence as they would for self-defence.[525] In some instances, it may be appropriate for the defence to argue putative self-defence without arguing self-defence.

1. Elements

There are two different ways in which an accused can qualify for putative self-defence. The first is if she believed, honestly but mistakenly, that she had to act in self-defence. The second is that she believed honestly that she had to act in self-defence but exceeded the lawful bounds of the defence. Thus, the elements of putative self-defence are:

- The accused believed honestly that she or he was acting in self-defence; and
- The belief was a mistake of fact; *OR*
- The accused exceeded the bounds of self-defence.[526]

(a) Honest belief

The most important element for putative self-defence is that the accused thought sincerely that she or he was acting in self-defence. If the accused was aware that she or he was acting unlawfully or foresaw that she or he could be acting unlawfully, the defence fails. The courts employ a subjective test to determine whether the belief was honest.[527] In cases in which women kill their abusers, the Supreme Court of Appeal explained that this test depends in part on the abuse victim's experiences, as well as on her gender:

> "Her decision to kill and to hire others for that purpose is… something which has to be judicially evaluated not from a male perspective or an objective perspective but by the court's placing itself as far as it can in the position of the woman concerned, with a fully detailed account of the abusive relationship and the assistance of expert evidence… Only by judging the case on that basis can the offender's equality right under s 9(1) of the Constitution be given proper effect. It means treating an abused woman accused with due regard for gender difference in order to achieve equality of judicial treatment."[528]

A subjective test that considers gender differences and gendered experiences gives advocates the opportunity to argue that women's socialization, disempowerment and their unequal size and strength are factors that must be evaluated when looking at their actions. The court also concluded that, when judging her circumstances, the evaluation must consider the rights infringed by the abuser, including the rights to dignity, bodily integrity and freedom from violence.[529]

Although the Supreme Court of Appeal decision in *Ferreira v S* involved a woman seeking mitigation of sentence, the case strongly resembles a case of putative self-defence. In *Ferreira*, the abused woman had suffered a long history – approximately 7 years – of abuse at the hands of her intimate partner, with whom she lived. He abused her mentally, physically, sexually and financially, using these tactics to control her. The abuse grew increasingly worse, was aggravated by alcohol and included threats with knives and a gun.

The abused woman tried to leave at least four times. Each time her partner found her and begged her forgiveness. Believing she could not escape and hoping the promises would prove true, she agreed to return home. She called the police on three occasions. Twice the police did not show up; once they told her she should sober up her abuser. They did not provide her with any meaningful assistance. She had no family and her partner had successfully isolated her from her friends. The neighbours were willing to do only so much to help her and no more.

Two weeks before his death, the abuser severely sexually abused the accused. He then threatened her with further sexual abuse, going so far as to threaten that he would find men to rape her if she tried to leave.

The combination of her intimate partner's control over her life, his ability to locate her when she fled and the refusal of the police to help her, convinced Ferreira that these threats were real and she could not escape. Believing she had no other alternative to stop the abuse, she hired two men to kill her intimate partner. Two weeks later, he was dead. The accused pleaded guilty to pre-meditated murder and was given a life sentence. The Supreme Court of Appeal overturned the sentence on appeal, giving her a six-year wholly suspended sentence.

In deciding whether to mitigate Ferreira's sentence, the court tested whether the killing was subjectively justifiable in order to determine whether any substantial and compelling circumstances existed for Ferreira.[530] Essentially, it asked whether, at the time of her abuser's death, the accused honestly believed she had no choice but to kill him in order to escape the violence, which is the test for putative self-defence. It canvassed the possible alternatives Ferreira could have used to stop the abuse other than killing him. The court seemed to be using this analysis to determine Ferreira's credibility.

When canvassing the alternatives, the Supreme Court of Appeal (SCA) explained that "the crucial question … was why she decided on murder rather than to leave the deceased."[531] It looked at whether she could have used the money with which she paid the contract killers to escape her abuser. Because the accused depended on the deceased financially, the court believed that the money came from him and that "the probable result of escaping with his money, however, would have been a theft charge and police pursuit."[532] It examined informal channels of help, such as friends, family and neighbours, and determined that they could not or would not have assisted the accused.[533]

Ferreira argued that her moral blameworthiness for killing her abuser should be decreased because the police failed in their duty to protect her from the violence when she called them. Despite three calls to the police, the SCA concluded that their duty to protect her may not have been activated because "the full extent of their knowledge of the appellant's plight was not proved."[534] The court seemed to suggest that the police could have provided an avenue for escaping the abuse. It also concluded that Ferreira could have sought legal advice and/or an interdict to stop the abuse. These conclusions seem to serve as the mistake of fact that excluded her from self-defence.

The SCA in *Ferreira* accepted the expert testimony that explained that persistent and pervasive abuse often leads abused women to develop the belief that they cannot leave their abusers safely, even if avenues for help objectively are open.[535] It seemed particularly influenced by the fact that Ferreira's belief and the action of hiring a contract killer conformed to the behaviour of other abused women in similar situations.[536] Ultimately, the court concluded: "Given her personal history and the pass to which her life had come, the reason for killing rather than leaving was adequately established by the evidence. She felt exposed to that risk (of rape) at the time when the killing occurred."[537] Ferreira essentially met the requirements for putative self-defence.

As the *Ferreira* decision shows, expert evidence regarding the psychological impact of abuse on the accused, as well as evidence of the circumstances that led her to believe sincerely that she could not escape the violence, can explain why the accused honestly believed she was acting in self-defence. Information regarding the pattern of abuse and the psychological impact of abuse can then be used to argue that her belief was reasonable in the circumstances.

(b) Mistake of fact
Putative self-defence should be argued when the accused believed mistakenly that she had to act in self-defence.[538] Typically, courts find putative self-defence when a person interprets an attack from suggestive circumstances though in reality there is none. One example of this is from *S v Naidoo* in which the accused believed that the noise he heard at the door was burglars. The accused lived in a dangerous neighbourhood, he had been a victim of crime previously and it was late at night. Fearing an attack, he fired through the screen door, killing his father. There was some basis for the accused to believe he was in danger, but his belief was mistaken. The accused in *Naidoo* succeeded in the defence.

At least one judge interviewed by the CSVR raised the concern that an accused can meet this element only if she can provide some objective evidence of an attack. This concern can be answered with the same evidence the accused would use to substantiate that she feared an imminent unlawful attack for self-defence – evidence of the pattern of abuse and/or pre-assault symbols that signify an imminent attack. Expert evidence can explain that abused women become sufficiently sensitized to their abusers to be able accurately to predict or anticipate an attack. After explaining this general point, the advocate and expert must highlight what it was about the deceased's behaviour that led the accused to believe she was in danger. Even if she was mistaken, this information will provide some basis for her belief.

Another mistake of fact an accused can make is that she wrongly believed that she had no alternative but to act in lethal self-defence. Essentially, the accused believed her act was necessary, when in reality she could safely have left the relationship or contacted the police. This is basically the approach the *Ferreira* court took when it decided that the appellant honestly believed she was acting to protect herself but that she could have contacted the police or received a protection order to stop the abuse.[539]

Finally, the arguments the advocate should use to explain why the abused women faced an imminent threat of deadly or gross bodily harm under self-defence could be used to explain why the woman's mistake was reasonable in light of her circumstances. The section on self-defence that describes the reasonableness requirement explains the importance of expert testimony and evidence of the pattern of abuse to this argument. The *Ferreira* decision supports each of these arguments.

(c) Exceeded bounds of self-defence

The second way in which an accused can succeed at putative self-defence is if she or he honestly believed that she or he was acting in lawful self-defence, but used too much force when defending him/herself.[540] Essentially, if the accused fails the proportionality test applied under self-defence, she or he may qualify for putative self-defence. An accused cannot rely on this defence, however, if she or he knew or suspected that she or he was using too much force.[541] If the accused succeeds in his or her argument for putative self-defence, the question then becomes whether the accused should have known that she or he exceeded the bounds of self-defence. If the court answers the question in the affirmative, the accused's action is negligent and she or he will be convicted of culpable homicide; if answered in the negative, the accused must be acquitted.[542]

Battered women who kill their passive abusers may have difficulty explaining how they did not realise they were exceeding the bounds of self-defence. Advocates should use the arguments and expert testimony described above under the element of proportionality to explain that their clients genuinely believed they needed to use lethal force to protect themselves, although their beliefs were mistaken.

2. Conclusion

Putative self-defence is one option advocates should consider in cases of abused women who kill in non-confrontational situations. It goes hand-in-hand with self-defence and is dependent on the same kinds of arguments and evidence. For women who believe they had no choice when they killed their abusers, this is another option to be used in the alternative to self-defence.

CHAPTER 5

Defences for women who lost control

Contents	Page
A. PROVOCATION/SEVERE EMOTIONAL STRESS/DIMINISHED CAPACITY NOT A SEPARATE DEFENCE	155
B. NON-PATHOLOGICAL CRIMINAL INCAPACITY	158
1. Elements of the defence	159
(a) Triggering event	160
(b) Lose the ability to distinguish between right and wrong or Lose the ability to act in accordance with right or wrong	163
(c) The unlawful act must have occurred during the period of incapacity	165
2. Conclusion	167
C. INSANITY DEFENCE	167
D. CONCLUSION	169

CHAPTER 5 EXAMINES the different defences abused women who kill can rely on when they killed because they lost control. Non-pathological criminal incapacity and insanity pertain to accused who lacked the capacity to control his or her behaviour. Non-pathological criminal incapacity applies when the accused killed because she or he lost all control and suffered from full incapacity as a result of a strong emotional stress or conflict, something environmental rather than pathological. Insanity pertains to those who have been diagnosed with a recognized mental impairment that made it impossible for them to control their actions.

At this stage, it is important to caution that many women who kill will describe that they suddenly snapped and killed for that reason. While by itself this description would suggest that this category of defences will be most appropriate, practitioners need to dig deeper to assure themselves that the woman did not kill because she thought she was defending her life e.g. that she snapped because she thought he was going to kill her.

A. PROVOCATION/SEVERE EMOTIONAL STRESS/ DIMINISHED CAPACITY NOT A SEPARATE DEFENCE

South Africa no longer recognizes a partial-excuse defence of provocation or severe emotional stress/diminished capacity.[543] Accused argued this defence when their emotions caused them to lose self-control sufficiently to decrease their mental capacity but stopped short of fully incapacitating them. Full incapacity belongs under the defence of non-pathological criminal incapacity. An accused who acted under diminished capacity could not have acted intentionally when she or he killed, which reduced the criminal charge from murder to culpable homicide. The partial defence "understood" human weakness and that "emotion hinders the individual's ability to act reasonably."[544]

The provocation/severe emotional stress defence was abolished as a measure to keep short-tempered persons from benefiting from their impulsive behaviour. Instead, through the change in law, the justice system hoped to encourage self-control.[545] The Supreme Court of Appeal decision in *S v Eadie* restated the intention to abolish the partial defence in its *obiter dicta*.[546] It explained that unless the accused was provoked to the point of acting under non-pathological criminal incapacity, she or he must have retained some control over his or her actions. If she or he acted with at least some control, she or he acted with intent:

> When an accused acts in an aggressive goal-directed and focused manner, spurred on by anger or some other emotion, whilst still able to appreciate the difference between right and wrong and while still able to direct and control his actions, it stretches credulity when he then claims, after assaulting or killing someone that at some stage during the directed and planned manoeuvre, he lost his ability to control his actions. Reduced to its essence it amounts to this: the accused is claiming that his uncontrolled act just happens to coincide with the demise of the person who prior to the act was the object of his anger, jealousy or hatred.[547]

The trigger event, instead, should be considered as part of mitigation of sentence. Earlier decisions provide the basis for the *Eadie dicta*: "Criminal conduct arising from an argument or some or other emotional conflict is more often than not preceded by some sort of provocation. Loss of temper in the ordinary sense is a common occurrence. It may in appropriate circumstances mitigate, but it does not exonerate."[548] Despite these decisions, some criminal law practitioners argue that an accused can continue to use a provocation/severe emotional stress defence to negate the intention element of murder.[549]

The defence in the *Engelbrecht* decision, fully described in Chapter 4, attempted to create a special type of diminished capacity defence for abused women who kill that the Witwatersrand Local Division refused to adopt. As a reminder, in *Engelbrecht*, a woman killed her abusive husband while he was sleeping after suffering repeated physical, sexual, psychological and economic abuse at his hands. She initially argued self-defence, which failed, and was sentenced to imprisonment until 'the rising of the court'.

In addition to self-defence, the accused argued for the application of a new type of excuse defence, which essentially would admit that she intended to act unlawfully, but that would "excuse" her unlawful behaviour because the average person or the reasonable person in her circumstances would have acted in the same way. The proposed defence depends heavily on the psychological theory of the effects of abuse described as coercive control in Chapter 2 and blends the elements of necessity of defensive action and reasonableness from self-defence into diminished capacity. The defence described the elements of the new defence as follows:

"If a person ('the victim') acts with lethal force against another ('the abuser'), and the victim:-
1. has been subjected to forms of domestic violence as defined in the Domestic Violence Act, 1998, by the abuser over a sustained period of time and which forms of domestic violence, through a pattern of coercive control, has reasonably induced a state of psychological and or physical captivity in the mind of the victim;
2. has reasonably explored reasonable avenues of escape from the abuser, the reasonableness thereof being determined with reference to, *inter alia*:-
   2.1. reasonable attempts to end contact between the victim and abuser;
   2.2. reasonable attempts to gain the assistance and/or protection of the police or other institutions or family and friends; and
   2.3. any other relevant fact; and
   3. reasonably apprehended the threat of death or serious injury to him/herself, a family member, or some other legitimate and commensurate interest at the hands of the abuser if he/she did not so act, notwithstanding that such threat was not discernibly imminent;
   4. has had his or her conative power to act in accordance with his or her appreciation of right and wrong greatly weakened or severely eroded by virtue of the domestic violence perpetrated by the abuser;

then the victim will not be held liable for the killing of the abuser since the law cannot expect the victim to have endured the threat of the possibility of a sacrifice of his or her life or other commensurate interest; the victim's conduct will not be unreasonable."

Under her argument, if the accused could provide sufficient evidence of each element of their new excuse defence, she could not be convicted of murder.

The court in *Engelbrecht* rejected the proposed new defence for a variety of reasons. First, the court felt it was unnecessary to create a special defence for abused women when they already have access to self-defence.[550] Adoption of the special defence then would give abused women a separate and second chance to avoid criminal liability that would not exist for other accused.[551] In addition to the privilege this could accord, a special defence for abused women would exclude women's experiences from informing the reasonableness standard of self-defence, essentially it would suggest that there is something inherently unreasonable about their decisions to kill.[552]

The court further explained that it rejected the proposed defence because the elements reflect the test already applied in self-defence, which essentially requires testing the accused's actions against how a reasonable person in his or her circumstances would have reacted.[553] If the accused failed the test the first time, how could she prove it the second time?[554] This approach confuses justification defences which explain why seemingly criminal behaviour is lawful with excuse defences that conclude that while the behaviour was unlawful, the actions were understandable and should be excused. Reasonableness is mostly irrelevant to the latter category of defences. The court also rejected the application of a full defence that would excuse unlawful behaviour based on diminished capacity when South African law currently considers diminished capacity only at the sentencing stage.[555]

No longer a separate partial defence, accused can argue provocation/severe emotional stress as part of a defence of non-pathological criminal incapacity or as a mitigating factor to be considered after conviction. The next section of the chapter describes provocation/severe emotional stress as it relates to non-pathological criminal incapacity. Mitigation of sentence is examined in Chapter 6.

B. NON-PATHOLOGICAL CRIMINAL INCAPACITY

Non-pathological criminal incapacity is a criminal defence that explains that the accused did not act voluntarily when she or he killed the deceased, which is a required element for a criminal conviction.[556] To act voluntarily, "the human mind must be in control of the act which he has performed."[557] Under this defence, the accused asserts that she or he did not have self-control at the time she or he acted – that she or he was incapacitated.[558] She or he also argues that the incapacity did not result from a pathological problem or disease, such as insanity, but from something temporary in nature, such as stress or anger. If the accused's argument succeeds, she or he must be acquitted of murder.

The legal theory behind this defence is that the law should punish a person only if she or he acted voluntarily and was able to understand that his or her action was wrong at the time of the crime and to act accordingly. If the accused suffered from incapacity at the time she or he killed, she or he is not criminally responsible for the crime. South African courts have expressed fear that this defence is too easily abused by criminally accused.[559] As a result, they use a very strict standard to test for it that makes it increasingly unlikely that any criminal accused will succeed with the defence.

Non-pathological criminal incapacity is the only defence that abused women who kill in non-confrontational situations have successfully argued in South Africa. It is by far the most common defence argued for them. It should not be viewed, however, as the only defence that abused women should use. Instead, it is just one of several and it applies only to those women who felt they lost all control at the time they killed their abusers.

1. Elements of the defence

The decision in *S v Eadie* greatly restricts the defence of non-pathological criminal incapacity.[560] Under this decision, an accused can succeed with the defence only if she or he was acting in an automatic fashion, making this the same defence as sane automatism. The court explained: "It must now be clearly understood that an accused can only lack self-control when he is acting in a state of automatism."[561] This judgment sounds a sobering note of caution that a defence of non-pathological incapacity will not be accepted lightly. Additionally, the *Eadie* decision added an objective element to the determination of non-pathological criminal incapacity. The decision requires courts to consider whether a reasonable person would have lost control in the accused's circumstances when testing the accused's credibility.[562] Both of these new requirements increase the burden on those accused who wish to invoke the defence.

To prove non-pathological criminal incapacity, the accused must lay the foundation for:

- A triggering event that caused the accused,
- To lose the ability to distinguish between right and wrong, or to act in accordance with what she or he knows is right and wrong.
- The unlawful act must have occurred during the period of incapacity.

The prosecution is responsible for disproving the accused's claim. It is aided in this burden by "the natural inference that in the absence of exceptional circumstances a sane person who engages in conduct which would ordinarily give rise to criminal liability, does so consciously and voluntarily."[563]

(a) Triggering event
The first element of the defence of non-pathological incapacity is that the accused killed the deceased in response to a triggering event. The Supreme Court of Appeal in *S v Henry*, 1999 (1) SACR 13, explained that a:

> Trigger mechanism... was required to induce a state of psychogenic automatism. There had to be some emotionally charged event or provocation of extraordinary significance to the person concerned and the emotional arousal that it caused had to be of such a nature as to disturb the consciousness of the person concerned to the extent that it resulted in unconscious or automatic behaviour with consequential amnesia.

Because this defence is non-pathological criminal incapacity, the trigger must be something other than a diagnosed mental disorder or disease. This raises the first caution when using this defence on behalf of abused women who kill. Battered Women's Syndrome and Post-Traumatic Stress Disorder may be treated as pathological disorders. If experts rely on either of these two theories to describe the effects of abuse on the accused, she may not be able to argue this defence. Instead, the abused woman could be forced to argue an insanity defence.

Under South African law, there are no particular requirements for what the emotional trigger event should be. The non-capacity could result from:

- Emotional collapse
- Emotional stress
- Total disintegration of the personality
- Shock
- Fear
- Anger
- Tension

- Insulting or oppressive conduct of another person
- Pre-menstrual stress
- Provocation
- Stress
- Overwhelming and debilitating social conditions.[564]

Any combination of these factors also could be sufficient, as well as any of these factors combined with intoxication.

South African courts hesitate to find non-pathological criminal incapacity as a result of a single incident of stress or provocation.[565] Courts seem to expect that only a build up of stress or cumulative provocation will cause a person to lose control to the point of incapacity:

> The chances of X (accused) succeeding with this defence if he became emotionally disturbed for only a brief period before and during the act are slender. It is significant that in many of these cases in which the defence succeeded or in which the court was at least prepared to consider it seriously, X's act was preceded by a very long period – months or years – in which his level of emotional stress increased progressively. The ultimate event which led to X's firing the fatal shot can be compared with the last drop in the bucket which caused it to overflow.[566]

Snyman explains that under circumstances of prolonged stress or provocation, the accused may grow mentally or physically exhausted, which "increasingly strain(s) his powers of self-control, until these powers eventually snap."[567] He noted that these circumstances may exist in an unhappy marriage.

For practitioners representing women who kill their abusers in non-confrontational situations, this understanding of cumulative stress and provocation is helpful. Unfortunately, it is not enough – courts want to know what made this session of abuse different from those in the past that did not result in killing. In *S v Ingram*, the Appellate Division could not locate a sufficiently strong triggering event to justify a loss of capacity.[568] In *Ingram*, the husband shot his abusive wife after she became drunk and verbally abusive. In the past, the husband and their children had been able to subdue the wife by locking her in the bedroom or the bathroom. As their children struggled to do this, the husband retrieved his gun and shot his wife. The court rejected non-pathological criminal incapacity because "The appellant had on previous occasions failed to isolate and restrain the deceased. There is no rational reason why on this particular occasion such failure should have operated as a trigger mechanism when it had not done so before."[569]

An advocate for an abused woman who kills must find out what the trigger event was and what made it different from past events. The triggering event need not be the last incident of violence alone, but could also include the continuing threat of abuse. In fact, this may be the preferable argument for a woman who killed when there was a long lapse between the last bout of violence and her action. Either way, the advocate will need to explain as clearly as possible the turning point in the woman's mind. As Chapter 3 explains, women typically kill because they believe they cannot survive more abuse or because the abusers escalated the violence too far beyond what they could accept. The advocate can support this with evidence of the pattern of abuse in the relationship and through expert testimony that explains the cumulative fear and stress that made the last incident of abuse (and the continuing threat) "the last drop in the bucket."

In some instances, abused women kill in response to what objectively looks like a minor act or gesture with little significance. As explained in the Chapter 4 discussion of the unlawful act requirement of self-defence, something insignificant to an outsider may signal the start of abuse.[570] Evidence on the pattern of abuse typically substantiates these arguments. Two judges on the High Court of Australia highlighted this point:

> There may be cases in which a matter of apparently slight significance is properly to be regarded as evidence of provocation when considered in light of expert evidence as to the battered woman's heightened arousal or awareness of danger. And evidence of that may also be relevant to the gravity of the provocation, as may the history of the abusive relationship.[571]

The defence does not specifically require expert testimony about the accused's state of mind; however, it should be treated as essential. The Supreme Court of Appeal highly recommends using such testimony to explain the triggering event and the accused's response to it.[572]

Although difficult to avoid, advocates should be cautious when arguing provocation because it could be a double-edged sword. Instead of negating the accused's intention to kill, courts sometimes find that the provocation confirms it:[573]

> "Facts which can be relied upon as indicating that a person was acting in a state of automatism are often consistent with the reasons for the commission of a deliberate, unlawful act. Thus – as one knows – stress, frustration, fatigue and provocation, for instance may diminish self-control to the extent that, colloquially put, a person snaps and a conscious act amounting to a crime results."[574]

(b) Lose the ability to distinguish between right and wrong or lose the ability to act in accordance with right or wrong

There are two ways in which an accused can provide the foundation for a finding of non-pathological criminal incapacity: (1) if she or he can provide evidence that she or he lost the ability to distinguish between right and wrong, or (2) if she or he could distinguish between right and wrong but could not act based upon that knowledge. While this second method has been a part of South African law for a long time, the *Eadie* decision contends that this argument should succeed only on rare occasions.[575] The Court wrote: "Whilst it may be difficult to visualize a situation where one retains the ability to distinguish between right and wrong yet loses the ability to control one's actions, it appears notionally possible."[576] What is now only "notionally possible" was the predominant explanation for a finding of non-pathological criminal incapacity.

Additionally, no longer is it enough for the accused to argue that she or he had "an inability to restrain oneself, or an inability to resist temptation, or an inability to resist one's emotions" to prove loss of control.[577] The Supreme Court of Appeal concluded that to allow an accused to argue "the devil made me do it" to escape criminal liability "does violence to the fundamentals of any self-respecting system of law."[578] Instead, the courts must look for evidence of sane automatism to prove incapacity.

South African courts apply a subjective test to determine whether the accused suffered from non-pathological criminal incapacity. The *Eadie* decision warned, however, that courts should not be quick to accept the accused's self-serving claims. Instead, they should add an objective test to determine the accused's credibility.[579] The test is whether in the accused's circumstances it was reasonable for him/her to lose control.[580] The more unreasonable the accused's response, the less likely she or he lost control. For example, the *Eadie* decision involved an accused who claimed that he was incapacitated by road rage at the time he killed the deceased. One of the deciding factors against finding incapacity was that "hundreds of thousands of people daily find themselves in similar or worse situations, yet they do not go out clubbing fellow motorists to death when their anger may be provoked."[581]

Courts look for certain behavioural clues to determine whether an accused killed because of non-pathological criminal incapacity. In particular, they watch for goal-directed behaviour before, during, and immediately after the unlawful act. Goal-directed behaviour indicates self-control. For example, in *S v. Kali*, the court noted that the accused had shot and killed his girlfriend and members of her family, but not everyone else in the room.[582] Although the court accepted that the accused acted in rage, the court found that "his actions were directed at certain individuals only and do not reflect an involuntary or uncontrollable course of conduct."[583]

The court may find non-pathological incapacity despite apparently controlled behaviour if the actions were something the accused regularly performed.[584] South African courts accept that a person maintains motor functions while acting automatically. However, automatons perform these functions based on muscle memory. If the action is not something the person typically performs, she or he could not have been acting automatically.[585]

In addition to erratic behaviour, courts look for evidence that the accused was dazed and confused before, after and during the killing. Persons emerging from a state of automatism typically are confused.[586] A person who appears focused and clear-headed is likely to have been in control.

Amnesia also signals courts that a person suffered from non-pathological criminal incapacity at the time she or he killed. Courts caution, however, that the accused must have "true absence of memory rather than a retrograde loss of memory after the event."[587] They recognize that traumatic events often result in amnesia and are wary of finding incapacity on this basis alone.[588]

Battered women who kill in non-confrontational situations, particularly those who hire contract killers, will have the most difficulty proving that their behaviour was not goal-directed and focused. Much of their argument will depend on expert testimony explaining the psychological effects of abuse on these women and particularly on the accused. The expert testimony must address the appearance of goal-directed behaviour and how, despite that, the woman acted without control.

Prior to the *Eadie* decision, some women successfully argued that they killed their abuser while in a state of non-pathological criminal incapacity.[589] The expert evidence proved pivotal in each of these cases. In one of the few reported cases, *S v Campher*, one of the judges on appeal rejected the accused's claim of incapacity because she did not provide expert testimony:

> "From her evidence it is not possible to infer that she had lacked the ability to appreciate the wrongfulness of her act. It may be that she had acted on a subconscious impulse and had not at that moment realized that she was acting wrongfully, but since there was no psychiatric evidence in the case, I will assume that, when she fired the shot, she appreciated that she was acting wrongfully and that she thus had the necessary power of distinction."[590]

The court in *S v Wiid*, highlighted an important problem with these cases.[591] In *Wiid*, the husband had beaten his wife, leaving her with a broken nose, broken teeth and bruises on her face, and had threatened to kill her just before she shot him. Before concluding that the accused suffered from non-pathological criminal incapacity, the court analyzed whether the husband could have carried out the threat. The husband's capacity to carry out his threat is irrelevant to whether the threat triggered a total loss of control. This decision suggests that courts may test for capacity using a purely objective test, rather than subjective test in which the credibility of the claim is tested objectively, at least as it applies to abused women. Advocates should watch for this.

(c) The unlawful act must have occurred during the period of incapacity

The next requirement of non-pathological criminal incapacity is that the accused must have been suffering from the incapacity at the time she or he killed the deceased. While this is typically an implicit requirement, it can serve as a barrier to the defence for women who kill their abusers in non-confrontational situations. Courts are reluctant to find incapacity when there is a long lapse in time between the triggering event and the woman's response, particularly if the accused performed complex actions during the lapse.[592] Women who hire killers will have the most difficulty meeting this element.

One way around this hurdle is for the woman to argue that because of the cumulative provocation and fear, she had no time to "cool down." This is where the understanding of domestic violence as a process becomes particularly important. Domestic violence and the threat of violence continue unabated where there is a pattern of abuse. It continues even during apparent calm in the relationship. If the court can understand that the woman lives in constant fear of her abuser and that the triggering event is, in part, the constant threat to her, then it may be able to understand that there was no time for the woman to regain her self-control. The Supreme Court of Kentucky took a similar approach in one of these cases, finding:

> "Extreme emotional disturbance may be more gradual than the flash point normally associated with sudden heat of passion . . . The fact that the triggering event may have festered for a time in Springer's (the accused's) mind before the explosive event occurred does not preclude a finding that she killed her husband while under the influence of extreme emotional disturbance."[593]

Advocates can bolster this argument with expert evidence that women are socialized not to act in "the heat of passion", which this defence expects, but through a slow burn of emotion that eventually flares.[594] For the criminal justice system to be fair, it must include women's experiences with and responses to violence within defences. Ignoring that women are socialized to respond to provocation, stress and other triggering events differently from men perpetuates the bias in the law in favour of men. Experts can testify about the effect of the power imbalance in the relationship on the accused, particularly that an abused woman is fearful of her abuser at all times because she knows he can abuse her at will. The combination of socialization, women's disempowerment by the abuser, and the size-differential between the abuser and his victim temper heat-of-passion responses; these factors are more likely to lead an abuse victim to respond in a slow burn of emotions.

2. Conclusion

Non-pathological criminal incapacity is the appropriate defence for women who killed their abusers because they lost all self-control. A few women who killed in non-confrontational situations have been successful at the defence. However, it is not the only defence they can argue. Unfortunately for this category of women, the *Eadie* decision seems to severely limit the defence.

C. INSANITY DEFENCE

The insanity defence will apply only rarely to abused women who kill their batterers, as most do not suffer from a mental illness or disorder sufficient for the defence. It has strict requirements set out in Criminal Procedure Act 51 of 1977, ss 77–79. The defence is nearly identical to non-pathological criminal incapacity except that a diagnosed mental illness or disorder must have caused the accused to act unlawfully. The statute reads:

> "A person who commits an act which constitutes an offence and who at the time of such commission suffers from a mental illness or mental defect which makes him incapable
>
> *(a)* of appreciating the wrongfulness of his act; or
> *(b)* of acting in accordance with an appreciation of the wrongfulness of his act,
>
> shall not be criminally responsible for such act."[595]

An accused who argues this defence must provide psychiatric evidence of the underlying mental problem.[596] A diagnosis under the Mental Health Act by itself is insufficient to prove loss of capacity necessary for the defence, although courts consider it a factor.[597] Even if the accused proves she or he suffered from insanity, she or he must submit evidence that the insanity resulted in the unlawful act.[598] If the court concludes that insanity caused the unlawful act, the accused will be acquitted of murder but must be detained in a state hospital for the duration of the insanity.[599]

Women who kill because they are suffering from Battered Women's Syndrome or Post-Traumatic Stress Disorder may be able to argue insanity defence if the psychological effects of abuse are sufficiently severe. For example, a statute in Ohio provides:

> "If a defendant is charged with an offense involving the use of force against another and the defendant enters a plea to the charge of not guilty by reason of insanity, the defendant may introduce expert testimony of the 'battered woman syndrome' and expert testimony that the defendant suffered from that syndrome as evidence to establish the requisite impairment of the defendant's reason, at the time of commission of the offense, that is necessary for a finding that the defendant is not guilty by reason of insanity."[600]

Women suffering from BWS or PTSD, however, may find that their disorders are too pathological for a finding of non-pathological criminal incapacity and yet not sufficiently pathological for insanity. They could be excluded from both defences on the basis of such a diagnosis.

Even if BWS or PTSD are sufficient to meet the element of a pathological impairment, defence counsel needs to question strongly whether this is the appropriate defence for an abused woman who kills. First of all, a woman's decision to kill her abuser may be rational in context of the violence she faces. Arguing insanity both incorrectly reflects the choices she made and stigmatizes what is potentially a normal reaction to an abnormal situation. Insanity should be argued only rarely and only after the woman's advocate assures him/herself that it appropriately reflects the woman's behaviour based on her description of events.

D. CONCLUSION

Non-pathological criminal incapacity and the insanity defences to murder are open to women who kill their abusers because they lost control. Advocates defending an abused woman who kills should be cautious when choosing these arguments. They also must not immediately assume that any woman who kills her abuser in a non-confrontational situation did so as a result of non-pathological criminal incapacity or insanity. This assumption stigmatizes women and treats their responses to domestic violence as abnormal. They must also assure themselves that the woman did not kill because she thought her life was at risk.

Women who have killed in non-confrontational situations have been able to argue successfully non-pathological criminal incapacity based on a build-up of fear and provocation. The *Eadie* decision strongly indicates that it will be increasingly more difficult for these women to prove the defence. The Supreme Court of Appeal equates non-pathological criminal incapacity with sane automatism, which could be exceedingly difficult to prove. Expert testimony must be utilized to explain that the woman acted without control, even in the face of goal-directed behaviour. The *Eadie* decision also injected an objective test of credibility to the test for the defence, again seemingly throwing up more barriers to the use of the defence.

Insanity may be far more difficult to prove, but there appears to be no reason these women cannot access the defence. Battered Women's Syndrome or Post-Traumatic Stress Disorder could serve as the basis for the pathological impairment that resulted in the loss of control, although there may be some barriers to this argument.

CHAPTER 6
Post-conviction Relief

Contents	Page
A. MITIGATION OF SENTENCE	171
1. Substantial and compelling circumstances	171
2. Provocation and severe emotional stress that results in diminished capacity	177
3. Provocation that does not result in diminished capacity	179
4. Conclusion	180
B. PRESIDENTIAL CLEMENCY AND PARDON POWERS	180
1. Executive pardon or clemency	181
2. Legal arguments	183
3. Political arguments and arguments for mercy	184
4. Additional arguments and information	185
5. Conclusion	185

There are two avenues of post-conviction relief in South Africa: mitigation of sentence and clemency. This chapter describes both those mechanisms. Mitigation of sentence is particularly important for women who kill their abusers, as South African criminal law does not provide partial defences to murder for provocation or severe emotional stress that results in diminished capacity. Unless abused women can meet the stringent tests for self-defence, putative self-defence or non-pathological criminal incapacity, they will be convicted of murder. Mitigation of sentence then becomes the only easily accessible tool these women can use to avoid lengthy imprisonment.

Clemency also has the potential to be an important tool for South African women convicted of killing their abusers, although it has yet to become one. In the United States in particular, clemency campaigns on behalf of these women have been successful, resulting in the release of many women from prison. Each of these mechanisms of relief is described below.

A. MITIGATION OF SENTENCE

The Criminal Law Amendment Act 105 of 1997 establishes a mandatory minimum sentence for certain murder convictions. The purpose of the mandatory sentences is to "ensure a severe, standardized and consistent response from the courts."[601] Many battered women who kill their abusers in non-confrontational situations or through a hired killer plead guilty to, or are convicted of, pre-meditated murder. Under the sentencing statute, convictions for pre-meditated murder result in life sentences unless the convicted accused can show that "substantial and compelling" circumstances exist to mitigate the sentence.[602]

1. Substantial and compelling circumstances

An accused convicted of murder may be relieved of the harsh mandatory life sentence if she or he can prove that substantial and compelling circumstances exist that reduce his or her moral blameworthiness.[603] Until the Supreme Court of Appeal decision in *S v Malgas*, the meaning of "substantial and compelling" was ambiguous and inconsistently applied by South African courts.[604] A strict interpretation required evidence of exceptional or shocking circumstances to justify decreasing a sentence. The less strict interpretation required evidence that the mandatory minimum sentence would lead to an injustice in the particular case; the injustice did not need to be shocking for the court to lessen the sentence.

The *Malgas* decision clarified the ambiguity in the Criminal Law Amendment Act concerning substantial and compelling circumstances. It refused to define the terms; instead it explained how to determine whether those circumstances exist. Using instinct, courts should determine substantial and compelling circumstances based on the less strict interpretation of the statute – whether injustice would occur if the court imposed the mandatory sentence on the convicted accused:

> "Once a court reaches the point where unease has hardened into a conviction that an injustice will be done, that can only be because it is satisfied that the circumstances of the particular case render the prescribed sentence unjust or, as some might prefer to put it, disproportionate to the crime, the criminal and the legitimate needs of society. If that is the result of a consideration of the circumstances the court is entitled to characterise them as substantial and compelling and such as to justify the imposition of a lesser sentence."[605]

Overall, however, the *Malgas* decision explained that the mandatory minimum sentences are "generally appropriate" for the convictions and that the court should depart from them only with a "weighty justification."[606] It warned that:

> "Speculative hypotheses favourable to the offender, maudlin sympathy, aversion to imprisoning first offenders, personal doubts as to the efficacy of the policy implicit in the amending legislation, and like considerations were equally obviously not intended to qualify as substantial and compelling circumstances."[607]

The Supreme Court of Appeal clarified that courts can continue to look at what were treated as extenuating circumstances prior to the Criminal Law Amendment Act to determine substantial and compelling circumstances.[608] It declined, however, to list circumstances that should be included in any definition. This means there are no theoretical limits to what could be considered a mitigating circumstance for purposes of sentencing as long as the convicted accused was less blameworthy as a result of it.[609] The most commonly accepted circumstances that result in mitigation – provocation and extreme emotional stress/diminished capacity – are described separately below.

To help determine whether any substantial and compelling circumstances exist, "A court may, before passing sentence, receive such evidence as it thinks fit in order to inform itself as to the proper sentence to be passed."[610] Advocates for women convicted of murder for killing their abusers should include evidence of the pattern and history of abuse between the accused and the deceased, the social context evidence contained in chapters 1 through 3 above, as well as evidence of other acts of abuse against the convicted accused when arguing mitigation of sentence. Expert testimony should use all of this information to explain the convicted accused's mindset at the time she killed. As described below, advocates have successfully used evidence of the psychological effects of abuse and the abused woman's motive for killing to provide a factual foundation for a finding of substantial and compelling circumstances.

The Criminal Law Amendment Act gives courts discretion to deviate from the prescribed sentence if they find substantial and compelling circumstances. Courts can impose shorter periods of imprisonment, suspend the sentence entirely or in part, or impose correctional supervision with or without conditions.

When deciding whether to order non-custodial sentences, the courts consider "whether the particular offender, having regard to his personal circumstances, the nature of the crime and the interests of society must be removed from the community."[611] South African courts have ordered correctional supervision or have suspended sentences entirely if the accused killed because of a "special relationship between the actor and the victim."[612] Women who kill their abusers have benefited from such a finding and have received non-custodial sentences.[613] Typically, however, these cases involved an accused who had been mentally or physically abused just prior to the time she or he killed his or her intimate partner and who committed the killing him/herself.[614] The Supreme Court of Appeal decision in *Ferreira v S* described below removes this limitation.

Although some abuse victims have received non-custodial sentences, women who have killed their abusers have generally suffered from disproportionately high sentences for murder. A recent study completed by the Centre for the Study of Violence and Reconciliation on sentencing for convictions for the murder of an intimate partner found that 21% of women received sentences of over 21 years while only 8% of men received such high sentences.[615] Many of the women in this category killed using hired killers. Men and women nearly equally received sentences of between 10 and 21 years. The majority of women receiving the highest and medium range sentences stated that they killed in response to ongoing abuse. By contrast, the largest proportion of men killed because of jealousy or because their victim had left them, yet they were less likely to receive the highest range sentences. The courts seem more willing to understand men's violent responses to jealousy and separation than women's experiences with abuse.[616] They treated the method of killing as more important than the motive.

Ferreira v S,[617] the most recent decision on appropriate sentencing for a woman who kills her abuser in a non-confrontational situation, begins to correct this bias in sentencing law. It highlights the importance of understanding the social context of abuse, particularly the psychological effects on the woman and the circumstances in which she killed, for purposes of deciding whether any substantial and compelling circumstances exist that justify mitigation of sentence.

The facts of the decision are described fully in Chapter 4. As a brief reminder, Ferreira suffered a long history of mental, physical, sexual and economic abuse at the hands of her intimate partner. Believing she had no other way to escape continued violence, Ferreira hired two men who killed her partner. She pleaded guilty to murder and was sentenced to life imprisonment under the mandatory minimum sentencing law. The lower court concluded that hiring a killer was a sufficiently aggravating factor to erase the mitigating circumstances of the abusive relationship.

The Supreme Court of Appeal heard the appeal of the lower court's decision that no substantial and compelling circumstances existed that justified reducing Ferreira's sentence. The appellant argued that the fact that she honestly believed she had no other way to escape the abuse but to kill her husband was a substantial and compelling circumstance that should mitigate her sentence. She argued that her motive for her husband's death was self-preservation, which should lessen her moral blameworthiness.

The court differentiated Ferreira's argument from provocation, noting: "This was not a killing, from her point of view, perpetrated in the heat of, or very shortly after, the grossly abusive events of the day of the rape."[618] The court determined that the test for substantial and compelling circumstances in her case was whether the killing was "subjectively seen as justifiable."[619] Significantly, the Court concluded that the accused's state of mind at the time she killed

> "… has to be judicially evaluated not from a male perspective or an objective perspective but by the court's placing itself as far as it can in the position of the woman concerned, with a fully detailed account of the abusive relationship and the assistance of expert evidence… Only by judging the case on that basis can the offender's equality right under s 9(1) of the Constitution be given proper effect. It means treating an abused woman accused with due regard for gender difference in order to achieve equality of judicial treatment."[620]

The court decision recognizes explicitly that women's experiences must inform mitigation of sentence in order to ensure equality. As Chapter 4 describes, much of the court analysis mirrored an analysis of putative self-defence.

Ultimately, the court accepted that the appellant honestly believed that she could not escape her husband's abuse unless she killed him: "This is not a case where the first appellant's motive was anything other than to end the relationship so as to preserve her bodily integrity."[621] The court relied heavily on expert testimony in reaching this conclusion.[622] It seemed particularly influenced by the fact that Ferreira's belief and the action of hiring a contract killer conformed to the behaviour of other abused women in similar situations.[623]

Women who kill using contract killers stand to benefit most from the *Ferreira* decision. The court specifically questioned whether hiring killers inherently increases a convicted accused's moral blameworthiness. The court refused to rule that in all cases contract killing is an aggravating factor for purposes of sentencing. Instead, "the moral blameworthiness of the procurer, however, must depend on the motive and subjective state of mind with which a contract killer is engaged."[624] This changed a long line of cases consistent with the lower court ruling that refused to treat abuse as a significant mitigating factor because of the contract aspect of the killing.[625]

The court in *Ferreira* underscored its approach in *obiter dicta* using a hypothetical. In this hypothetical, A, B and C are battered women who killed their abusers after a long history of violence. After a triggering event, each believed she had no other avenue to protect herself from the abuse. A killed her husband a day later. B summoned up the strength to kill her husband a week after the triggering event. Feeling mentally and physically frail, C hired men to kill her husband two weeks after the event.[626] The court explained that the question is not whether "C is more morally blameworthy than the others because she had more time to reflect and appears to have shown callousness by getting others to commit the crime."[627] Instead, the question is whether through the period between the triggering event and when her husband was killed, the abused woman continued to believe she had no choice but to kill him to protect herself.[628] As long as the answer to the question is yes, then the court should not treat these women differently from each other, despite the difference in time lapses and methods for killing.[629]

The court explained that killing because the accused believes she or he is acting in self-preservation could justify imposing a non-custodial sentence. The court based this conclusion on the idea that in the hypothetical "the homicide committed will have been not too far across the borderline between lawful and unlawful conduct."[630] There is nothing in the court's decision, however, that restricts a court from imposing a non-custodial sentence for women who killed their abusers because of diminished capacity.

The decision is an important victory for abused women who kill in non-confrontational situations and for those who use hired killers. Importantly, the court shifted the focus of the mitigation analysis towards the woman's motive and away from her method of killing. It allows courts to give non-custodial sentences to a woman who kills her abuser using a contract killer. The decision accepts that women's experiences with abuse must be considered before a court can decide whether substantial and compelling circumstances exist to justify mitigation of sentence. It forces courts to recognize that men and women respond differently to violence and that women cannot be judged on a male standard for purposes of determining a sentence. Importantly for each of the criminal defences, as well as mitigation of sentence, the decision accepts that women remain fearful of continued abuse long after the occurrence of the triggering event that leads her to believe her life/bodily integrity is at risk.[631]

2. Provocation and severe emotional stress that results in diminished capacity

South African criminal law does not recognize provocation or severe emotional stress resulting in diminished capacity as separate defences to murder. Accused who kill because they lost control and whose arguments fall short of non-pathological criminal incapacity can provide a factual foundation for diminished capacity as a mitigating circumstance for sentencing purposes.[632] The analysis of diminished capacity is similar to the analysis of non-pathological criminal incapacity, except the accused need not act as an automaton to qualify for mitigation. The important elements for proving diminished capacity are:

- a triggering event that
- diminished the accused's ability to differentiate between right and wrong; or
- diminished the accused's ability to act in accordance with what she or he knew was right and wrong; and
- the unlawful act occurred during the period of diminished capacity.

The first step of the inquiry is whether there was a triggering event that caused the accused to act with less than full self-control. The triggering event could be any of the factors listed under non-pathological criminal incapacity in Chapter 5. It need not have been substantially different from anything the accused experienced before, as is required for full defence.[633] A minor act may be sufficient to cause diminished capacity, as long as the accused responded with intense emotion. Women who kill their abusers could benefit from this, particularly if they viewed the triggering event as the "last straw."[634]

Women who kill their abusers also can argue that the psychological effects of abuse caused the killing. Women can rely on the same types of evidence and arguments described in Chapter 5 under the trigger event element of non-pathological criminal incapacity to meet this requirement for diminished capacity.

South African courts do not apply a rigid test to determine whether an accused acted under diminished capacity such as they do for non-pathological criminal incapacity. Regardless, the types of evidence and arguments described in Chapter 5 can aid the accused in meeting the diminished capacity standard for mitigation of sentence.

As with non-pathological criminal incapacity, women who kill their abusers in non-confrontational situations may find that the time-lapse between the triggering event and when they killed excludes them from a finding that they killed while suffering from diminished capacity. The *Ferreira* decision goes a long way towards helping women clear this hurdle, as it accepts that a woman may continue to suffer from fear and other effects of abuse long after the conclusion of the triggering event. Essentially, it accepts that there is nothing inconsistent between a lapse of time between the trigger event and the killing and a finding that the woman acted under diminished capacity. An advocate for an abused woman who kills can apply the same types of evidence and arguments described under non-pathological criminal incapacity to deal with a time-lapse.

Many women who kill because they suffered from diminished capacity should qualify for non-custodial sentences, particularly since in many of the cases imprisonment will not serve any of the three goals of punishment: deterrence, prevention and retribution. Firstly, courts in foreign jurisdictions have recognized that imprisonment does not serve deterrence goals in cases of battered women who kill their abusers:

> "The court is in no way excusing or licensing women who kill their husbands or men who kill their wives because of such (abusive) circumstances, but to suggest that a particular sentence will deter others, in my opinion is meaningless if the person is in the circumstances which Ms. Whitton was in.
>
> * * *
>
> I therefore find, certainly in this case and possible in other cases, that where there has been spousal abuse, general deterrence does not appear to be meaningful."[635]

Secondly, women who kill their abusers, regardless of the circumstances, do not pose a high risk to society, which negates the preventive goal of sentencing. Studies in the United States show that these women have low rates of recidivism.[636] A third and perhaps most common reason courts give to justify non-custodial sentences is that the abusive circumstances in which the killing occurred suggests that these women deserve to be treated with mercy.[637] Retribution only continues the victimization started by the abuser.[638] As the Constitutional Court wrote:

> "Retribution ought not to be given undue weight in the balancing process (for sentencing). The Constitution is premised on the assumption that ours will be a constitutional State founded on the recognition of human rights. The concluding provision on National Unity and Reconciliation contains the following commitment: 'The adoption of this Constitution lays the secure foundation for the people of South Africa to transcend the divisions and strife of the past, which generated gross violations of human rights, the transgression of humanitarian principles in violent conflicts and a legacy of hatred, fear, guilt and revenge. These can now be addressed on the basis that there is a need for understanding but not for vengeance, a need for reparation but not for retaliation, a need for ubuntu but not victimization."[639]

A court that considers the goals of punishment in light of the circumstances in which the abused woman killed should be able to justify non-custodial punishment for some women who kill their abusers as a result of diminished capacity.

3. Provocation that does not result in diminished capacity

An accused convicted of murder also can argue provocation as a mitigating circumstance, even if it did not result in diminished capacity. Courts treat "a crime committed impulsively" as "morally less blameworthy than one committed with premeditations."[640] To qualify for mitigation of sentence on this basis, the convicted accused must show that the provocation affected the accused such that she or he acted unlawfully.[641] South African courts use a subjective test to determine whether the accused acted under provocation, which includes consideration of his or her "personal characteristics, such as a quick temper, jealousy or a superstitious turn of mind."[642]

Factors such as shock, fear, anger, oppressive conduct or almost any of the factors that serve as a triggering event for non-pathological criminal incapacity could serve as the provoking event and therefore as a substantial and compelling circumstance. The arguments for this type of provocation are identical to those described under diminished capacity. Rather than suffering from the effects of diminished capacity, the convicted accused would argue that they were suffering from cumulative rage and/or cumulative fear at the time of the killing, which explains any time lapse and negates that she or he acted in a cold-blooded manner.

4. Conclusion
Women who kill their abusers, even in non-confrontational situations, should have few obstacles in the way of proving substantial and compelling circumstances that justify a reduction in sentence following a conviction for premeditated murder, particularly in light of the *Ferreira* decision. *Ferreira* opened up mitigation of sentence to women who hire contract killers, a group historically excluded from this form of post-conviction relief. The decision forces courts to examine a woman's motive for killing rather than rely solely on her method of killing to determine her moral blameworthiness. The decision also requires courts to consider women's separate experiences when determining punishment. This decision is an important step to ensuring that women no longer suffer from the male bias found in criminal law.

B. PRESIDENTIAL CLEMENCY AND PARDON POWERS

Another avenue of post-conviction relief is a clemency application. Clemency is the discretional power given to the executive leader of a country to correct any harsh or unjust result of a criminal conviction or sentence.[643] The executive can grant a complete pardon, which releases the applicant from the conviction; or it can use the clemency power to relieve him/her of some or all of the consequences of a conviction, including by commuting the sentence.

Over the past 15–20 years, United States governors in Massachusetts, California, New York, Ohio, Maryland, Florida, Illinois and North Carolina, among others, have used their clemency powers to release from prison women convicted of killing their abusive intimate partners.[644] One study showed that these governors exercised their clemency powers for similar reasons, including:

- The women did not receive a fair trial because they were not allowed to argue evidence of the psychological effects of abuse that led to their convictions.[645]
- The women received ineffective assistance of defence counsel because counsel did not place the evidence of abuse and its effects before the court.[646]
- The women were suffering from psychological effects of abuse that led them to believe they had no way out.[647]
- The governors felt compassion and sympathy for the women who killed because of abuse, particularly if the women had already served at least some prison time.[648]
- The sentences were disproportionate to the crime.[649]
- The women believed they had no choice but to kill their abuser.[650]

There are two different types of argument that advocates could assert on behalf of abused women who kill – political/mercy arguments and legal arguments. Applicants, however, must be careful about balancing their arguments: "Focusing too much on justice would transform the petition into an appeal; asking only for mercy would transform the petition into an application for parole."[651] The South African Department of Justice refused to recommend a pardon for one woman who killed her abuser because of the predominant focus on legal arguments. Instead, it concluded that it would be more appropriate for courts to reconsider these cases. With this in mind, advocates should ensure that clemency applications include a significant number of political arguments.

1. Executive pardon or clemency

Section 84(2)*(j)* of South Africa's Constitution gives the president the power to use a pardon or clemency on behalf of convicted persons. The president can use this power at his or her discretion and with few limitations. One important limitation is that the power cannot be used to violate the Constitution or Bill of Rights.[652] A court can review the pardon, although in practice judicial review should occur only rarely.

The decision in *RSA v Hugo* set out some practical guidance for review of presidential pardons.[653] In *Hugo* the President ordered the release of incarcerated women who were mothers of young children. Male prisoners argued that the pardon discriminated unfairly against them. The Constitutional Court explained that the pardon gave women with young children an advantage and that men were disadvantaged as a result. Because no one was entitled to the pardon, however, the president's action did not limit any of the prisoners' rights.[654] The Constitutional Court provided the following guidance for the exercise of the pardon power:

- The power to pardon must be used in good faith;[655]
- it must not be used arbitrarily, meaning that it should be used for the benefit of society;
- it cannot be used to discriminate or otherwise violate the Bill of Rights.

Another possible limitation to the presidential power to grant pardons and clemency is that executives typically grant them only if the convicted person has exhausted all legal remedies. A woman who does not meet this criterion may need to explain why an appeal is either not possible or is unlikely to succeed because of problems such as ineffectual counsel or poverty.

While the President has broad discretion to grant pardons or clemency to prisoners, whether she or he will use that power will depend on many considerations, particularly political considerations. One of the first is whether the prisoner is likely to be a danger to society.[656] Fortunately, there is research in the United States which shows that abused women who kill have low rates of recidivism.[657] Of 27 women released in two states under the executive clemency power, only one woman returned to prison and that was for a drug charge.[658] The low rate of recidivism suggests that these women constitute a low risk to society.

Another possible political concern is whether the granting of a pardon will be viewed as second-guessing the judiciary, which could appear to be a violation of separation of powers.[659] Some believe that if a large number of prisoners receive a pardon, it will appear that the executive is usurping the power of the courts over criminal cases.[660] This consideration suggests that abused women who kill could be more likely to receive a pardon if their clemency applications were based on something other than legal failures at trial or in the court's use of its discretion.

When arguing for clemency, it is important to keep in mind that the applicant is "begging" for mercy and is not entitled to it. Applicants should be wary of appearing to demand or suggesting entitlement to it.[661]

2. Legal arguments

There are a variety of legal arguments an abused woman can make in an application for clemency. These arguments focus on the violation of the woman's right to a fair trial as a result of pervasive gender discrimination by courts. The main arguments concentrate on (1) the unwillingness of courts to take account of the circumstances in which these women kill; and (2) trial advocates' ignorance of the importance of leading evidence about the history of abuse and its effects on the woman. Advocates should review the trial records to see to what extent evidence of the history of violence was led and how the court responded to it.

The first argument has proved to be very strong. For example, Canada undertook an entire executive review process of cases of women convicted of murder or a lesser crime for the death of their abusive partners in the period before the Canadian Supreme Court ruling in *Lavallee*, which paved the way for appropriate use of psycho-social research.[662] Similarly, the governor of Ohio who commuted the sentences of 28 women convicted of killing their abusive intimates partners explained:

> "I believe that the power to commute was designed wisely by early generations for precisely a situation like this, where women find themselves in prison under circumstances where had they been given the chance to defend themselves with the facts, brutal, shocking facts about their life experiences, they almost certainly would not have been convicted or would have been convicted of a lesser crime."[663]

For South African cases, even if the court heard evidence of the abuse, applicants could argue that without expert testimony, the court could not understand why the abused women killed and why they did not leave or turn to the police.[664] Advocates for these women should watch for any other stereotypes used by the court or the prosecution that affected their trials and which expert testimony could have countered.

The second argument is based on arguments of ineffective assistance of counsel. Many abused women who kill are advised to plead guilty to murder because their advocates did not know how to build a defence on their behalf. They could not see how these women's situations fit within the traditional interpretations of criminal defences. Additionally, some legal counsel carry biases against these women or apply stereotypes to these clients, rendering them unable to assist them properly. For example, some legal practitioners interviewed by the Centre for the Study of Violence and Reconciliation opined that abused women who kill their batterers in non-confrontational situations are inherently unreasonable.[665] Again, these arguments will depend on the individual circumstances surrounding the woman's trial.

3. Political arguments and arguments for mercy

The main political argument on behalf of abused women who kill is that they form a vulnerable segment of society that is deserving of mercy. Clemency for these women could be argued as an extension of the commitment the government made towards stopping domestic violence and ensuring that women have the full benefit of the rights to bodily integrity, dignity and freedom from violence enshrined in the Constitution.[666] Focusing on this point, rather than on systemic problems in law enforcement and the courts, could forestall a defensive response from the government.[667]

Using the information contained in Chapter 1, the application could highlight the fact that, despite the efforts the government has made on behalf of domestic violence victims, legal mechanisms and police do not provide enough support to stop the violence. The application should be careful about blaming the government; instead, it should focus on the extent and complexity of the problem that makes it difficult to protect these women.[668]

Another political argument that could be made is that the criminal law is gendered in application. As former Constitutional Court judge, Justice Kriegler explained, criminal defence law was made by men for men.[669] The Canadian decision in *Lavallee* discussed in Chapter 4 provides further support for this position. The gender bias in the law compounds the disadvantages of domestic violence victims, as does poverty. For example, many women use pro deo counsel who often lack the time and resources to mount the type of defence necessary to ensure their clients receive a fair trial.[670] Further, misunderstandings of women's experiences with and responses to violence lead many South African courts to withhold sympathy for women who kill their abusers, particularly if they contracted killers.[671] The *Ferreira* decision described in Chapters 4 and 5 supports the contention that the motive for killing is far more important than the method of killing.

4. Additional arguments and information

Applications for clemency should also include information about the personal circumstances of the accused. Advocates should emphasize:

- the abuse the woman suffered at the hands of the man she killed; this should be detailed, clear and not legalistic;
- the attempts the woman made to seek help, including information about the failure of the police or the criminal justice system to provide assistance;
- whether the woman killed because she thought she had no choice;
- the time the woman has already served;
- any good behaviour in prison, including efforts to overcome effects of abuse and/or develop new skills;
- whether the abused woman had any previous criminal record (if she had, the application must confront the information directly);
- whether she suffers from a physical illness;
- The likelihood of rehabilitation;
- Whether she has young children who need her support;
- Any skills she has that will allow her to find work to support herself;
- That she will be moving into a stable environment that will provide her with support;
- Who will be in her support network.[672]

5. Conclusion

Clemency could be a useful tool for abused women convicted of killing their abusers. Unfortunately, it is fully discretionary, which means it should not be relied on for most of these women.[673] Applications for clemency must clearly articulate political and legal arguments, as well as the personal circumstances of the convicted woman that could justify clemency.

CHAPTER 7

Evidentiary requirements

Contents	Page
A. REQUIREMENTS FOR ADMISSION OF EVIDENCE UNDER SOUTH AFRICAN LAW	187
B. HISTORY AND PATTERN OF ABUSE IN THE RELATIONSHIP	188
C. HISTORY OF VIOLENCE AGAINST OTHERS	190
D. SOCIAL CONTEXT EVIDENCE	190
1. Admission of expert testimony	191
(a) Women's options for avoiding abuse	191
(b) Psychological effects of domestic violence on its victims	192
2. Evidence regarding why the woman did not leave and dispelling myths of abuse	194
E. EVIDENCE OF PRIOR ACTS OF VIOLENCE AGAINST THE WOMAN	195
F. TESTIMONY OR EVIDENCE GATHERED FROM THE ACCUSED WOMAN	195
G. CONCLUSION	196

THERE ARE FOUR MAIN TYPES OF EVIDENCE that advocates should provide on behalf of a woman who kills her abuser. These are:
- history and pattern of abuse in the accused's relationship with the deceased;
- other violent acts of the abuser of which the accused was aware;
- social context evidence as described in Chapters 1 through 3; and
- evidence of other acts of abuse perpetrated against the accused.

Each of these types of evidence supports different elements of the defences and/or a conclusion of substantial and compelling circumstances sufficient to justify mitigation of sentence. They ensure that women's experiences inform criminal defence law. Significantly, many criminal law practitioners in South Africa believe that without such evidence, women tried for murdering their abusers cannot provide a factual foundation for the defences or justify mitigation of sentence.

Chapter 7 presents a general overview of the evidence. The application of the evidence to the individual elements of the defences and/or mitigation of sentence is more fully described within their respective chapters.

A. REQUIREMENTS FOR ADMISSION OF EVIDENCE UNDER SOUTH AFRICAN LAW

South African law distinguishes between the relevance and the admissibility of evidence. All irrelevant evidence is automatically inadmissible.[674] Relevant evidence may be admissible, but by no means is all relevant evidence admissible. Rather, the bulk of the law of evidence consists of rules excluding relevant evidence for some specific reason. The strict formalism of the common law of evidence, however, is being appreciably relaxed.

When deciding whether to admit evidence, South African courts look at whether the evidence can give rise to inferences about the facts and issues of the trial.[675] Courts determine relevancy "based upon a blend of logic and experience lying outside the law."[676] This approach can be problematic if the judicial officer's common sense about domestic violence is based on myths and stereotypes.[677] Courts around the world are calling for expert testimony on the effects of abuse on victims and for the social context of abuse to correct these perceptions: "the expert testimony 'is aimed at an area where the purported common knowledge of the jury may be very much mistaken, an area where jurors' logic, drawn from their own experience, may lead to a wholly incorrect conclusion."[678] While South Africa does not have a jury system, this statement applies to all finders of fact who need to understand experiences outside their own in order to fairly decide the facts in their cases.[679]

Evidence tangential to the issues or too remote will not be admitted.[680] Nor will courts admit evidence if its probative value is outweighed by the prejudice to a party at trial.[681] Other important factors courts consider before admitting evidence at trial is whether it will cause "confusion of the issues, undue delay, waste of time, needless presentation of cumulative issues, the investigation of collateral issues that beg the very issue that the court has to decide, unnecessary expense and other prejudicial factors."[682]

Importantly for women who kill their abusers, courts consider any evidence relating to the accused's motive relevant and admissible at trial regardless of its prejudicial effects or whether it is tangential in nature.[683] This means that the evidence of the history and pattern of abuse as well as the psychological effects on the woman and other social context evidence should be admitted easily.

B. HISTORY AND PATTERN OF ABUSE IN THE RELATIONSHIP

The history and pattern of abuse between the accused and deceased are very important to a woman raising a defence to murder or requesting mitigation of sentence, particularly for a woman who killed her abuser in a non-confrontational situation.[684] They help to explain the woman's state of mind when she killed.[685] In particular, they can explain why the woman honestly and reasonably feared for her life and safety for purposes of self-defence and putative self-defence.[686] The history and pattern of abuse can also support the woman's belief that the attack against which she was defending was imminent.[687] For example, Kentucky enacted legislation that explains: "'Imminent' means impending danger and, in the context of domestic violence and abuse as defined by Kentucky Revised Statutes, ... belief that danger is imminent can be inferred from a past pattern of repeated serious abuse."[688]

The history and pattern of abuse also assist in explaining the trigger event or the cumulative fear, stress and/or provocation that caused non-pathological criminal incapacity, provocation or diminished capacity.[689] For mitigation of sentence, they provide the basis for a finding of "substantial and compelling" circumstances. It must be emphasized, however, that the abuse by itself does not justify an otherwise unlawful action or reduce the accused's moral blameworthiness. Instead, it helps explain her actions for purposes of the defences and mitigation of sentence.

A history and pattern of abuse fall within the category of similar fact evidence. Typically, the prosecutor produces this type of evidence to prove an accused's propensity for committing the type of crime for which she or he is currently charged.[690] Because it is suggestive but not determinative of whether the accused committed the particular crime in the particular instance, courts reject this evidence.[691] If, however, "the similar fact evidence does not go to show guilt on the part of an accused, prejudice is a far less sensitive issue."[692] Because women use the evidence to provide a factual foundation for their defences or to mitigate a sentence, there seems to be no reason why a court would exclude it.[693]

This evidence may also be regarded as character evidence, as it relates to the character of the deceased. While character evidence is often excluded as a prejudicial attempt to damage the credibility of a plaintiff, defendant, accused or complainant,[694] in trials of abused women who kill, it is used to support the woman's subjective and/or reasonable fears of her abuser or the trigger event that caused her to lose control. Because this evidence directly targets the issues and facts at trial, as well as explains the woman's motive for killing her abuser, the cogency of the evidence should easily outweigh its prejudicial effects.

Advocates for women who kill their abusers should be careful to gather as much information about the nature, duration and extent of abuse as possible. This information should be detailed, including specific incidents of abuse. The advocate should also try to substantiate the abuse with medical records, testimony of family, neighbours and friends, police reports, court records, and any other evidence that supports the existence of abuse. Expert testimony regarding the psychological effects of abuse, as described below, should discuss the importance of the history and pattern of abuse to the woman's perceptions as they relate to her state of mind or other elements of the defences.

C. HISTORY OF VIOLENCE AGAINST OTHERS

The history of the deceased's violence against others helps explain the woman's reasonable fear of death or serious bodily injury at his hands.[695] Only instances of which the accused was aware would be relevant to her claim.[696] For example, if a woman knows that her partner stabbed a co-worker in a fit of anger, she has reason to fear him when he threatens her with a knife or other violence. She could assert that she feared a threat consistent with the abuser's prior behaviour.

This type of evidence is character evidence. Often courts exclude this type of evidence when it is used merely to prove that a party to an action or a complainant is a bad person. However, this is not the purpose of the testimony. Instead, an abused woman seeks to admit evidence of the deceased's prior bad acts and reputation for violence to support an element of her defence or mitigation of sentence – that she reasonably and/or subjectively feared her abuser. For this reason, this evidence should be admissible.

D. SOCIAL CONTEXT EVIDENCE

As Chapters 1 through 3 describe, there are three types of social context evidence necessary to the success of a defence or mitigation of sentence for an abused woman on trial for killing her battering intimate partner. The first type focuses on how women are treated by the government, courts, police, society, friends and family. The evidence explains abuse victims' limited options for escaping the violence. The second type of social context evidence is the psycho-social evidence. The expert testimony should focus on the psychological effects of abuse on women. However, other types of psycho-social evidence are relevant to the legal defences or mitigation of sentence. Evidence of the psychology of batterers supports the reasonableness of the effects of abuse on women; while evidence of the social judgment theory explains what leads abused women to kill.

The third type of social context evidence serves to destroy the common myths and stereotypes about abused women. In particular, it helps the court understand why an abused woman cannot simply leave the abusive relationship and why she is not to blame for the abuse. Combined, all of this evidence can explain the context within which these women live and is relevant to the reasons they kill. There should be no impediments to the admission of social context evidence.

1. Admission of expert testimony

South African courts admit evidence from experts when "by reason of their special knowledge and skill they are better qualified to draw inferences than the judicial officer" or simply if the evidence could help the court reach its decision.[697] The expert testimony must be relevant to the issues at trial.[698] The court is responsible for qualifying a person as an expert: "the court must be satisfied that the witness possesses sufficient skill, training or experience to assist it. His qualifications have to be measured against the evidence he intends to give in order to determine whether they are sufficient to enable him to give relevant evidence."[699]

When testifying before the court, the expert who gives his or her opinion must explain the basis for it, including whether it is based on personal knowledge or facts she or he heard in court.[700] Experts should be cautious about relying solely on information gathered from the accused. If the court rejects the accused's testimony on the facts that underpin the opinion, it may be compelled to reject the expert's conclusions.[701] Advocates also need to ensure that the facts underlying the expert's testimony are submitted as evidence at trial or as the court in *S v Engebrecht* wrote: "the opinion offered to the court must be proved by admissible evidence, either facts within the personal knowledge of the expert or on the basis of facts proven by others."[702] Failure to do that will affect how the court treats the evidence. When the expert opinion is based on facts proved by admissible evidence, the court will treat that evidence as possibly true. Opinions based on facts not admitted into evidence will be given less weight; and opinions founded on facts that were proved untrue will be given no weight at all.[703]

(a) Women's options for avoiding abuse

Chapters 1 through 3 describe the variety of options courts and society assume are open to battered women to escape the abuse as well as the limitations of those options. For purposes of a trial of a woman for killing her intimate partner, the information contained in these chapters often supports the woman's belief that few or none of those options was truly open to her. This information establishes, at least in part, the mindset of the woman and begins to place the court in her circumstances, knowing what she knows and seeing what she sees.[704] For self-defence and putative self-defence, this evidence elucidates why the woman felt she had no other option but to kill her abuser to stop the abuse.[705] For self-defence, it explains why this belief is reasonable.[706] It also supports the credibility of the abused woman who argues that she suffered from diminished capacity or incapacity because of the violence. Finally, evidence of the lack of real options afforded to women to stop abuse also is important for mitigation of sentence because it describes some of the circumstances that could be deemed substantial and compelling and that justify a more lenient sentence.

An advocate for an abused woman who kills will need to find out about whether the abused woman ever sought help or tried to leave (keep in mind that most women will have tried something) and why those attempts failed. The advocate should canvass each of the options open to women to escape the abuse, detailing each request for help and the reactions the woman received, as well as each attempt to leave. The generalized information in Chapters 1, 2 and 3 will support the woman's experiences and the difficulties she faced leaving her abuser. However, it cannot stand on its own.

(b) Psychological effects of domestic violence on its victims

Abused women who kill who are charged with murder need to provide expert testimony of the psychological effects of abuse on women generally, and the accused particularly, in order to provide the factual foundation for a defence or mitigation of sentence. Without this information, it may be impossible for a court to understand how a woman's actions fit within any of the defences or why her circumstances justify mitigation of sentence.[707] For example, the Witwatersrand Local Division in *S v Engelbrecht* quoted the Supreme Court of Canada decision in *Lavallee v Queen*, fully described in Chapter 4, to explain the importance of this type of expert testimony in cases of abused women who kill:

"Expert evidence on the psychological effect of battering on wives and common law partners must, it seems to me, be both relevant and necessary in the context of the present case. How can the mental state of the appellant be appreciated without it? The average member of the public (or of the jury) can be forgiven for asking: why would a woman put up with this kind of treatment? Why would she continue to live with such a man? How could she love a partner who beat her to the point of requiring hospitalisation? We would expect the woman to pack her bags and go. Where is her self respect? Why does she not cut loose and make a new life for herself? Such is the reaction of the average person confronted with the so-called 'battered wife syndrome'. We need help to understand it and help is available from trained professionals."[708]

For self-defence and putative self-defence, the effects of abuse on its victims explain women's heightened sensitivity to abuse, which they develop as a survival technique to avoid it.[709] This evidence provides the basis for the belief that the women faced an imminent or inevitable threat, even if an objective observer could not see it.[710] It also provides a factual foundation for proof that these women's beliefs were reasonable and credible.[711]

A woman's heightened sensitivity to her abuser developed by her experience with him could also explain the triggering event that resulted in the woman losing control for non-pathological incapacity, diminished capacity and provocation. The effects of abuse on the woman are vital to explaining both that she lost control at the time she acted and how her actions reflected the loss. Expert testimony could counter the appearance of goal-directed behaviour that normally suggests full capacity. It also helps courts understand how a seemingly minor act could have triggered such a severe reaction.[712]

All of these arguments are aided by other psycho-social testimony. Testimony on the psychology of the batterer bolsters the view that domestic violence is a self-perpetuating process rather than a once-off explosion of rage or anger.[713] It explains that the primary goal of domestic violence is control. Understanding domestic violence in this way explains why a woman could reasonably and subjectively fear abuse between episodes of violence and why she could not leave. The process of domestic violence as well as testimony about women's socialization away from sudden responses to violence explains that some abused women respond to it with a slow burn of emotions, rather than with an immediate reaction, which is important for women who kill in non-confrontational situations and differently from men.

Advocates must be careful when using testimony of the psychological effects of abuse. They have to avoid treating women's experiences as pathological and abnormal. The importance of the testimony is to ensure that the court sees that a woman's response to abuse is normal in the face of an abnormal situation, which means that it may be reasonable in her circumstances even if it resulted in a loss of control. For example, the coercive control theory and Stockholm syndrome explain that prisoners and hostages react to conditions of violence and control in much the same way as abused women. Therefore, the psychological effects of abuse are dependent not only on the individual's psychology or gender but also on the circumstances.

Finally, for self-defence and putative self-defence claims, advocates need to be careful that the expert testimony does not suggest diminished capacity. The psychological testimony should aid these women's defences, not hinder them. As the Canadian Supreme Court wrote in *R v Malott*:[714]

> "The legal inquiry into the culpability of a woman who is, for instance, claiming self-defence must focus on the reasonableness of her actions in the context of her personal experiences, and her experiences as a woman, not on her status as a battered woman and her entitlement to claim that she is suffering from 'battered woman syndrome'."[715]

Overall, the experts need to describe the individual effects of the abuse on the psychology of the woman who killed and then place her as a member of a vulnerable group of society because courts need to understand the particular mindset of the accused as well as her experiences as a member of a neglected group. Experts can strengthen their testimony with other forms of psycho-social research.

2. Evidence regarding why the woman did not leave and dispelling myths of abuse

The last category of social context evidence an abused woman who kills will need to admit in her trial is evidence dispelling myths and stereotypes of abused women, particularly that they can always leave.[716] The advocate should use the research contained in Chapter 1 through 3 to support the subjective reasons the woman provides for why she did not leave.

E. EVIDENCE OF PRIOR ACTS OF VIOLENCE AGAINST THE WOMAN

To some degree, evidence of prior acts of violence against the accused should be covered in the expert testimony about the psychological effects of abuse on the particular woman. The information is particularly helpful for diminished capacity or non-pathological criminal incapacity as it could be another aspect of the trigger that caused the woman to lose control and kill her abuser.

F. TESTIMONY OR EVIDENCE GATHERED FROM THE ACCUSED WOMAN

Whether or not the accused chooses to testify at her trial, her advocate must ensure that the following facts are gathered to provide the foundation for the defences or for mitigation of the sentence. In each case, the woman needs to provide information about:

- the history of abuse, including specific details of incidents of violence;
- names of people or facilities that could corroborate the abuse;
- what caused her to kill her abuser;
- whether there was something different about the abuse that led her to kill;
- whether she felt threatened through the entire period between when she perceived an imminent attack and when she killed her abuser.

For self-defence, the advocate must also inquire into the following:

- why the woman believed she faced an imminent attack, or alternatively, why she believed the attack was inevitable;
- why she thought she had no other options to escape the abuse;

- why she believed she could not survive the attack or that it would result in serious bodily harm.

For non-pathological criminal incapacity and diminished capacity, the advocate needs to ask:

- why the woman killed her husband;
- whether there was a triggering event;
- how the woman behaved before, during and after the killing;
- when she feels she started to become incapacitated; e.g. in *Ferreira*, the diminished capacity started at the time of the sexual abuse, two weeks before the murder;
- whether she regained capacity at any point between when she first suffered from incapacity and when she killed.

G. CONCLUSION

Each type of evidence described above is invaluable to the defences or the mitigation of sentence of a woman who kills her abuser. Without information about the history of abuse, the social context of domestic violence, and the deceased's acts of violence against others, a court is unlikely to understand how a woman who killed in a non-confrontation situation fits into criminal defences or within the category of convicted accused deserving of mitigation of sentence. Admission of this evidence drives courts to account for women's experiences with violence, which historically have been excluded from criminal defence law.

ENDNOTES

INTRODUCTION

1. In 2001 he was quoted as saying that the DVA was "made for a country like Sweden, not South Africa" and was not practical or implementable (Louis Oelofse and Siyabona Mkhwanazi, "Well-meaning laws can't be policed – Selebi", *The Star*, 14 August 2001; Jeremy Michaels, "Selebi summoned for domestic violence remarks", *The Mercury*, 22 August 2001).
2. Former Justice Kriegler at the launch of Legal Defences for Battered Women who Kill their Abusers, Centre For the Study of Violence and Reconciliation, Johannesburg, South Africa, 13 November 2003.
3. *Ferreira, Chilambo and Koesyn v The State* 1 April 2004 SCA 245/03 at 19 para 40.
4. H Ludsin, "South African Criminal Law and Battered Women Who Kill (Discussion Document 2)", Centre for the Study of Violence and Reconciliation (2003) at 6.1.

CHAPTER 1

5. Dutton, M A (1996) "Validity of Battered Woman Syndrome in Criminal Cases Involving Battered Women." Review paper edited by Malcolm Gordon, National Institute of Mental Health, US Department of Justice. http://www.ojp.usdoj.gov/ocpa/94Guides/Trials/Valid/ p 4 of printout.
6. Coker, D (1992) "Heat of passion and wife-killing: Men who batter and men who kill." *Southern California Review of Law and Women's Studies* Fall.
7. The DVA refers to "controlling or abusive behaviour where such conduct harms, or may cause imminent harm to the safety, health or well-being of the complainant".
8. Okun, L (1986) *Woman Abuse: Facts Replacing Myths*. New York, State University of New York Press; Graham, D L R, Rawlings, E and Rimini, N (1988) "Survivors of Terror: Battered Women, Hostages and the Stockholm Syndrome" in Kersti Yllo and Michele Bograd (eds) *Feminist Perspectives on Wife Abuse*. Newbury Park, Sage; Dobash, R E and Dobash, R (1983) *Violence Against Wives*. The Free Press.
9. Okun, L (1986) op cit.
10. Dutton, M A (1996) op cit, p 5 of printout.
11. Nussbaum, M (1999) *Sex and Social Justice*. New York, Oxford University Press at 218
12. See Krug, E G, Dahlberg, L L, Mercy, J A, Zwi, A B and Lozano, R (eds) (2002) *World report on violence and health*. Geneva, World Health Organization at 101.
13. Dunkle, K, Jewkes, R, Brown, H, McIntyre, J, Gray, G and Harlow, S (2003) *Gender-based Violence and HIV Infection among Pregnant Women in Soweto*. Gender and Health Group, Medical Research Council.
14. Mathews, S, Abrahams, N, Martin, L J, Vetten, L, Van der Merwe, L and Jewkes, R (2004) "'Every six hours a woman is killed by her intimate partner': A national study of female homicide in South Africa." MRC Policy brief no 5, June 2004.
15. See Jewkes, R, Penn-Kekana, L, Levin, J, Ratsaka, M and Schrieber, M (1999) *He Must Give Me Money, He Mustn't Beat Me: Violence Against Women in Three South African Provinces*. Pretoria, CERSA (Women's Health) Medical Research Council at 11.
16. Ibid. at 13.
17. Artz, L (1999) *Violence Against Women in Rural Southern Cape: Exploring Access to Justice Through a Feminist Jurisprudence Framework*. Institute of Criminology, University of Cape Town at 114.
18. Abrahams, N, Jewkes, R and Laubsher, R (1999) "I do not believe in democracy in the home: Men's relationships with and abuse of women." Pretoria, CERSA Medical Research Council at 8.
19. Mathews, S, Abrahams, N, Martin, L J, Vetten, L, Van der Merwe, L and Jewkes, R (2004) "'Every six hours a woman is killed by her intimate partner': A national study of female homicide in South Africa." MRC Policy brief no 5, June 2004.
20. *Commonwealth v Stonehouse* 521 Pa 41, 62 (Sup Ct Pa 1989) ("It is widely acknowledged that commonly held beliefs about battered women are subject to myths and ultimately place the blame for battering on the battered victim.")
21. A sample of some myths and facts about domestic violence can be reviewed at the following sites: Crisis Support Network, www.crisis-support.org; Protective Order

Project, University of Indiana, www.law.indiana.edu/pop/doemsticviolence/mythsfacts.shtml; Education Wife Assault, www.womanabuseprevention.com/html/myths/html; Boston Public Health Fact Sheet, www.bpfc.org

22 Abuse Counseling and Treatment, Inc, Alcohol and Domestic Violence: http://www.actabuse.com/alcoholdv.html
23 Dutton, M A (1996) "Battered women's strategic response to violence: The role of context" in Jeffrey L Edleson and Zvi C Eisikovits: *Future Interventions with Battered Women and their Families*. London, Sage Publications at 111.
24 Dutton, M A (1996) op cit at 111–18.
25 Dobash, R E and Dobash, R (1983) *Violence against Wives*. New York, The Free Press at 75.
26 Hoff, L A (1990) *Battered Women as Survivors*. London, Routledge at 78.
27 Blumberg, J M, Swartz, L and Roper, K (1996) "Possibilities for intervention in wife abuse: discourses among care givers in a community health project" in Lorraine Glanz and Andrew Spiegel (eds) *Violence and Family Life in a Contemporary South Africa: Research and Policy Issues*. Pretoria, HSRC Publishers, at 186.
28 Blumberg, J M, Swartz, L and Roper, K (1996) op cit at 173–5.
29 Blumberg, J M, Swartz, L and Roper, K (1996) op cit at 176–7.
30 Blumberg, J M, Swartz, L and Roper, K (1996) op cit at 194.
31 Hoff, L A (1990) *Battered Women as Survivors*. London, Routledge at 42–3.
32 It is unclear whether the man must have paid lobola before the marriage is legally recognized.
33 Bennett, T W *Customary Law in South Africa* 235, 250.
34 These problems led a counsellor working for a domestic violence organization to remark:
    "It is culturally acceptable to hit a woman when you are angry. If a woman makes a man angry she must apologise and has to respect the man. Culturally [it is acceptable] to beat a woman with a stick or a sjambok and not with an open hand (slap). If he has paid *lobola* she can't go back to her family unless he tells her to 'go home'. Then her family has to repay the *lobola*."
    (Rasool, S, Vermaak, K, Pharaoh, R, Louw, A and Stavrou, A (2002) *Violence Against Women*. Institute for Security Studies at 57).
35 Jewkes, R, Penn-Kekana, L, Levin, J, Ratsaka, M and Schrieber, M (1999) *He Must Give Me Money, He Mustn't Beat Me: Violence Against Women in Three South African Provinces*. Pretoria, CERSA (Women's Health) Medical Research Council at 9.
36 Ibid.
37 Ibid.
38 Ibid.
39 Curran, E and Bonthuys, E (2004) "Customary law and domestic violence in rural South African communities". Centre for the Study of Violence and Reconciliation at 17–18 (citing Lillian Artz, (1999) 42 *Agenda* 58).
40 Curran, E and Bonthuys, E (2004) op cit (citing Olivier et al *Indigenous Law* par 55).
41 *S v Mvamvu* (case no 350/2003, delivered on 29 September 2004) para 16.
42 Ferraro, K J (1983) "Rationalising vViolence: How battered women stay." *Victimology* 8, 203–212 at 210.
43 Ferraro, K J (1983) op cit at 205.
44 "Domestic violence against women and girls." *Innocenti Digest* No 6, June 2000, http://www.unicef-icdc.org/publications/pdf/digest6e.pdf, at 7.
45 Rasool, S, Vermaak, K, Pharaoh, L, Louw, A and Stavrou, A (2002) *Violence Against Women*. Institute for Security Studies.
46 Bollen, S, Artz, L, Vetten, L and Louw, A (1999) "Violence against women in metropolitan South Africa: A study on impact and service delivery." Institute for Security Studies Monograph Series No 41, Table 14.
47 Novitz, T *The Prevention of Family Violence Act 1993*. University of Cape Town: Law, Race and Gender Research Unit (1996) at 23. See also Human Rights Watch, Global Report on Women's Human Rights, "Violence Against Women in South Africa" http://www.hrw.org/about/projects/womrep/index.htm #Top of page.
48 Novitz, T op cit at 23 (citing the Criminal Law Amendment Act 4 of 1992, which amended the Criminal Procedure Act 56 of 1955, s 384).
49 Prevention of Family Violence Act section 5. A few months prior to its enactment, a decision of the Ciskei Supreme Court in *S v Ncanywa* 1993 (2) SA 567 (Cka) abolished the exemption for the former homeland. See also Hansson, D, Russell, D and Harmes, R "An international bibliography on marital rape with a comment on the current legal position in South Africa," (1992) *SAJHR* 587.
50 Sec 1(2).
51 Novitz , T (1996) op cit at 9.
52 Novitz , T (1996) op cit at 26–9.
53 See e.g. Human Rights Watch, Global Report on Women's Human Rights, "Violence Against Women in South Africa" http://www.hrw.org/about/projects/

	womrep/index.htm #Top of page.		*Women*. Institute for Security Studies at 136.
54	Sec 1(vii).	84	Sec 2, read together with s 4(2) and regulations 2–3.
55	Sec 4.		
56	Sec 7(2).	85	Human Rights Watch, South Africa (1997) *Violence Against Women and the Medico-Legal System*.
57	Sec 7 (1)*(c)*, (3) and (4).		
58	Sec 7(6).		
59	Sec 8.	86	Ibid
60	Sec 4(5).	87	See Chapter 2 for a description of the real risks to women who attempt to leave relationships.
61	Sec 5(2).		
62	Sec 5(1).		
63	Sec 5(3) and sec 6(5).	88	*Commonwealth v Stonehouse* 521 Pa 41, 63 (Sup Ct Pa 1989).
64	Parenzee, P, Artz, L and Moult, K (2001) *Monitoring the Implementation of the Domestic Violence Act: First Research Report 2000–2001*, Institute of Criminology at 24.		
		89	Sec 2.
		90	Sec 2.
		91	Sec 2.
		92	Sec 3.
65	Ibid.	93	Sec 5(3) and s 6(5).
66	Parenzee, P, Artz, L and Moult, K (2001) op cit at 20.	94	Parenzee, P, Artz, L and Moult, K (2001) op cit at 81. See also the comments of national police Commissioner Jackie Selebi on p4 of the Introduction.
67	Parenzee, P, Artz, L & Moult, K (2001) op cit at 107.		
68	Human Rights Watch, South Africa (1997) *Violence Against Women and the Medico-Legal System*.	95	Parenzee, P, Artz, L and Moult, K (2001) op cit at 80; Independent Complaints Directorate *Domestic Violence Report to Parliament* 2001.
69	Parenzee, P, Artz, L and Moult, K (2001) op cit at 95–6.		
70	Parenzee, P, Artz, L and Moult, K (2001) op cit at 94.	96	Ibid
		97	Human Rights Watch, South Africa (1997). *Violence Against Women and the Medico-Legal System*.
71	Parenzee, P, Artz, L and Moult, K (2001) op cit at 84.		
72	Parenzee, P, Artz, L and Moult, K (2001) op cit at 80.	98	Parenzee, P, Artz, L and Moult, K (2001) op cit at 82.
73	Parenzee, P, Artz, L and Moult, K (2001) op cit at 97.	99	Parenzee, P, Artz, L and Moult, K (2001) op cit at 85.
74	Ibid.	100	Ibid.
75	Justice College, which provides magistrates with training, offers a week-long course on family law, of which one day is dedicated to the Domestic Violence Act. See eg, Parenzee, P, Artz, L and Moult, K (2001) op cit at 97.	101	Artz, L (1999) *Violence Against Women in Rural Southern Cape: Exploring Access to Justice Through a Feminist Jurisprudence Framework*, Institute of Criminology, University of Cape Town at141.
		102	Artz, L (1999) op cit at 142.
		103	Artz, L (1999) op cit at 144.
76	Parenzee, P, Artz, L and Moult, K (2001) op cit at 66.	104	Olckers, I. (1997) "Safety and Security, Justice and Correctional Services" in D Budlender (ed) *The Second Women's Budget*. Cape Town: IDASA at 131.
77	Sec 7(1)*(c)* and 7(2).		
78	Artz, L (2003) *Magistrates and the Domestic Violence Act: Issues of Interpretation*. Institute of Criminology at 31–2.		
		105	Artz, L (1999) op cit at 125–6. One study in the Western Cape highlighted that: "The majority of women's stories depicted experiences of contact with the police as being fraught with frustration, claiming they have lost all 'confidence' in the ability of the police service to provide adequate assistance. Many spoke about the police with a sense of helplessness and despair, describing police officials as being 'careless and corrupt'." Mathews, S & Abrahams, N (2001) *An Analysis of the Impact of the Domestic Violence Act (No 116 of 1998) on Women*. The Gender Advocacy Programme & The Medical Research Council at 26.
79	Parenzee, P, Artz, L and Moult, K (2001) op cit at 23.		
80	Parenzee, P, Artz, L and Moult, K (2001) op cit at 24.		
81	See Chapter 2 for a description of the real risks to women who attempt to leave relationships.		
82	Fedler, J "Lawyering domestic violence through the prevention of the Family Violence Act 1993 – An evaluation after a year in operation" (1995) 112 *SALJ* 231 at 235.		
83	Rasool, S, Vermaak, K, Pharaoh, R, Louw, A & Stavrou, A (2002) *Violence Against*		

106 Rasool, S, Vermaak, K, Pharaoh, R, Louw A & Stavrou, A (2002) *Violence Against Women*. Institute for Security Studies at 112.
107 Department of Safety and Security. (1998). *White paper on Safety and Security "In Service of Safety" 1999–2004*. Available at http://www.gov.za/whitepaper/1998/safety.htm Site accessed December 2003.
108 See Mathews, S and Abrahams, N (2001) op cit at 26.
109 *S v Baloyi* 2000 (1) SACR 81 para. 12.
110 Rasool, S, Vermaak, K, Pharaoh, R, Louw A & Stavrou, A (2002) op cit at 78.
111 Rasool, S, Vermaak, K, Pharaoh, R, Louw A & Stavrou, A (2002) op cit at 79.
112 Jacobs, T & Suleman, F (1999) *Breaking the Silence: A Profile of Domestic Violence in Women Attending a Community Health Centre*. Durban: Health Systems Trust at 15.
113 Mmatshilo Motsei (1993) *Detection of woman battering in health care settings: The case of Alexandra Health Clinic*. Women's Health Project: University of the Witwatersrand at 17.
114 Jacobs, T & Suleman, F (1999) op cit at 14–15.
115 Rasool, S, Vermaak, K, Pharaoh, R, Louw A & Stavrou, A (2002) op cit at 89.
116 Rasool, S, Vermaak, K, Pharaoh, R, Louw A & Stavrou, A (2002) op cit at 90.
117 Vetten, L & Khan, Z (2002)*"We're doing their work for them": An Investigation into Government Support to Non-profit Organisations Providing Services to Women Experiencing Gender Violence*. Johannesburg: Centre for the Study of Violence and Reconciliation at 5.
118 Ibid.
119 Rasool, S, Vermaak, K, Pharaoh, R, Louw A & Stavrou, A (2002); Artz, L (1999) op cit.
120 See Artz, L, (1997) 'Access to Justice for Rural Women: Special Focus on Violence Against Women.' Report prepared for the Black Sash. Institute of Criminology.
121 Artz, L (1997) 'Access to Justice for Rural Women : Special Focus on Violence Against Women'. Report prepared for the Black Sash. Institute of Criminology.
122 Why Battered Women Stay, http://www.stopviolence.com/domviol/whytheystay.htm
123 Park, Y J, with Peters, R and De Sa, C (2000) "More than simply a refuge: Shelters for abused women in South Africa" in Yoon Jung Park, Joanne Fedler and Zubeda Dangor (eds) *Reclaiming Women's Spaces: New Perspectives on Violence Against Women and Sheltering in South Africa*. Johannesburg: Nisaa Institute for Women's Development at 248.
124 The first shelter specifically for abused women was opened by POWA in 1984.
125 Park *et al* (2000) op cit at 248.
126 Parenzee, P, Artz, L & Moult, K (2001) *Monitoring the Implementation of the Domestic Violence Act* First Research Report 2000–2001, Institute of Criminology at 84.
127 Rasool, S, Vermaak, K, Pharaoh, R, Louw A & Stavrou, A (2002); Artz, L (1999) op cit at 100.
128 Rasool, S, Vermaak, K, Pharaoh, R, Louw A & Stavrou, A (2002); Artz, L (1999) op cit at 101.
129 Herman, J L (1992) *Trauma and Recovery*. New York, Basic Books at 61.
130 Rasool, S, Vermaak, K, Pharaoh, R, Louw A & Stavrou, A (2002); Artz, L (1999) op cit at 101.
131 Artz (1999) at 128.
132 Ibid.
133 Artz (1999) at 123.
134 Ibid.
135 "Domestic violence against women and girls" (2000) *Innocenti Digest* No 6, June 2000. http://www.unicef-icdc.org/publications/pdf/digest6e.pdf, at 8.
136 Commission on Gender Equality Annual Report (1999) at 8.
137 'South Africa Tackles Social Inequalities,' *Africa Recovery* vol 14(4) at 14.
138 Aliber, M (2002) *Overview of the Incidence of Poverty in South Africa for the 10-Year Review*, Human Sciences Research Council at 3.
139 Aliber, M (2002) op cit at 5.
140 Aliber, M (2002) op cit at 10.
141 Oranje, M (2002) *A comparative Analysis of 1996 and 2001-Census Data on vulnerable and Special Target Groups*. University of Pretoria at 64.
142 Labour Force Survey, Statistics South Africa, March 2004 as ii.
143 Labour Force Survey, Statistics South Africa, March 2004 at xi.
144 Oranje, M (2002) op cit at 61.
145 Bennett, T W (1999) *Human Rights and African Customary Law* at 122, 126.
146 Ibid.
147 Bennett, T W (1999) op cit at 125.
148 Social Assistance Act 59 of 1992.
149 Nedlac, Report on Social and Economic Developments in South Africa 1997.
150 *Stonehouse* (1989) Pa. at 69. Unfortunately, it is a myth that South African courts have used against abused women who kill. See *Kgafela* Case No 429/2002 (Supreme Court of Appeal) para 9.
151 Parenzee, P, Artz, L & Moult, K (2001) *Monitoring the Implementation of the Domestic Violence Act* First Research Report

152 Ibid.
153 Sec 2.
154 Sec 15 (reinforcing common-law duty of support of children). *Petersen v Maintenance Officer, Simon's Town Maintenance Court, and Others* 2004 (2) SA 56 (C) (duty of support owed by grandparents to grandchildren); Muslim marriages, which are currently not recognized statutorily as marriages, but are treated as marriages for purposes of maintenance and support. *Daniels v Campbell* 2004 (5) SA 331 (CC).
155 South African Law Commission, Discussion Document 106: Domestic Partners (2003) at 5.2.3. The Constitutional Court concluded, however, that the parties of any of these types of relationship could agree to a reciprocal duty of support, which could serve as the basis for a maintenance order. *Satchwell v President of the Republic Of South Africa and Another* 2002 (6) SA 1 (CC).
156 Sec 6.
157 Sec 16.
158 Secs 26, 27, 28 and 30.
159 Sec 31.
160 Mills, S (2004). "Women's poverty and the failure of the judicial system" in Debbie Budlender & Bhekinkosi Moyo (eds) *What about the Children? The Silent Voices in Maintenance*. Johannesburg, Tshwaranang Legal Advocacy Centre.
161 Community Agency for Social Enquiry. (2004) *Implementation of the Maintenance Act in the South African Magistrate's Courts*. Report researched for the Commission on Gender Equality at 107.
162 Community Agency for Social Enquiry (2004) op cit at 111.
163 Divorce Act, s 7(2).

CHAPTER 2

164 Dutton, D G with Golant, S K (1995) *The Batterer*. New York, Basic Books at 13.
165 Dobash, R E & Dobash, R P (1983) *Violence Against Wives*. New York, The Free Press at 93.
166 Abrahams, N, Jewkes, RP & Laubsher, R (1999) *I Do Not Believe in Democracy in the Home: Men's Relationships With and Abuse of Women*. CERSA Medical Research Council (1999) at 16.
167 Meaning that she attempted to challenge his authority in the home, or failed to show what he perceived to be the required respect for his authority.
168 Abrahams, N, Jewkes, R & Laubsher, R (1999) at 15.
169 James, K, Seddon, B & Brown, J *"Using it" or "Losing it": Men's Construction of Their Violence Towards Female Partners*. Australian Domestic & Family Violence Clearinghouse at 16.
170 James, K, Seddon, B & Brown, J op cit at 16.
171 James, K, Seddon, B & Brown, J op cit at 12.
172 Ibid.
173 James, K, Seddon, B & Brown, J op cit at 18.
174 James, K, Seddon, B & Brown, J op cit at 19.
175 Gondolf, E (1988) *Battered Women as Survivors: An Alternative to Treating Learned Helplessness*. New York, Lexington Books at 65–6.
176 Tweed, R & Dutton, D G (1998) "A comparison of instrumental and impulsive subgroups of batterers." *Violence & Victims* 13, 3, 217–30, page 2 of printout.
177 Ibid.
178 Ibid.
179 Okun, L (1986) *Woman Abuse: Facts Replacing Myths*. New York, State University of New York Press at 120.
180 Tweed, R & Dutton, D G (1998) op cit, page 8 of printout.
181 Tweed, R & Dutton, D G (1998) op cit, page 2 of printout.
182 Ibid.
183 Tweed, R & Dutton, D G (1998) op cit, page 4 of printout.
184 Tweed, R & Dutton, D G (1998) op cit, page 7 of printout.
185 James, K, Seddon, B & Brown, J op cit at 4.
186 James, K, Seddon, B & Brown, J op cit at 7.
187 James, K, Seddon, B & Brown, J op cit at 9.
188 James, K, Seddon, B & Brown, J op cit at 7.
189 James, K, Seddon, B & Brown, J op cit at 5.
190 Ibid
191 James, K, Seddon, B & Brown, J op cit at 6.
192 James, K, Seddon, B & Brown, J op cit at 7.
193 Schelling, T (1963) *The Strategy of Conflict*. London, Oxford University Press at 16–18.
194 Jacobson, N S & Gottman, J M "Anatomy of a violent relationship" 1998 *Psychology Today* March–April, p 3 of printout.
195 Jacobson, N S & Gottman, J M op cit, p 4 of printout.
196 Ibid.
197 Jacobson, N S & Gottman, J M op cit, p 5 of printout.
198 Ibid.
199 Jacobson, N & Gottman, J (1998) *Breaking the Cycle: New Insights into Violent Relationships*. London, Bloomsbury at 28–30.
200 Dobash, R E & Dobash, R P (1998) "Violent men and violent contexts" in R Emerson Dobash & Russell P Dobash (eds) *Rethinking Violence Against Women*. London, Sage Publications at 156–60.
201 Dobash, R E & Dobash, R P (1998) op cit at 158.
202 Dobash, R E & Dobash, R P (1998) op cit

at 162.
203 Dobash, R E & Dobash, R P (1998) op cit at 147.
204 Motz, A (2001) *The Psychology of Female Violence*. East Sussex, Brunner-Routledge at 223.
205 Ibid.
206 Motz, A (2001) op cit at 222.
207 Dutton, D G & Kerry, G *Modus Operandi and Personality Disorder in Incarcerated Spousal Killers* at 3. The Alabama Court of Criminal Appeals surveyed recent court decisions in the state, noting the growing number of cases in which men were charged with killing their female intimate partners. Based on this survey, it concluded: "It has become increasingly clear that leaving an abusive relationship may not, in fact, mean that the victim's safety is no longer threatened. As our own cases show, domestic violence often escalates to deadly levels." *State v Harrington* 858 So 2d 278, 298 (2003).
208 Dutton, D G & Kerry, G op cit at 2.
209 Dutton, D G & Kerry, G op cit at 3.
210 Vetten, L (2005) *Gunning for You: The Role of Guns in Men's Killing of their Intimate Female Partners*. CSVR Gender Programme, Policy Brief No 02.
211 Hart, B J (1990) *Assessing Whether Batterers Will Kill*. Pennsylvania Center Against Violence and Abuse.
212 Department of Justice, Canada, A Review of Section 264 (Criminal Harassment) of the Criminal Code of Canada, http://www.justice.gc.ca/en/ps/rs/rep/wd96-7a-e.pdf, 5 (quoting Susan Bernstein "Living under siege: Do stalking laws protect domestic violence victims?" (1993) 15 *Cardozo L Rev* 525 at 529).
213 Department of Justice, Canada, op cit at 26.
214 Department of Justice, Canada, op cit at 5.
215 Dobash, R E & Dobash, R P (1998) op cit at 146.
216 Stark, Evan (1995) "Re-presenting woman battering: From battered woman syndrome to coercive control" (1995) 58 *Albany L Rev* 973 at 5.
217 Bollen, S, Artz, L, Vetten, L and Louw, A (1999) "Violence against women in metropolitan South Africa: A study on impact and service delivery" Institute for Security Studies Monograph Series No 41 at 26.
218 Downs, D A (1996) *More than Victims: Battered Women, the Syndrome, Society and the Law*. Chicago, the University of Chicago Press at 5–7.
219 Ferraro, K J (2003) "The words change but the melody lingers: The persistence of the battered woman syndrome in criminal cases involving battered women" (2003) *Violence Against Women* 9(1) 110 at 129.
220 Summary taken from Walker, L E (1989) at 42–51.
221 Griffith, M F (1995) "Battered woman syndrome: A tool for batterers?" (1995) 64 *Fordham L Rev* 141 at 172; Stark, E (1995) "Symposium on reconceptualizing violence against women by intimate partners" (1995) 58 *Albany L Rev* 973 at 998.
222 Allard, S A (1991) "Rethinking battered woman syndrome: A black feminist perspective" (1991) 1 *UCLA Women's LJ* 191 at 192.
223 Faigman, D L & Wright, A J "The battered woman syndrome in the age of science" (1997) 39 *Arizona L Rev* 67 at 82–88; *Osland v Queen* (1998) HCA 75 para 169 (High Court Aust); *R v Mallot*, (1998) 1 SCR 123 para 20 (Sup Ct Canada).
224 *R v Thornton* (1996) 2 LAC (Eng Crim Ct) 679.
225 *R v Ahluwalia* (1992) 4 All ER 889; *R v Thornton* (1996) 2 LAC (Eng Crim Ct) 679.
226 *Lavallee v Queen* (1990) 55 CCC3d 97 (Sup Ct Canada).
227 *Lavallee v Queen* (supra); Wannop, A L (1995) "Battered woman syndrome and the defense of battered women in Canada and England" (1995) 19 *Suffolk Transnational L Rev* 251 at 268.
228 *Lavallee v Queen* (supra); *Osland v Queen* (supra) at para 169; *R v Mallot* (supra) at para 20; Wannop, A L ibid.
229 *State v Kelly* 478 A ed 364 (1984); *Weiand v State* (1998) 732 So ed 1044.
230 *Commonwealth v Stonehouse* (1989) 521 Pa 41 (Sup Ct Pa).
231 Griffith, M F (1995) op cit at 161–2.
232 *Lavallee v Queen* (supra); Griffith, M F (1995) op cit at 161–2
233 Griffith, M F (1995) ibid.
234 Griffith, M F (1995) ibid; *Commonwealth v Stonehouse* (supra).
235 Allard, S A (1991) op cit at 195–6; Margulies, P "Identity on trial: Subordination, social science, evidence, and criminal defense" (1998) 51 *Rutgers L Rev* 45 at 47–8.
236 *R v Mallot* (supra) at para 4.
237 Maguigan, H (1991) "Battered women and self-defense: Myths and misconceptions in current reform proposals" (1991) 140 *Univ Pa L Rev* 379 at 444–5.
238 *Griffin v State* (1998) 749 P 2d 246, 249 (Sup Ct Wy).
239 Chan W (1997) "Legal equality and domestic homicides" (1997) 25 *Int J Soc L* 203 at 206.
240 Kazan, P "Reasonableness, gender difference and self-defense law" (1997) 24 *Manitoba L J* 549 at para 24.

241 See *Osland v Queen* (*supra*) at para 161.
242 *Osland v Queen* (*supra*) at para 161; Peter Margulies (1998) op cit at 48.
243 *Commonwealth v Stonehouse* (*supra*) at 41 note 10.
244 Browne, A (1987) *When Battered Women Kill*. New York, Free Press at 183.
245 Aliber, M (2002) *Overview of the Incidence of Poverty in South Africa for the 10-Year Review*, Human Sciences Research Council at 5.
246 Rasool, S, Vermaak, K, Pharaoh, R, Louw, A & Stavrou, A (2002) *Violence Against Women*. Institute for Security Studies at 58.
247 *Osland v Queen* (*supra*) at para 164.
248 Barnett, O W & LaViolette, A D (1993) *It Could Happen to Anyone: Why Battered Women Stay*. London, Sage Publications at 16–18.
249 *Clemency for Battered Women in Michigan: A Manual for Attorneys, Law Students and Social Workers*. Michigan, ACLU, October 1998 [hereinafter *1998 Manual*].
250 Including those subjected to thought reform techniques (popularly – though misleadingly – termed 'brainwashing').
251 The term originates from a 1973 bank robbery in Stockholm, Sweden, which resulted in three women and a man being taken hostage. During their six days of captivity, the four hostages came to bond with their captors – even seeing them as protecting them from the police. This bonding, which occurs between both parties, has been noted since in a number of hostage situations. It is often encouraged by those who negotiate with captors, as it improves the chances of the survival of the hostages.
252 Herman, J L (1992) *Trauma and Recovery*. New York, Basic Books at 74.
253 Herman, J L (1992) op cit at 75.
254 Okun, Lewis (1986). *Woman Abuse: Facts Replacing Myths*. New York, State University of New York Press at 119.
255 Herman, J L (1992) op cit at 74.
256 See the *Ferreira* and *Engelbrecht* cases; Okun L (1986) op cit at 122.
257 Okun, L (1986) op cit at 119.
258 Ibid.
259 Herman, J L (1992) op cit at 76.
260 Amnesty International (1973) *Report on Torture*. London, Duckworth at 53.
261 Stark, E "Symposium on reconceptualizing violence against women by intimate partners" (1995) 58 *Albany L Rev* 973 at 976.
262 Herman, J L (1992) op cit at 77.
263 Okun, L (1986) op cit at 118.
264 Herman, J L (1992) op cit at 77.
265 Mathews, S & Abrahams, N (2001) *An Analysis of the Impact of the Domestic Violence Act (No 116 of 1998) on Women*. The Gender Advocacy Programme and the Medical Research Council at 20.
266 Mathews, S & Abrahams, N (2001) op cit at 20.
267 Bhana, K & Hochfeld, T (2001) *"Now We Have Nothing": Exploring the Impact of Maternal Imprisonment on Children whose Mothers Killed an Abusive Partner*. Johannesburg, The Centre for the Study of Violence and Reconciliation at 26.
268 Artz, L (1999) *Violence Against Women in Rural Southern Cape: Exploring Access to Justice Through a Feminist Jurisprudence Framework*. Institute of Criminology, University of Cape Town at 127.
269 Okun, L (1986) op cit at 121–2.
270 Mathews, S & Abrahams, N (2001) op cit at 20; see also the *Ferreira* and *Engelbrecht* cases.
271 Herman, J L (1992) op cit at 77.
272 Graham, D L R, Rawlings, E I & Rigsby, R K (1994) *Loving to Survive: Sexual Terror, Men's Violence, and Women's Lives*. New York, New York University Press at 37–9.
273 Okun, L (1986) op cit at 125.
274 Rasool, S, Vermaak, K, Pharaoh, R, Louw, A & Stavrou, A (2002) op cit at 35.
275 Okun, L (1986) op cit at 124–6.
276 Ferraro, K J "Rationalising violence: How battered women stay" (1983) 8 *Victimology* 203 at 209.
277 Okun, L (1986) op cit at 116–17.
278 Ferraro, K J op cit at 208.
279 Okun, L (1986) op cit at 117.
280 Okun, L (1986) op cit at 130–2.
281 Herman, J L (1992) op cit at 79.
282 Russell, D E H (1990) *Rape in Marriage*. Bloomington and Indianapolis, Indiana University Press at 285.
283 Herman, J L (1992) op cit.
284 See the *Engelbrecht* case.
285 See the *Engelbrecht* case.
286 Herman, J L (1992) op cit at 79.
287 Bhana, K & Hochfeld, T (2001) op cit at 24.
288 See the *Engelbrecht* case.
289 Herman, J L (1992) op cit at 77.
290 Okun, L (1986) op cit at 120.
291 Herman, J L (1992) op cit at 76.
292 Herman, J L (1992) op cit at 92.
293 Herman, J L (1992) op cit at 83.
294 See the *Engelbrecht* case.
295 Herman, J L (1992) op cit at 83.
296 Herman, J L (1992) op cit at 87–89.
297 Herman, J L (1992) op cit at 84.
298 Dutton, D & Painter, S (1993). "Emotional attachments in abusive relationships: A test of traumatic bonding theory" 8(2) *Violence and Victims* 105 at 105.
299 Dutton, D & Painter, S (1993) op cit at 107.

300 Herman, J L (1992) op cit at 78.
301 Dutton, D & Painter, S (1993) op cit at 108.
302 Dobash, R E & Dobash, R P (1979) *Violence against Wives* 95 at 96.
303 Dutton, D & Painter, S (1993) op cit at 106.
304 Dutton, D & Painter, S (1993) op cit at 117–18.
305 Dutton, D & Painter, S (1981) "Traumatic bonding: The development of emotional attachments in battered women and other relationships of intermittent abuse" 6(1–4) *Victimology* 139 at 139.
306 Barnett, O W & LaViolette, A D (1993) op cit at 95.
307 Hughes, M J & Jones, L "Women, domestic violence and post-traumatic stress disorder" http://www.csus.edu/calst/government_affairs/reports/ffp32.pdf, 15.
308 Hughes, M J & Jones, L op cit at 17.
309 Hattendorf, J, Ottens, A J & Lomax, R G (1999) "Type and severity of abuse and post-traumatic stress disorder symptoms reported by women who killed abusive partners" (1999) *Violence Against Women* 5(3) 292 at 310.
310 Herman, J L (1992) op cit at 121.
311 Hughes, M J & Jones, L op cit at 18–19.
312 Hughes, M J & Jones, L op cit at 15–16.
313 Amnesty International. (1973) *Report on Torture*. London, Duckworth at 53.

CHAPTER 3

314 *Ferreira, Chilambo and Koesyn v The State* CCT Case 245/03 (1 April 2004) at para 13.
315 Mills (1985) cited in Judith Wuest & Marilyn Merritt-Gray (1999) "Not going back: Sustaining the separation in the process of leaving abusive relationships" 5(2) *Violence Against Women* 110 at 111.
316 Landenburger (1989) in Judith Wuest & Marilyn Merritt-Gray (1999). "Not going back: Sustaining the separation in the process of leaving abusive relationships" 5(2) *Violence Against Women* 110 at 112.
317 Ferraro, K J (1983) "Rationalising violence: How battered women stay" (1983) 8 *Victimology* 203 at 207.
318 Dobash, R E & Dobash, RP (1979) *Violence Against Wives* at 97.
319 Stark, E (1995) "Symposium on reconceptualizing violence against women by intimate partners" 58 *Albany L Rev* 973 at 981.
320 Barnett, O W & LaViolette, A D (1993) *It Could Happen to Anyone: Why Battered Women Stay*. London, Sage Publications at 53.
321 Ferraro, K J (1983) op cit at 204.
322 Ferraro, K J (1983) op cit at 207–9.
323 Hoff, L A (1990) *Battered Women as Survivors*. Routledge, London at 64–5.
324 Wuest, J & Merritt-Gray, M (1999) "Not going back: Sustaining the separation in the process of leaving abusive relationships" (2) *Violence Against Women* 110 at 115–18.
325 Wuest, J & Merritt-Gray, M (1999) op cit at 120.
326 See eg *Engelbrecht's* case.
327 1993, in Judith Wuest and Marilyn Merritt-Gray (1999). "Not going back: Sustaining the separation in the process of leaving abusive relationships" 5(2) *Violence Against Women* 110 at 112.
328 Herman, J L (1992) *Trauma and Recovery*. New York, Basic Books at 90.
329 Stark, E (1995) op cit at 1021.
330 Okun, L (1986) *Woman Abuse: Facts Replacing Myths*. New York, State University of New York Press at 74.
331 This notion of funnelling was put forward during expert testimony in the *Engelbrecht* matter and was accepted by the judge as a description of this particular defendant's circumstances.
332 Hoff, L A (1990) op cit at 70.
333 Hoff, L A (1990) op cit at 72.
334 See also Radford, L "Pleading for time: Justice for battered women who kill" in J Bridgeman and S Millins (1998) *Feminist Perspectives on Law: Law's Engagement with the Female Body* at 630.
335 See Browne, A (1987) *When Battered Women Kill*. New York, Free Press at 128.
336 Carden, A D (1994) "Wife abuse and the wife abuser: Review and recommendations" 22(4) *The Counseling Psychologist* 539 at 551.
337 See Browne, A (1987) op cit at 129.
338 Ibid. at page 130.
339 *Lavallee* at 119.
340 See Maguigan, H (1991) "Battered women and self-defense: Myths and misconceptions in current reform proposals"140 *Univ Pa L Rev* 379 at 397.
341 The remaining 5% of cases could not be classified, as court records did not include sufficient details about the incident.
342 Not one of the male perpetrators killed their female partners in response to ongoing abuse. However, at least a third of the men routinely abused their female partners before killing them.
343 Vetten, L & Ngwane, C (In press). *Sentencing Men and Women Convicted of Spousal Homicide: Findings from Three Gauteng Courts*. Research report in preparation for the Centre for the Study of Violence and Reconciliation.
344 Browne, A (1987) op cit at 183.

345 Certainly as Browne herself notes (op cit at 157) all factors were not present in all cases included within her sample.
346 Leonard, E A D (1997) "Convicted survivors: The imprisonment of battered women who kill" http://www.freebatteredwomen.org/pdfs/convsurv.pdf, 25.
347 Browne, A, Williams, K R & Dutton, D G (1999) "Homicide between intimate partners" in M Dwayne Smith & Margaret A Zahn (eds) *Studying and Preventing Homicide*. London, Sage Publications at 59.
348 Browne, A, Williams, K R & Dutton, D G (1999) op cit at 64.
349 Browne, A, Williams, K R & Dutton, D G (1999) op cit at 74.
350 *Lavallee* (*supra*) at 112.

CHAPTER 4

351 Constitution of the Republic of South Africa Act 108 of 1996 ("the Constitution") s 12. See also *Ferreira v S* CCT Case 245/03 (1 April 2004) (SCA) and *S v Baloyi* 2000 (1) BCLR 86 (CC) at para 11. (February 2005)
352 See Chapter 2. See also *S v Engelbrecht* Case No 64/2003 (WLD).
353 Constitution s 10. *Ferreira v S* (*supra*) and *S v Baloyi* (*supra*) at para 11.
354 Constitution s 9.
355 *S v Baloyi* (*supra*) at para 12
356 Constitution s 12.
357 See Chapter 2.
358 *Ferreira v S* (*supra*) at para 40. In *Ferreira*, the court considered these violations when looking at whether any substantial and compelling circumstances existed to justify mitigation of sentence for a woman convicted of murdering her husband. Because this information speaks to a woman's motive for killing, a court hearing a woman's defence should still consider this information.
359 *S v Baloyi* (*supra*) at para 11. See also *Carmichele v Minister of Safety and Security* 2001 (4) SA 938 (CC).
360 Unfortunately, with regard to domestic violence, the Supreme Court of Appeal applied this duty narrowly. In *S v Ferreira*, an abused woman who killed her violent partner argued that the police breached its duty to protect her after she called it on three occasions. Of the three times the accused called, the police showed up only once. On the one occasion, the police officer told her simply to sober up her husband. The Court concluded that the accused had not shown that the police had sufficient knowledge of the violence to activate the duty and that she should have taken other legal measures to stop the abuse. Para 42.
361 *S v Baloyi* (*supra*) at para 12.
362 Ludsin, H (2003) "South African Criminal Law and Battered Women Who Kill (Discussion Document 2)", Centre for the Study of Violence and Reconciliation section 6.1. This is despite efforts of women's advocates to locate appropriate cases in which to argue other defences.
363 *S v Engelbrecht* (*supra*) at paras 335, 336, 337.
364 Taylor, L J (1986) "Provoked reason in men and women: Heat-of-passion manslaughter and imperfect self-defense" 33 *UCLA L Rev* 1679 at 1681; Justice Kriegler, Launch of Legal Defences for Battered Women Who Kill Their Abusers and South African Criminal Law and Battered Women Who Kill, Centre for the Study of Violence and Reconciliation, 13 November 2003.
365 Ibid. See also, Vetten, L & Ngwane, C (In press) *Sentencing Men and Women Convicted of Spousal Homicide: Findings from Three Gauteng Courts*. Research report in preparation for the Centre for the Study of Violence and Reconciliation.
366 See, generally, Schneider, E M (2000) *Battered Women and Feminist Lawmaking*. New Haven Yale University Press.
367 *S v Engelbrecht* (*supra*).
368 *Ferreira v S* (*supra*) at para 40.
369 *S v Engelbrecht* (*supra*) at para 469.
370 Shaffer, M "*R v Lavallee*: A review essay" (1990) 22 *Ottawa L Rev* 607 at para 26.
371 *Carmichele v Minister of Safety and Security* (*supra*) at paras 34 and 40.
372 *Carmichele v Minister of Safety and Security* (*supra*) at para 36.
373 *S v Engelbrecht* (*supra*) at para 336.
374 *S v Engelbrecht* (*supra*) at para 340 (Satchwell J, who was responsible for establishing the law for the case, ultimately found that a woman who suffocated her abusive husband in his sleep met the elements for private defence. The two assessors in the trial disagreed, which made Satchwell J's opinion a dissenting one.
375 Taylor, L J (1986) op cit at 1699–1700.
376 Snyman, C R (2002) *Criminal Law* (4 ed) Butterworths at 102;
377 Snyman, C R (2002) op cit at 101.
378 Snyman, C R (2002) op cit at 104.
379 Ibid.
380 *Discussion Doc 2*, sec 2.1.1.
381 *Witt v State*, (1995) 892 P 2d 132, 189 (quoting *State v Richardson*, 189 Wis 2d 418 (App Ct Wis 1994). See also, Colorado Revised Statutes 18-6-801.5, Domestic Violence – <u>Evidence of Similar Transactions</u> ("The general assembly hereby finds that

domestic violence is frequently cyclical in nature, involves patterns of abuse, and can consist of harm with escalating levels of seriousness. The general assembly therefore declares that evidence of similar transactions can be helpful and is necessary in some situations in prosecuting crimes involving domestic violence"; Official Code GA section 16-3-21 Use of Force in Defense of Self or Others; Louisiana Code of Evidence Article 404, Relevancy and its Limits.
382 *S v Engelbrecht (supra)* at para 344.
383 *Engelbrecht (supra)* at para 361 and subsequent discussion.
384 *Engelbrecht (supra)* at para 342.
385 *Engelbrecht (supra)* at para 380.
386 *State v Gallegos* (1986) 104 New Mexico 247 (Ct of Apps NM) (disapproved of on other grounds); *Lavallee v Queen* 55 CCC3d 97 (1990); *R v Petel*, 1 SCR 3, 87 CCC3d 97 (Sup Ct Can 1994); *R v Malott*, 1 SCR 123 (Sup Ct Can 1998). The following cases applied the same principle to situations that did not involve battered women: *R v Nguyen* AJ No 129 (Alberta Ct of App 1997) and *R v Plain* OJ No 4927, 121 CCC3d 199 (Ontario Ct of Justice 1997); *R v Currie*, 166 CCC3d 190 (2002) ("The Supreme Court of Canada in *Cinous* confirmed the principle established in *R v Petel* (1994) 1 SCR 3 (SCC) that the existence of an actual assault is not a prerequisite for a defence under s 34(2). The question that the jury must ask itself is not whether the accused was unlawfully attacked but, whether he reasonably believed in the circumstances that he was being unlawfully attacked."); *Osland v Queen* (1998) HCA 75 (High Court of Australia); *R v Secretary* (1996) 107 Northern Territory Reports 1.
387 Arkansas Code s. 5-2-607.
388 Louisiana Code of Evidence, Article 404(2) and Maryland Code 10-916(3).
389 Snyman, C R (2002) op cit at 104.
390 Burchell, J M (1997) *South African Criminal Law and Procedure* vol 1 (3rd ed) Juta at 72.
391 Ibid.
392 *Ferreira (supra)* at para 40. See also *R v Van Vuuren* 1961 (3) SA 305 (E) (rights to dignity and personal freedom are legally protected interests). Chapter 4 describes the constitutional rights that domestic violence violates.
393 *S v Engelbrecht (supra)* at para 345.
394 See Chapter 1.
395 *S v Engelbrecht (supra)* at para 345.
396 Snyman, C R (2002) op cit at 105; *S v Mokonto* 1971 (2) SA 319, 324.
397 Burchell, J M (1997) op cit at 76.
398 Ibid; Snyman, C R (2002) ibid.
399 See Ludsin *Discussion Document 2* at 2.1.1 and 6.1.
400 *Engelbrecht (supra)* at para 349.
401 *Engelbrecht (supra)* at para 348.
402 Fletcher, G "Self-defense and relations of domination: Moral and legal perspectives on battered women who kill: Domination in the theory of justification and excuse" (1996) 57 *U Pittsburgh L Rev* 553 at 559–60.
403 Nourse, V F "Self-defense and subjectivity" (2001) 68 *U Chicago L Rev* 1235 at 1263.
404 *Lavallee (supra)* at para 116.
405 The woman's action also is not revenge because she was responding to her perception of a current threat rather than the last incident of abuse.
406 1967 (1) SA 488 (A).
407 *Engelbrecht (supra)* at para 347.
408 As translated in Burchell, J & Milton, J (2000) *Cases and Materials on Criminal Law* (2nd ed) Juta at 158. A third judge agreed with this conclusion.
409 See eg *Robinson v State* 308 SC 74, 417 SSE2d 88, 91 (Sup Ct SC 1992).
410 *Engelbrecht (supra)* at paras 389 –90.
411 See Chapter 2.
412 Krause, J H (1994) "Of merciful justice and justified mercy: Commuting the sentences of battered women who kill" 46 *Florida L Rev* 699 at 711–12.
413 1982 (2) SA 587 (T).
414 *S v Mogohlwane* 1982 (2) SA 587 (T) (as translated by CSVR).
415 *Engelbrecht (supra)* at para 397 (footnotes removed).
416 *Engelbrecht (supra)* at para 395.
417 The second assessor, Professor Naude, simply concluded that the domestic violence was inevitable.
418 The criminal law experts also expressed concern that if the definition of imminence was broadened or exchanged for evidence that self-defence was necessary, many criminally accused would make spurious claims of self-defence. These fears should be assuaged by the difficulty accused persons would have meeting a standard of inevitability and providing a foundation that explains why there were no other options available to protect against an unlawful attack. There are very few situations outside of the abuse context that would allow for this argument.
419 *Engelbrecht (supra)* at para 348.
420 *Engelbrecht (supra)* at para 350.
421 RS 1985, c C-46, s 34 (1992).
422 55 CCC3d 97 (1990)
423 At 120 (per Wilson J).
424 At para 53.
425 At para 116. See also *R v Petel (supra)*; *R v*

426 *Cinous* 162 CCC3d 129 (Sup Ct Can 2002). *Lavallee* at 120–1.
427 *R v Petel* (*supra*) at 97; *R v Malott* (*supra*) at 123; *R v Nguyen* AJ No 129 (Alberta Ct of App 1997) and *R v Plain* OJ No 4927, 121 CCC3d 199 (Ontario Ct of Justice 1997); *R v Currie*, 166 CCC3d 190 (2002) See also *Osland v Queen* (*supra*) at 75.
428 Kentucky Revised Statutes Section 503.010.
429 Utah Statutes, s 76-2-402.
430 (1986) 104 New Mexico 247 (Ct of Apps NM) (Disapproved of on other grounds.)
431 At 250.
432 at 250. See also *State v Gaethe-Leonard* (2001) Wash App LEXIS 2488 (Ct Apps Wash). But see *State v Stewart* (1988) 243 Kansas 639, 646 (Sup Ct Kansas) ("In order to instruct a jury on self-defense, there must be some showing of an imminent threat or a confrontational circumstance involving an overt act by an aggressor. There is no exception to this requirement where the defendant has suffered long-term domestic abuse and the victim is the abuser."); *Jahnke v State*, (1984) 682 P2d 991 (Sup Ct Wyoming) (Requiring some showing of a confrontation before allowing an accused to argue self-defence); *Robinson v State* 308 SC 74, 417 SE2d 88 (Sup Ct SC 1992).
433 *State v Janes* 121 Wn2d 220 at 241–2 (1993). See also *State v Smullen* 844 A2d 429 (Ct App Md 2003); *People v Humphrey* 921 P2d 1, 8-9 (Sup Ct Ca. 1996); *Robinson v State* (*supra*) at 91; *State v Burtzlaff*, 493 NW2d 1 (Sup Ct SD 1992). But see *State v Norman* 324 NC 253, 261 (Sup Ct NC 1989); *State v Stewart* (*supra*) at 639.
434 107 N Territory Reports 1 (Sup Ct NT 1996).
435 Snyman, C R (2002) op cit at 105.
436 Burchell, J M (1997) op cit at 105–6.
437 *Engelbrecht* (*supra*) at para 355.
438 *Engelbrecht* (*supra*) at para 351, quoting Snyman, C R (2002) op cit at 106
439 *Engelbrecht* (*supra*) at para 352.
440 *Engelbrecht* (*supra*) at para 355.
441 Informal support networks may be able to discuss the violence with the abusers and hope to convince them to stop the violence or obtain treatment. This potential solution, however, relies heavily on people who have no obligation to help the abuse victim and may cause the abuser to respond violently. It also is likely to prove ineffective when one considers the psychology of abusers and the cycle of abuse. Expecting the woman to wait to see if these informal support networks can accomplish what she and the police could not is both unrealistic and unfair, as it places her in continuing danger.
442 *Engelbrecht* (*supra*) at para 352, footnote 118.
443 Ludsin *Discussion Document 2* sec 6.1.
444 *Engelbrecht* (*supra*) at para 354
445 Snyman, C R (2002) op cit at 106.
446 Snyman, C R (2002) op cit at 107. But see Burchell, J M (1997) op cit at 77 ("Where the threat is one of personal injury the obvious possible way of avoiding the attack is to flee. Thus, if the harm can be avoided by flight the accused should flee").
447 *Engelbrecht* (*supra*) at para 354. See also, *Robinson v State* (*supra*) at 88, 92: "Under ... self-defense, a defendant must show that she had no other means of avoiding the danger than to act as she did. A battered woman who is held hostage by her batterer may have no other means of avoiding a battering than to kill her batterer in self-defense. Moreover, a battered woman often may be able to claim the inapplicability of this element of self-defense because she acts while on her own premises and has no duty to retreat."
448 *Lavallee* (*supra*) at 121.
449 CC67/97. On file with the Centre for the Study of Violence and Reconciliation.
450 *S v Mogohlwane*, 1982 (2) SA 587 (T) (as translated by CSVR).
451 Nourse, V F (1998) Book review: "The new normativity: The abuse excuse and the resurgence of judgment in the criminal law" 50 *Stanford L Rev* 1435 at 1454–5.
452 *Engelbrecht* (*supra*) at para 355; *Lavallee* (*supra*) at para 121.
453 *Engelbrecht* (*supra*) at para 356.
454 See also, *Lavallee* (*supra*) at para 121.
455 *Engelbrecht* (*supra*) at para 404. See also, factual findings of Advocate Opperman at para 434. Advocate Opperman explained that the accused failed to meet the proportionality requirement in part because ending the relationship seemed to remain an option: "She was able to (and did) order him out of her life on a number of occasions and was equally able to invite him back into her life."
456 Nourse, V F (2001) "Self-defense and subjectivity" 68 *Univ Chi LR* 1235 at 1236.
457 *Engelbrecht* (*supra*) at para 410.
458 At para 413. See also para 86.
459 At para 72.
460 At para 415.
461 At para 90.
462 At para 366. Both assessors, as well as the judge, concluded that the accused suffered from this behaviour. (Para 34).

463 *Engelbrecht* (*supra*) at paras 424 and 427.
464 *Engelbrecht* (*supra*) at para 403: "Domestic violence is a serious matter and someone who institutes such proceedings should not merely sit back and wait for the process to take its course. She should have tried to find out when her case was going to be heard or reinstituted the action"; and at para 407: Advocate Opperman: "It cannot be expected of society or the State to actively pursue Mrs Engelbrecht in order to ensure that she appears in Court. Mrs Engelbrecht is an autonomous, competent and intelligent decision maker and is capable of herself enquiring about this important event."
465 *S v Baloyi* (*supra*) at para 12.
466 At para 352.
467 At para 446.
468 See Chapter 1.
469 Van Wyk (in translation) – Burchell & Milton (1997) *Cases and Materials on Criminal Law* (2 ed, Juta) at 154. But see *S v Naidoo* 1997 (1) SACR 62 (T).
470 Snyman, C R (2002) op cit at 109.
471 *S v Moyo* (1999) JOL 5048, 4 (T); *R v Patel* (*supra*) at 123.
472 *S v Dingaan* (2001) JOL 8949, 9 (Ck) (citing *R v Attwood*, 1946 AD 331); *R v Patel* (*supra*) at 123 (citing *R v Attwood* 1946 AD 331); *S v Jackson* 1963 (2) SA 626, 628 (A).
473 *Ex parte Minister van Justisie: In re S v Van Wyk*, 1967 (1) SA 488 (A). It is doubtful that this decision would be upheld under South Africa's new Constitution.
474 At para 357 (quoted but not referenced).
475 The court attached the following footnote to this factor:
"The onus should not always be on the victim to terminate unlawful actions by an abuser but the onus is on those bodies and individuals – medical practitioners, individual policeman, magistrates, employers, prosecutors, social workers – to proactively intervene to ensure that Constitutional rights have meaningful content and that the law is obeyed and enforced." (Para 357.)
476 At para 357.
477 See *Lavallee* (*supra*) at para 121.
478 At para 424. Advocate Naude also claimed that the accused had the option of throwing her husband out of the house to end the violence, despite his earlier finding of fact (along with Judge Satchwell and Advocate Opperman) that:
"The threat of violence or psychological or emotional cruelty endures beyond the immediate proximity of Mr and Mrs Engelbrecht. It reached past each one of their separations since Mr Engelbrecht was adept at finding Mrs Engelbrecht at work, in the shops, asleep in her flat, socialising with her friends, at her new residence and at her proposed employment in another town. Each time he did so another act of domestic violence was perpetrated by him." (Para 359.) Finally, Advocate Naude used myths about abuse victims to justify his conclusion that there was no proportionality between the accused's response and the threatened attack. He concluded that Mrs Engelbrecht was an intelligent woman capable of working, which assumes that she has options that may not exist. (Para 424.)
479 At paras 429, 430, 431 and 432. Advocate Opperman never explains what kind of help the accused could have received from her friends, although she highlighted an instance where a friend loaned the accused money to move into a new apartment.
480 See Ludsin *Discussion Document 2* at 18.
481 See eg *Lavallee* (*supra*) at 125 ("Expert testimony relating to the ability of an accused to perceive danger from her mate may go to the issue of whether she 'reasonably apprehended' death or grievous bodily harm on a particular occasion.")
482 See eg *State v Norman* (*supra*) at 265 ("Such predictions of future assaults to justify the defendant's use of deadly force in this case would be entirely speculative, because there was no evidence that her husband had ever inflicted any harm upon her that approached life-threatening injury").
483 *Lavallee* (*supra*) at 119 quoting Julie Blackman (1986) "Potential uses for expert testimony: Ideas toward the representation of battered women who kill" (1986) 9 *Women's Rights Law Reporter* 227 at 229.
484 *Lavallee* (*supra*) at 119 quoting Julie Blackman (1986) "Potential uses for expert testimony: Ideas toward the representation of battered women who kill" (1986) 9 *Women's Rights Law Reporter* 227 at 229.
485 *Lavallee* (*supra*) at 119.
486 *Engelbrecht* (*supra*) at 304 and 305.
487 *Engelbrecht* (*supra*) at 386.
488 Faigman (1987) "Discerning justice when battered women kill" 39 *Hastings LJ* 207 at 217; Ewing, C P *Battered Women Who Kill* at 85.
489 See eg *State v Smullen* 844 (*supra*) at 429 ("The fact that the defendant's perception either of imminent harm or the amount of force necessary to deal with the threat is inaccurate does not necessarily make the perception unreasonable."); *Lavallee v Queen* (*supra*) at 97.
490 *Engelbrecht* (*supra*) at 328.
491 *Mokonto* (*supra*) at 323; *S v Patel* (*supra*)

(citing *R v Attwood*, 1946 AD 331); Snyman, C R (2002) op cit at 111 note 13; *Burchell* 78. Burchell describes this as an objective test. *Burchell* 79. The authors disagree with this categorization on the basis that once a court is asked to consider reasonableness based on a woman's circumstances, it is required to consider her actions based on some degree of subjectivity and, therefore, has both subjective and objective elements. *Dingaan v S* (*supra*) agreed this is a mixed test, quoting Snyman that "normally, an act of self defence is judged objectively but there is always an element of subjectivity which (sic) relates to the persons and circumstances involved in the act." (At 9).

492 *Mokonto* 1971 (2) SA at 323; *Patel* 1959 (3) SA at 123 (Citing *R v Attwood*, 1946 AD 331); Snyman, C R (2002) op cit at 111 note 13; Burchell op cit at 78 note 18.

493 *Engelbrecht* (*supra*) at para 327 (quoting *S v Motleleni* 1976 (1) SA 403, 406 A).

494 *Engelbrecht* (*supra*) at para 329.

495 *Dingaan v S* (*supra*) at 9; An American court provides a particularly instructive statement of the point:
"The subjective aspects ensure that the jury fully understands the totality of the defendant's actions from the defendant's own perspective. Such a consideration is especially important in battered person cases. As one court has explained: 'The subjective perceptions of an individual, brutalized regularly by domestic violence, are especially critical to the determination of whether her actions in purported self-defense were reasonable.' Victims of a battering relationship live in a hopeless vacuum of 'cumulative terror'."
(*State v Janes* 121 Wn 2d 220, 239 (Sup Ct Wash 1993)).

496 *Burchell* at 79. See also Snyman, C R (2002) op cit 111–12; *S v Sataardien* 1998 (1) SACR 637 (C). See also *R v Patel* (*supra*) at 123, quoting Gardiner and Lansdown: "The danger may in truth not have been great, but the jury must consider whether a reasonable man, in the circumstances in which the accused was placed could have thought that he was in great danger. A weapon less dangerous than the one used may have been at hand (sic) which would have sufficed to ward off the threatened assault but the jury must not expect too nice a discrimination or too careful a choice of weapons from a man called upon in a sudden emergency to act promptly and without opportunity for reflection."

497 *Engelbrecht* (*supra*) at para 332.

498 245/03.

499 At para 333.

500 *Engelbrecht* (*supra*) at paras 330, 359.

501 Snyman, C R (2002) op cit at 111 note 13.

502 *Engelbrecht* (*supra*) at para 332.

503 *Engelbrecht* (*supra*) at para 336.

504 At para 335.

505 At para 358.

506 See eg *People v Humphrey* 921 P2d 1, 9 (Sup Ct Ca 1996).

507 (1 SCR 123 (SCC)).

508 At para 358 (quoting *Malott* (*supra*) at para 40). The Supreme Court of Washington in the United States reached a similar conclusion:
"The respondent was entitled to have the jury consider her actions in the light of her own perceptions of the situation, including those perceptions which were the product of our nation's 'long and unfortunate history of sex discrimination.' Until such time as the effects of that history are eradicated, care must be taken to assure that our self-defense instructions afford women the right to have their conduct judged in light of the individual physical handicaps which are the product of sex discrimination. To fail to do so is to deny the right of the individual woman involved to trial by the same rules which are applicable to male defendants."
State v Wanrow 559 P 2d 548, 559 (Sup Ct Wash 1977) (statutorily amended on other grounds).

509 At para 359.

510 Alexander Reilly (1998) "The heart of the matter: Emotion in criminal defences" (1997–98) 29 *Ottawa L Rev* 117 at para 65. See also *Lavallee* (*supra*) at 120–1.

511 *R v Malott* (*supra*) at para 43 ("To fully accord with the spirit of *Lavallee*, where the reasonableness of a battered woman's belief is at issue in a criminal case, a judge and jury should be made to appreciate that a battered woman's experiences are both individualized, based on her own history and relationships, as well as shared with other women, within the context of a society and a legal system which has historically undervalued women's experiences.")

512 *Robinson v State* (*supra*) at 91.

513 At paras 18, 361, 362, 363 and 364.

514 At para 374.

515 At para 403 and 405.

516 At para 443.

517 *S v Baloyi* (*supra*) at para 11. See also *Carmichele v Minister of Safety and Security* (*supra*).

518 *S v Baloyi* (*supra*) at para 11. See also *Carmichele v Minister of Safety and Security* (*supra*).

519 *Engebrecht* (*supra*) at para 451.

520 Nevada Revised Statutes Annotated, s 200.150.

521 *Engelbrecht* (*supra*) at para 452.

522 Ferreira (supra) at para 45.
523 Ferreira (supra) at para 45.
524 Engebrecht (supra) at para 350.
525 S v Naidoo 1997 (1) SACR 62, 68 (T).
526 One important danger of arguing putative self-defence in the alternative is that judges may focus on this defence and avoid the more difficult question of self-defence. The primary objective in these cases is to lay an evidential basis and then to argue the applicability of self-defence to abused women who kill in non-confrontational situations.
527 Burchell op cit at 265.
528 Burchell op cit at 265–6.
529 Ferreira (supra) at para 40 (citing cf R v Malott (supra) at paras 38 and 40).
530 At para 40.
531 At para 38 ("What has to be borne in mind in each case, however, as remarked by Wilson J in Lavallee is that abused women may well kill their partners other than in self-defence and that the issue in each case is not whether the accused is an abused woman but whether the killing was objectively justifiable in self-defence. I would add: or subjectively seen as justifiable in mitigation of sentence.")
532 At para 13.
533 At para 28.
534 At paras 28, 42.
535 At para 42.
536 At para 37.
537 At para 35.
538 At para 39.
539 S v Naidoo (supra) at 67.
540 It is unclear what type of evidence Ferreira would have needed to provide to show that she had no real alternatives to avoid self-help. Her claim related to mitigation of sentence, not self-defence.
541 Burchell 265–6.
542 S v Ntuli 1975 (1) SA 429, 437.

CHAPTER 5

543 S v Ntuli (supra) at 436.
544 Snyman, C R (2002) Criminal Law (4 ed) Butterworths at 235;
545 Taylor, L J "Provoked reason in men and women: Heat-of-passion manslaughter and imperfect Self-defense" (1986) 33 UCLA L Rev 1679 at 1679; Reilly, A "The heart of the matter: Emotion in criminal defences" (1997-98) 29 Ottawa L Rev 117 at para 59.
546 S v Kensley 1995 (1) SACR 646, 658 (A).
547 2002 (3) SA 719.
548 S v Eadie 2002 (1) SACR 663 (C) at para 61.
549 See S v Henry 1999 (1) SACR 13 (SCA) at 20.
550 See Ludsin Discussion Doc 2 at sec 3.3.
551 S v Engelbrecht Case No 64/2003 (WLD) at paras 461, 463.
552 At para 466.
553 At para 469.
554 At para 463.
555 At para 463.
556 At para 464.
557 S v Laubscher 1988 (1) SA 163 (A) as translated in Burchell, J & Milton, J (2000) Cases and Materials on Criminal Law (2 ed) at 181.
558 S v Pederson 1998 (2) SACR 383 (N) at 386.
559 S v Henry 1999 (1) SACR at 19; Pederson (supra).
560 Burchell (2000) op cit at 185.
561 2002 (3) SA 719 (SCA).
562 S v Eadie 2002 (1) SACR 663 (C) at para 70.
563 Arguably this credibility test has always existed. Its restatement in Eadie suggests that the test will be only more strict.
564 S v Eadie 2002 (1) SACR 663 (C) at para 2; see also Francis 1999 (1) SACR 650 at 652; S v McDonald 2000 (2) SACR 493 (N) at 500; S v Pederson (supra) at 391.
565 Snyman, C R (2002) at 165, Burchell, J (2000) op cit at 211, S v Pederson (supra) at 391; S v Eadie 2002 (1) SACR 663 (C) at para 65.
566 S v Eadie (supra) at para 65; Snyman, C R (2002) at 165, 237.
567 Snyman, C R (2002) at 166; see also Burchell, J (2000) op cit at 211.
568 Snyman, C R (2002) at 165.
569 1995 (1) SACR 1 (A).
570 S v Ingram (supra) at 7.
571 Taylor, L J "Provoked reason in men and women: Heat-of-passion manslaughter and imperfect Self-defense" (1986) 33 UCLA L Rev 1679 at 1716.
572 Osland v Queen (1998) HCA 75 (High Ct Aust 1998) at para 55; see also R v Thornton [1996] 2 All ER 1023 (UK Ct App Crim).
573 S v Henry 1999 (1) SACR at 20.
574 Snyman, C R (2002) op cit at 239, Burchell, J (2000) op cit at 264.
575 Francis, 1999 (1) SACR at 652.
576 Eadie (supra) at para 65.
577 Eadie (supra) at para 59.
578 Eadie (supra) at para 60.
579 Eadie (supra) at para 60.
580 Eadie (supra) at para 64.
581 Pather, S (2002) "Provocation: Acquittals provoke a rethink" 15 SACJ 337 at 343; "S v Eadie: Road rage, incapacity and legal confusion" (2001) 14 SACJ 206 at 207.
582 Eadie (supra) at para 39 (based on lower court decision in S v Eadie (1) SACR 172 (C).
583 (2000) 2 All SA 181 (Ck).
584 S v Kali (supra) at 204.

585 Henry (supra) at 23.
586 S v Nursingh 1995 (2) SACR 331 (D) at 336 (disapproved of on different grounds in Eadie).
587 S v Pederson (supra) at 399; Henry (supra) at 20.
588 S v Pederson (supra) at 390; Henry (supra) at 20.
589 Snyman, C R (2002) op cit at 166; Carstens, P A & Le Roux, J (2000) "The defence of non-pathological incapacity with reference to the battered wife who kills her abusive husband" 14 SAJC 180 at 188.
590 See Ludsin Discussion Document 2 sec 3.6.3
591 S v Campher 1987 (1) SA 940 (A), as translated in Burchell & Milton (1997) Cases and Materials on Criminal Law (2 ed) Juta at 307.
592 1990 (1) SACR 561 (A).
593 Ingram (supra) at 7.
594 Springer v Kentucky (1999) 998 SW2d 439 at 452. See also R v Ahluwalia [1992] 4 All ER 889 (UK) Ct App Crim).
595 Alexander Reilly, A (1998) op cit at para 60.
596 Sec 78(1).
597 Snyman, C R (2002) op cit at 169.
598 Snyman, C R (2002) op cit at 164.
599 Snyman, C R (2002) op cit at 169; Burchell, J (2000) op cit at 216.
600 Snyman, C R (2002) op cit at 173.

CHAPTER 6

601 Ohio Revised Code, section 2945.392, Battered woman syndrome testimony.
602 S v Malgas 2001 (2) SA 1222 (SCA) at para 8; See also Van Zyl Smit, D (1999) "Mandatory minimum sentences and departures from them in substantial and compelling circumstances" 15 SAJHR 270 at 273: ("The statutorily prescribed South African penalties appear to have been instituted as a short-term deterrent designed to deal in a crisis with offences that are usually very serious and deserving of heavy punishments.")
603 Criminal Law Amendment Act 105 of 1997 s 51(1)(a) read with Part 1 of Schedule 2.
604 Sec 51(3) of the Criminal Law Amendment Act 105 of 1997:
"If any court referred to in subsection (1) or (2) is satisfied that substantial and compelling circumstances exist which justify the imposition of a lesser sentence than the sentence prescribed in those subsections, it shall enter those circumstances on the record of the proceedings and may thereupon impose such lesser sentence."
605 2001 (2) SA 1222 (SCA).
606 Malgas (supra) at para 22.
607 Malgas (supra) at para 18.
608 Malgas (supra) at para 9.
609 Ibid.
610 Snyman, C R (2002) Criminal Law (4 ed) Butterworths at 239.
611 Criminal Procedure Act No 51 of 1977, s 274(1).
612 S v Maleka, 2001 (2) SACR 366, para 5 (SCA).
613 Kensley 1995 (1) SACR at 660-1.
614 Engebrecht (supra); Potgieter 1994 (1) SACR at 88; Ingram 1995 (1) SACR at 9; Vetten, L & Ngwane, C (In press) Sentencing Men and Women Convicted of Spousal Homicide: Findings from Three Gauteng Courts. Research report in preparation for the Centre for the Study of Violence and Reconciliation.
615 Potgieter (supra) at 85; S v Larsen 1994 (2) SACR 149 (A) at 157; Ingram (supra) at 9.
616 Vetten, L & Ngwane, C (In press) Sentencing Men and Women Convicted of Spousal Homicide: Findings from Three Gauteng Courts. Research report in preparation for the Centre for the Study of Violence and Reconciliation.
617 See also Ludsin, H Discussion Document 2, sec 6.1.
618 Case No 245/03 (1 April 2004).
619 At para 33.
620 At para 38.
621 At para 40 (comparing R v Malott (1998) 1 SCR 123 (SCC) at paras 38 and 40.)
622 At paras 33, 35.
623 At para 35.
624 Ibid.
625 At para 33.
626 Ludsin, H Discussion Document 2 at sec 6.1.
627 At para 44.
628 Ibid.
629 At para 45.
630 Ibid.
631 Ibid.
632 At para 45.
633 Laubscher 1988 (1) SA at 317; Criminal Procedure Act 51 0f 1977, s 78(7); Snyman, C R (2002) at 239, S v Maleka (2001) JOL 7707 (A).
634 Ingram (supra) at 9.
635 Osland v Queen (1998) HCA 75 (High Ct Aust 1998) at para 56; R v Thornton [1996] 2 All ER 1023 (Ct App Crim Eng); R v ST (1995) EWJ No 2539 (Ct App Crim Eng).
636 R v Bennett (1993) OJ No 1011 para 75 (Ontario Court of Justice). See also R v Getkate (1998) OJ No 6329 (Ontario Court of Justice). See also, R v Hayward (2001) EWJ 6404 (Eng & Wales Ct App); Veen v Queen (No 2) 164 CLR 465 (High Ct Australia).

637 Romero, B B, Collins, J, Johnson, C, Merrigan, J, Perkins, L, Sznyter, J & May, L D "The Missouri Battered Women's Clemency Coalition: A collaborative effort in justice for eleven Missouri women" (2004) 23 *St Louis Univ Public L Rev* 193 at 220.
638 See eg *R v DEC* (1995) BCJ No. 1074 (British Columbia Supreme Court); *R v Sangha* (1996) EWJ No 3447 (Eng Ct App Crim); *R v Higgins* (1995) EWJ No 970 (Eng Ct App Crim); *R v Howell* (1998) 1 Cr App Rep (S) 229; *R v Fell* (2000) EWJ 1603 (Eng & Wales Ct App).
639 See eg *R v DEC* (*supra*) ("I think it would be totally inappropriate that Miss C, who was victimized as a child, victimized in her first marriage, victimized in marriage which led to this tragedy, should be further victimized by a term of incarceration. I do not think that the ends of justice demand that she be incarcerated. Quite the contrary, I think that in the particular and unique circumstances of this case a suspended sentence is appropriate.").
640 *S v Makwanyane* 1995 (2) SACR 1 (CC) at para 130. See also *S v Williams* 1995 (2) SACR 251 (CC) at para 50 ("The Constitution now offers an opportunity for South Africans to join the mainstream of a world community that is progressively moving away from punishments that place undue emphasis on retribution and vengeance, rather than on correction, prevention and the recognition of human rights.")
641 Snyman, C R (2002) at 239.
642 Ibid.
643 Ibid.
644 Krause, J H (1996) "Of merciful justice and justified mercy: Commuting the sentences of battered women who kill" (1996) 46 *Fla L Rev* 699 at 706.
645 See Romero, B B et al (2004) op cit at 215.
646 Ammons, L L (2003) "Why do you do the things you do? Clemency for battered incarcerated women: A decade's review" (2003)11 *Am Univ J of Gender, Soc Pol & L* 533 at 552.
647 Ammons, L L (2003) op cit at 552–6.
648 Ibid.
649 Ibid.
650 Ibid.
651 St Joan, J & Ehrenreich, N (2001) "Putting theory into practice: A battered women's clemency clinic" (2001) 8 *Clinical L Rev* 171 at 172.
652 Romero, B B et al (2004) op cit at 208.
653 *RSA v Hugo* (*supra*).
654 1997 (6) BCLR 708 (CC).
655 At para 47
656 At para 42.
657 Albertyn, C *Legal Opinion* at 22.
658 Romero, B B et al (2004) op cit at 220.
659 Ibid.
660 Albertyn, C *Legal Opinion* at 22.
661 Martin E Veinsredideris "The prospective effects of modifying existig law to accommodate preemptive self-defense by battered women" (2001) 49 *Univ Pa L Rev* 613 at 643.
662 Romero, B B et al (2004) op cit at 208.
663 *Self-Defence Review: Final Report*, submitted to the Minister of Justice of Canada and to the Solicitor General of Canada, 1997. The Canadian Minister of Justice was looking to correct the injustice to women previously excluded from self-defence prior to the *Lavallee* decision that for the first time used psycho-social research to help explain that a woman may have acted in self-defence although she killed in a non-confrontational situation.
664 Ammons, L L (2003) op cit at 549.
665 St Joan, J & Ehrenreich, N (2001) op cit at 216.
666 Ludsin, H *Discussion Document 2* at sec 3.6.4.
667 Albertyn, C *Legal Opinion* at 23.
668 Ibid.
669 Albertyn, C *Legal Opinion* at 24.
670 Former Justice Kriegler at launch of Legal Defences for Battered Women Who Kill Their Abusers, Centre For the Study of Violence and Reconciliation, Johannesburg, South Africa 13 November 2003.
671 Albertyn, C *Legal Opinion* at 24.
672 See Ludsin, H *Discussion Document 2* at sec 2 6.1.
673 *Clemency for Battered Women in Michigan: A Manual for Attorneys, Law Students and Social Workers*, http://www.umich.edu/~clemency/; Ammons, L L (2003) op cit at 551.

CHAPTER 7

674 For more information about clemency projects for abused women who kill, see Romero, B B et al (2004) op cit at 171.
675 Section 210 of the Criminal Procedure Act 51 of 1977 provides as follows: "Irrelevant evidence inadmissible. – No evidence as to any fact, matter or thing shall be admissible which is irrelevant or immaterial and which cannot conduce to prove or disprove any point or fact at issue in criminal proceedings."
676 Hoffmann, L H & Zeffertt, D T (1998) *The South African Law of Evidence* (4th ed) at 21.
677 Ibid, quoting *R v Matthews* 1960 (1) SA 752 (A) at 758.
678 See Chapters 2 and 3. See also *People v*

679 *Humphrey* 921 P2d 1 (Sup Ct Ca 1996).

679 *State v Nemeth* 82 Ohio St 3d 202, 208 (Sup Ct Oh 1998); *People v Erickson* 57 Cal App 4th 1391 at 1401 (Ct of App Calif 1997) (Sup Ct denied appeal); *Lavallee v Queen* 55 CCC3d 97 (1990) at 112; *Oslund v Queen* (1998) HCA 75 (High Ct Aust 1998) at paras 54 and 169.

680 *S v Engelbrecht* (Case No 64/2003 (WLD)) at para 29.

681 Hoffmann, L H & Zeffertt, D T (1998) op cit at 22–3.

682 Hoffmann, L H & Zeffertt, D T (1998) op cit at 45.

683 Hoffmann, L H & Zeffertt, D T (1998) op cit at 47.

684 Schwikkard, Skeen & Van der Merwe (1997) *Principles of Evidence* at 47.

685 Statutes in some jurisdictions in the United States specifically ensure the admissibility of this information in criminal trials of persons in a violent relationship. See e.g. Kentucky Revised Statutes Annotated s 503.050, General Principles of Justification; Maryland Code s 10-916, Battered Spouse Syndrome; Oregon Revised Statutes s 40.172, rule 404.1 Pattern, practice or history of abuse; expert testimony.

686 Massachusetts enacted legislation explaining the importance of testimony of a past pattern of abuse:
Massachusetts Annotated Laws Chapter 233, s 23F, Admissibility of Evidence to establish Reasonableness of Force reads:
"In the trial of criminal cases charging the use of force against another where the issue of defense of self or another, defense of duress or coercion, or accidental harm is asserted, a defendant shall be permitted to introduce either or both of the following in establishing the reasonableness of the defendant's apprehension that death or serious bodily injury was imminent, the reasonableness of the defendant's belief that he had availed himself of all available means to avoid physical combat or the reasonableness of a defendant's perception of the amount of force necessary to deal with the perceived threat:
(a) evidence that the defendant is or has been the victim of acts of physical, sexual or psychological harm or abuse;
(b) evidence by expert testimony regarding the common pattern in abusive relationships; the nature and effects of physical, sexual or psychological abuse and typical responses thereto, including how those effects relate to the perception of the imminent nature of the threat of death or serious bodily harm; the relevant facts and circumstances which form the basis for such opinion; and evidence whether the defendant displayed characteristics common to victims of abuse."
See also Texas Code of Criminal Procedure, art 38.36 Evidence in Prosecutions for Murder; Code of Virginia Code Annotated s 19.2-270.6, Evidence of abuse admissible in certain criminal trials. But see *Engelbrecht* (supra) at para 325, in which one assessor expressly rejected the use of expert testimony as proof of the accused's state of mind.

687 *People v Humphrey* 921 P2d 1 (Sup Ct Ca 1996) at 8–9; *Commonwealth v Stonehouse* 521 Pa 41 (Sup Ct Pa 1989); Massachusetts codified the relevancy of expert evidence to criminal defence law. See also Massachusetts Annotated Laws Chapter 233, s 23F, Admissibility of Evidence to establish Reasonableness.

688 *State v Janes* 121 Wn 2d 220 (Sup Ct Wash 1993) at 241. See eg Arkansas Statutes, s 76-2-402, Force in defense of person – forcible felony defined.

689 Kentucky Revised Statutes s 503.010. See also Utah Statutes, s 76-2-402.

690 *Commonwealth v Stonehouse* (supra).

691 Schwikkard, Skeen & Van der Merwe (1997) op cit at 63.

692 Schwikkard, Skeen & Van der Merwe (1997) op cit at 63–4.

693 Ibid.

694 Ibid.

695 Hoffmann, L H & Zeffertt, D T (1998) op cit at 47.

696 See *Chapman v State* 258 GA 214 (Sup Ct Ga 1988); *State v Torres* 488 NYS2d 358 (Sup Ct NY 1985); Utah Section 76-2-402, Force in defense of person – forcible felony defined.

697 *State v Torres* (supra).

698 Hoffmann, L H & Zeffertt, D T (1998) op cit at 97, 100; see also Schwikkard, Skeen and Van der Merwe (1997) op cit at 86.

699 Hoffmann, L H & Zeffertt, D T (1998) op cit at 98.

700 Hoffmann, L H & Zeffertt, D T (1998) op cit at 100.

701 Hoffmann, L H & Zeffertt, D T (1998) op cit at 101. Schwikkard, Skeen and Van der Merwe (1997) op cit at 88.

702 *Pederson* 1998 (3) All SA 321 ("Such a finding, namely that the appellant's evidence was unreliable and false, immediately undermines the expert option sought to be expressed by Dr. LG Pillay. The result is that there was no credible evidence to substantiate the conclusion that the appellant had acted involuntarily or that he was incapable of distinguishing between right and wrong when he stabbed the deceased or that he was incapable of

modulating his actions according to his appreciation of what was wrong and what was right at the time.")
703 *Engebrecht* (*supra*) at para 26.
704 *Engebrecht* (*supra*) at para 324.
705 *State v Allery* 682 P2d 312 (Sup Ct Wash 1984).
706 *Engebrecht* (*supra*) at para 29.
707 *State v Walker* 700 P2d 1168 (Ct Apps Wash 1985) (petition for review by Supreme Court of Washington denied *State v Walker* 1004 Wn2d 1012).
708 *Engebrecht* (*supra*) at para 27. See eg *Commonwealth v Stonehouse* (*supra*); Nevada Revised Statutes Annotated, s 48.061, Witnesses and Evidence; South Dakota Code s 22-16-3, Relationship between accused and victim bearing on degree of homicide.
709 See also *State v Nemeth* 82 Ohio St 3d 202 (1998) at 208. The Supreme Court of Ohio wrote about a battered child who killed his father in a non-confrontational situation: "Testimony on the ... psychological effects of abuse is essential to proving the elements of a self-defense claim. Non-confrontational killings do not fit the general pattern of self-defense. Without expert testimony, a trier of fact my not be able to understand that the defendant at the time of the killing could have had an honest belief that he was in imminent danger of death or great bodily harm. Further, it is difficult for the average person to understand the degree of helplessness an abused child may feel. Thus, expert testimony would also 'help dispel the ordinary lay person's perception that a (person) in a battering relationship is free to leave at any time.' In either instance, the expert testimony 'is aimed at an area where the purported common knowledge of the jury may be very much mistaken, an area where jurors' logic drawn from their own experience, may lead to a wholly incorrect conclusion.' "
See also, *Ibn-Tamas v United States* 407 A2d 626 (Ct Apps DC 1979); *Chapman v State*, 258 GA 214 (Sup Ct Ga 1988) at 216; *State v Eng* 1994 Ohio App LEXIS 4655 (Ct App Oh 1994); *State v Kacsmar* 421 Pa Super 64 (Superior Ct Pa 1992); *State v Smullen* 844 A2d 429 (Ct App Md 2003); *Osland v Queen* (*supra*) at 167 (concurring opinion); Maryland Code s 10-916, Battered Spouse Syndrome; Missouri Revised Statutes s 563.033, Battered Spouse Syndrome evidence that defendant acted in self-defense or defense of another – procedure; Ohio Revised Code Annotated, s 2901.06, Battered Woman Syndrome Testimony as Evidence Relevant to claim of Self-Defense; South Carolina Code Annotated, s 17-23-170, Admissibility of evidence concerning battered spouse syndrome; foundation; notice; lay testimony; Texas Code of Criminal Procedure, s 38.36 Evidence in Prosecutions for Murder.
710 *Osland v Queen* (*supra*) at para 55; *State v Smullen* (*supra*); *Lavallee* (*supra*) at 125; see also *Osland* (*supra*) at paras 54 and 169.
711 See e.g. *Witt v State* 892 P2d 132 (Sup Ct Wy 1995); *People v Jaspar* 119 Cal Rptr 3d 470 (Ct App Ca 2002); *State v Smullen* (*supra*); Wyoming Statutes, s 6-1-203, Battered Woman Syndrome; *Lavallee* (*supra*) at 125; *Osland* (*supra*) at paras 54, 169.
712 *Engelbrecht* (*supra*) at para 29; *State v Steele* 178 W Va 330 (Sup Ct W Va 1987); *Witt v State* (*supra*); *People v Humphrey* (*supra*); *People v Jaspar* (*supra*); *State v Smullen* (*supra*); *Lavallee* (*supra*) at 125; See also *Osland* (*supra*) at paras 54 and 169. For statutes in the United States that support the role of expert evidence on the psychological effects of abuse in proving self-defence, see section 12.3 of Ludsin H (2003) "Legal Defences for Battered Women Who Kill Their Abusers (Discussion Document 1)", Johannesburg Centre for the Study of Violence and Reconciliation.
713 *R v Thornton* [1996] 2 All ER 1023 (Ct. App Crim Eng); *R v SR* (1995) EWJ No 3375 (Ct App Crim Eng).
714 See eg *Engelbrecht* (*supra*) at paras 146–51.
715 (1998) 1 SCR 123
716 At para 41.
717 *Engelbrecht* (*supra*) at 29.